The

Macintosh
Bible guide to
FileMaker
Pro 3

Charles Rubin

 Peachpit Press

The Macintosh Bible Guide to FileMaker Pro 3
Charles Rubin

Peachpit Press
2414 Sixth Street
Berkeley, CA 94710
510/548-4393
510/548-5991 (fax)

Find us on the World Wide Web at:
http://www.peachpit.com

Peachpit Press is a division of Addison Wesley Longman
Copyright © 1996 by Charles Rubin

Editor: Nancy Davis
Copyeditor: Leslie Tilley
Cover design: YO, San Francisco
Cover illustration: John Grimes
Margin icons: Joe Crabtree, Art Parts; Lynda Banks, Lynda Banks Design
Production: Rick Gordon, Emerald Valley Graphics

ISBN 0-201-88356-2

9 8 7 6 5 4 3 2 1

Printed and bound in the United States of America

♻ Printed on recycled paper

Acknowledgments

My many thanks to the pleasant and energetic people at Peachpit Press and beyond who made this book a reality, including Nancy Davis, Leslie Tilley, Rick Gordon (at Emerald Valley Graphics), Mimi Heft, John Grimes, Cary Norsworthy, Roslyn Bullas, Keasley Jones, Hannah Onstad, Trish Booth, Gregor Clark, and of course, Ted Nace.

Charlie Rubin

Table of Contents

Introduction

~~~~~~

FileMaker Pro has been the best-selling Macintosh database since it appeared in 1985. It made its reputation by offering tremendous flexibility in managing data without requiring programming expertise. Now, version 3 extends FileMaker's power into the realm of relational database management, but the program remains simple enough for anyone to use.

This book is for anyone who wants to learn about FileMaker Pro, whether you're creating complex database applications or just trying to do a few simple things with a file somebody else has created. FileMaker Pro comes with its own manuals and an extensive online Help system, but this book offers extra assistance in several ways:

- It explains FileMaker Pro's basic features more quickly and clearly.

- It acknowledges confusing aspects of FileMaker Pro and helps you understand them.

- It points out FileMaker Pro's limitations so you don't waste your time trying to make it do things it can't.

- It anticipates common problems you'll have when using FileMaker Pro and provides quick solutions to them.

Why This Book Is Different

Like other documentation supplied by a program's manufacturer, FileMaker Pro's official manuals and online Help present it as if it's the only program in the universe and all its features and operations make perfect sense. Of course, you and I, who live in the real world, must try to learn about FileMaker Pro in the context of programs we already know, and things that make sense within the program can seem downright strange compared to the way other programs work. In this book, I've tried to put FileMaker Pro in perspective.

In deciding what to cover, I've embraced the basic truth that we learn best by doing. So rather than documenting every single variation of each command, I've spared you the extra pages—except where more examples were necessary to show something really important. As you use FileMaker Pro on your own, you'll undoubtedly find the best way to make its features suit your purposes.

Finally, I've saved a lot of space by assuming I don't have to repeat basic instructions endlessly. Rather than telling you about every single mouse click or command, I assume you're familiar with standard Macintosh operations, such as managing windows; selecting options with radio buttons, menus or checkboxes; and clicking buttons in dialog boxes.

What's New in FileMaker Pro 3

The last revision of FileMaker occurred at the end of 1992, so we have a right to expect some major improvements this time around. FileMaker Pro 3 doesn't disappoint. Here are the major improvements:

- Relational database management capabilities that allow you to work with information in many different files at once. In terms of basic data-handling power, this change alone brings FileMaker Pro into the "big leagues" of database management, with such programs as Microsoft Access and FoxPro.

- Larger data-handling capacities, including the ability to work with as many as 50 files at once, and with individual files as large as 320 megabytes.

- An online Help system.

- Improved, word processor-style formatting controls that make it much easier to dress up the output from your files.

- A much simpler method of merging data into form letters.

- Automatic file and field creation when you import data from another format.

- Dozens of new functions for manipulating data more flexibly.

- A beefed-up ScriptMaker, which now allows loops, conditional actions, and error-checking.

- A large collection of template files that let you quickly create files for dozens of common applications.

- Support for TCP/IP networks, Power Macintosh, and Windows 95.

All in all, these improvements address nearly all FileMaker's previous data-handling limitations, so if you've used an older version and have run into roadblocks with your database plans, FileMaker Pro version 3 will probably eliminate them.

Still, the program remains as easy to use as ever, proving once again that FileMaker leads all databases in combining power and simplicity.

How to Use This Book

This book was written for FileMaker Pro version 3 users, but much of the material applies to previous versions of FileMaker as well. If you're using an older version of FileMaker, you should upgrade. But even if you don't upgrade, you can still get a lot out of this book—you'll just have to ignore the explanations of features your version doesn't include.

If you're new to database programs, start with Chapter 1 to become familiar with basic database terms and concepts.

If you're not new to databases but new to FileMaker Pro, start with Chapter 2 to get an overall understanding of the program's operating style, features, and limitations. This overview will help you avoid a lot of confusion later.

If you're upgrading to FileMaker Pro version 3 from an earlier version, read Chapter 1 for an orientation about relational operations, and then look at Chapter 11 for details about FileMaker Pro's new relational capabilities. Also skim through the book and check the margins for the New Feature icon, to zero in on the program's new capabilities. Actually, you'll find three icons in the book:

New Feature

This icon appears next to sections describing features that are new to FileMaker Pro version 3.

Tip

This icon identifies tips or shortcuts that will help you make better use of FileMaker Pro.

Important Note

You'll see this icon next to sections covering special problems or especially crucial information.

If you need a quick solution to a specific problem, check the troubleshooting sections at the end of Chapter 2 and Chapters 4 through 16.

If you can't find the section you need, check the index for a cross-reference.

FileMaker Pro has been the best-selling Macintosh database program because it has always given most people the simplest possible way to manage data. Version 3 takes FileMaker's data-handling power to new heights, but new users and old-timers will still appreciate the ease with which they can access that power.

1 Basic Database Terms and Concepts

- What's a Database?
- Retrieving and Displaying information
- Sharing Files and Data

If you've never used a database program, there are certain fundamental concepts and terms you need to understand before you can make the most of FileMaker Pro. In this chapter, we'll look at how database programs work in general.

What's a Database?

A database is a collection of information, or *data*. The data could be names and addresses, sales orders, population statistics, or anything else. The point of keeping this information on a computer is to use the computer's ability to sort or arrange it, summarize it in a report, or locate a particular piece or group of data. For example, if you've got a thousand names and addresses in a computer database, you can quickly find a specific person's address or sort all the addresses by zip code for bulk mailing.

Computers are very orderly, and they can only manage information if it's kept in an orderly structure. Computers are also very stupid, and they can only tell one kind of information (such as a person's last name) from another kind (such as a street address) if you tell them which is which. Using a database program like FileMaker Pro, you can easily arrange information in a structure that your computer can understand and work with.

Organizing information

Database programs keep information in three basic levels of organization. The smallest level is the *field*, which is a category of information such as a person's last name or telephone number. The first challenge in setting up a database is to figure out the fields, or categories, you'll need to organize your data. In a database of names and addresses, for example, you might set up fields for first name, last name, street address, city, state, zip code, and phone number, as shown here:

Each field must have a unique name so the computer can tell one from another—and so you can remember which type of information goes in which field. Many people confuse fields with field names and with the data contained in fields, but there is a difference:

- *Fields* are the places where you put different kinds of data.

- *Field names* are the names you've given those places so you can tell one place from another by looking at your screen.

- *Data* is the information you store inside the fields.

Once you've created all the fields you need, you enter your data into them. Each set of filled-in fields is called a *record*. In an address database, each person's name and address is one record. Here's a list that shows five records:

			Record	Field Data			Field Label
First Name	**Last Name**	**Street**		**City**	**State**	**Zip**	**Phone**
Robert	Jones	33 Easy St.		New Orleans	LA	30567	715-555-5555
Henny	Waters	441 Liberty Square		Half Moon Bay	CA	94051	415-555-3456
Janet	Swanson	814 Harvard Ave.		Concord	MA	01280	516-555-8989
Meni	Wilson	20 Lentil Ave.		Berkeley	CA	94705	510-555-7653
George	Peters	80754 Towns Blvd.		Chicago	IL	60611	312-555-7612

A *file* is a collection of records containing a certain type of data (such as addresses). Different files can contain different types of data (one might hold addresses, and another, sales orders) or they can contain the same type of data and just store different groups of records (one address file for California and another address file for New York).

Defining fields

As mentioned above, creating a database file starts with setting up or *defining* fields to store your data in. Once you've done so, it's important to enter each piece of data into the field set up for it—and to avoid putting any other type of data there. For example, a First Name field should contain nothing other than first names. If you sometimes put people's last names there, and their first names somewhere else, you won't be able to find their records later when you try to look up their first names in the First Name field. It's like sorting fruit: The whole point is to put each kind of fruit in its own basket. If you don't do that, there's no point in having different baskets.

Since it's important to be consistent about where you put different types of data, most database programs let you define fields to handle specific types of information, such as text, numbers, dates, and times. For example, if you define an Amount Due field as a number field and then try to put words in that field, some programs will give you an error message.

Defining fields by type also helps the computer know how to handle information correctly after you've entered it. For example, if you define a field to contain dates in the mm/dd/yy format, and then ask the computer to find all entries after, say, 1/31/91, it will know you want records dated after January 31, 1991. If you'd defined the field to contain times (instead of dates) and tried the same search, you'd get the wrong group of records.

Database programs vary in the number of different types of data you can assign to fields. Some programs only let you choose between text and numbers, while others (such as FileMaker Pro) give you lots of options.

Retrieving and Displaying Information

Sorting and selecting information

Once you've stored information in a database, you can use the program's sorting and selecting features to find or display groups of data. *Sorting* arranges records in alphabetical or numerical order, based on the contents of one or more fields. For example, you might sort an address file in ascending order by zip code, like this:

First Name	Last Name	Street	City	State	Zip
Janet	Swanson	814 Harvard Ave.	Concord	MA	01280
Robert	Jones	33 Easy St.	New Orleans	LA	30567
George	Peters	80754 Towns Blvd.	Chicago	IL	60611
Henny	Waters	441 Liberty Square	Half Moon Bay	CA	94051
Meni	Wilson	20 Lentil Ave.	Berkeley	CA	94705

Selecting, on the other hand, lets you find certain records in a file and view or print only the records you found. To select records, you tell the computer to look up records by matching specific criteria in one or more fields. For example, you might want to select only address records where the last name begins with the letter *A*. To do this, you would tell the database program to find all records where the contents of the Last Name field begin with *A*.

Selecting only A-letter names to view or print doesn't mean the rest of your records are gone, though. They're still in the file; they're just temporarily hidden from view.

Indexing information

For a database program to find or sort records quickly, its data must be indexed. An *index* is an invisible table that stores every unique entry you type into a field and keeps track of every place it appears in the file.

For example, you might have several address records where the entry in the State field is "California." The index would contain the name "California," and would know the position of every record whose State field contained that name. If you wanted to select just these records, the database could quickly assemble them using the index. Without an index, the database would have to search through every record in the file to find specific data, which takes a lot longer.

Database programs handle indexes in various ways. Most programs that can work on several files at once only index fields when you tell them to. The assumption is that you don't want to bog down the database by making it index a lot of fields whose data you don't need to find quickly. These programs are harder to use, because you have to decide in advance which fields to index, and it's difficult or impossible to change your mind later. (Indexed fields are often called *key fields*.)

Other programs, such as FileMaker Pro, index every field automatically as needed. That makes setting up a file easier, and you don't have to worry about being able to find something quickly.

You can now make FileMaker Pro index a field constantly, if you like. See p. 60 in Chapter 4.

NEW FEATURE

Data and layouts: form vs. content

So far, we've talked about a database file's contents—how you set up fields and create records and how information is stored. But there's also the matter of form—the way fields, records, and data appear on your computer screen or on paper.

In the simplest database programs, you can only view or print data in rows and columns; each record is a row and each field is a column. In more sophisticated programs, such as FileMaker Pro, you can arrange fields any way you want. You can show some fields but not others, or you can make the same field's information appear in more than one place. FileMaker Pro calls such arrangements *layouts*. It lets you create as many different layouts as you like and switch between them easily.

Having flexibility with layouts makes it a lot easier to organize and collect data. For example, if you were typing information from paper forms into fields, you could create a layout that has fields arranged to match the form, making it easier to put data where it belongs. In another layout, you might include only certain fields—just the names and phone numbers from an address file, for example—so you can see the information you need more easily.

It's easy to get confused about the difference between the contents of a database and the way those contents appear on the screen. When you don't see a certain field, it seems as if the information's gone, when in fact it's only hidden from view on that particular layout. The potential for this type of confusion is greater with FileMaker Pro, because it allows you so much flexibility in arranging your data. For example, here are three different layouts of data from the same FileMaker Pro file:

Data entry layout

First Name	Janet
Last Name	Swanson
Street	814 Harvard Ave.
City	Concord
State	MA
Zip Code	01280
Phone Number	516-555-8989

Address directory layout

Janet	Swanson
814 Harvard Ave.	
Concord	MA 01280

Phone list layout

Last Name	First Name	Phone Number
Swanson	Janet	516-555-8989
Jones	Robert	715-555-5555

Some programs also let you control things like the font, type size, and style of the data shown. And if a program lets you define date or time fields, you can probably choose how you want dates or times displayed (between, for example, August 31, 1996 and 8/31/96); FileMaker Pro gives you this flexibility. But changing the way information is displayed doesn't affect the information itself.

Sharing Files and Data

Because people in business often need to share the same data, some database programs allow files to be worked on by more than one user at a time. With these *multi-user* databases, the files are available to many people on the same network, and all users have a copy of the program on their own computer. As long as a file is available, any user can access it. Several users can work on the same file at the same time, and each user's changes are saved to the shared copy of the file.

Multi-user databases usually have a *database administrator*, or someone who has overall responsibility for the file. The database administrator usually controls who can access information in the file. Some users might not be able to see fields containing salary information, for example. In some cases, users might not even be allowed to open a file.

Managing information in multiple files

Technically, the term *database* refers to a collection of files managed together. With the first widely used database manager programs, you created a series of files containing different sets of information and then used the program to compare, combine, separate, or otherwise manipulate the information in the files by specifying relationships between fields. Today, these programs are called *relational database* programs, because they let you work with data from different files by defining specific relationships between those files. With a non-relational (or *flat-file*) database program, you work with just one file's data at a time. FileMaker Pro version 3 is a relational database program; previous versions of the program were not.

NEW FEATURE

Relational database programs let you work with data more flexibly and economically. You can store different categories of information in different files, and yet still use the information whenever you need it. In addition, the information need only be stored once: If you need a particular category of information in another file, you can set up a relationship to the file where it's stored so that you can display that data in the new file without having to re-enter it.

For example, you might have a Personnel file with employee names, numbers, addresses, and years of experience, and a Salary file with employee names, numbers, and salaries. In a relational database, as shown below, the Salary file's employee name data can actually be stored in the Personnel file: You simply create a relationship to the Personnel file that lets you display the name in the Salary file.

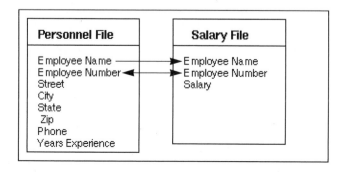

In this case, there's a relationship between the Employee Number fields in each file: When you type an employee number into the Salary file that matches an employee number in the Personnel file, that record's Employee Name information is displayed in the Salary file. With the employee name data stored only in the Personnel file, you only have to update that file when you add, change, or delete employee information—the Salary file is automatically updated as well.

Lookups are another way that database programs let you move information between files. Using a lookup, one file can be set to automatically look up and copy data from another file. Unlike a relational setup, in which one file's information can be displayed (but not stored) in other files, a lookup actually copies data from one file to the other so that it ends up being stored in both files.

Some flat-file databases (including previous versions of FileMaker Pro) offered lookups to give you more data-handling flexibility. But even in a relational program (like FileMaker Pro version 3), lookups are useful in that once data is copied from a lookup file it doesn't change. In a relational program, on the other hand, the data displayed in a related file will change each time the data is updated in the file where it's actually stored.

Here's an example of why you would use a lookup instead of a relational link. Suppose a lumber company has an order entry system that includes two files: a Products file that stores lumber names and prices, and an Invoices file that stores orders. Both the Invoices file and the Products file contain a field called Price, which shows the price of the item being ordered. Since lumber prices change frequently, it's important to charge each customer the price that's current for lumber at the time the order is placed. With a lookup, the Invoices file copies the current price for lumber from the Price field in the Products file, and the invoice thereby reflects the current price. If the Invoices file simply displayed Price field information from the Products file instead, the invoice price would change every time the Products file was updated.

Importing and exporting data

Once you've gone to the trouble of typing data into a database, you may want to use that information with other programs. For example, you might want to *export* data from a database and work with it in a spreadsheet file. On the other hand, you might *import* data from another program to make a database file out of it.

To enable importing and exporting of data between files and programs, databases and other programs use standard data interchange formats. The most common format is *ASCII* (for American Standard Code for Information Interchange), also known as *text format*. Text format is understood by virtually every program that stores information as letters and numbers (as opposed to graphics).

Text files consist of continuous streams of letters and numbers. This kind of information is pretty useless to a database program unless it's *delimited*, or separated, into fields and records, like the data in a database file.

The most common way of delimiting information into fields is to put a space, comma, or tab between two fields' information. Records are separated from each other by carriage returns, like this:

Waters	\<TAB\>	Henny	\<TAB\>	415-555-3546	\<CR\>
Swanson	\<TAB\>	Janet	\<TAB\>	516-555-8989	\<CR\>
Wilson	\<TAB\>	Meni	\<TAB\>	510-555-7653	\<CR\>

Different database programs vary in the kinds of standard data formats they can import or export. Some programs can only work with one type of delimiter, while others can handle spaces, tabs, or commas. Programs also vary in whether they let you control which fields to export or import, and what order the fields should be in: Some programs allow you complete control, while others give you no choice at all.

These are the basic features of database programs. Beginning in Chapter 3, we'll see how FileMaker Pro uses them to manage data.

2

Installing and Configuring FileMaker Pro

- Installing FileMaker Pro
- Configuring FileMaker Pro
- Troubleshooting

The complete FileMaker Pro package includes a set of floppy disks containing many different files. In this section, we'll see how to install these on your Mac system. A hard disk is required to install FileMaker Pro, and you must have about 10 megabytes of free space on it to perform the full installation.

FileMaker Pro uses an Installer program to make installation easier. Many of the files on the installation disks are compressed, and you must use the Installer to decompress them and install them in the right places on your hard disk drive.

Installing FileMaker Pro

Using the Installer

To use the Installer, find the disks that came with your copy of FileMaker Pro and insert Disk 1 in your floppy disk drive. Double-click the FileMaker Pro Installer icon in the disk's window. The Installer's title screen appears. Click the OK button or press the (Return) key, and the Installer's main dialog box appears, like this:

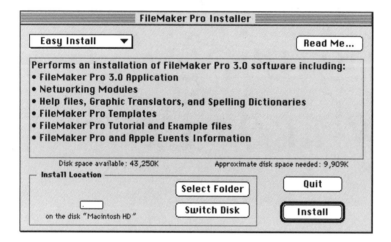

The Installer assumes you want to install all FileMaker Pro's utility, template, and tutorial files, so it presents the Easy Install option, which performs the full installation. For a full installation, you need about 10 megabytes of free space on your hard disk. The hard disk you currently have selected is named in the window as the Install Location.

If you want to perform the full installation on the current hard disk, just click the Install button or press (Return) or (Enter). The Installer will then prompt you to insert the various floppy disks in your FileMaker Pro package as it performs the installation.

If you want to install FileMaker Pro on a different disk, click the Switch Disk button until the name of the disk you want is showing in the dialog box. You can also click the Select Folder button to install the program inside a particular folder on your hard disk.

The Installer won't install FileMaker Pro on a network server if you're running it from another Mac on the network. To install the program on a server, you must run the Installer on the server itself.

The Read Me button at the top of the dialog box displays information about how to use the Installer dialog box.

Performing a partial installation

Easy Install is the simplest installation method, but you may not want to install all the FileMaker Pro files on your disk. For example, if you're an individual user and you want to conserve space on your hard disk, you probably won't want to install the FileMaker networking modules (which let you share files over a network), or you might want to omit the template, tutorial, or example files.

To install a partial set of FileMaker Pro files with the Installer, choose Custom Install from the pop-up menu in the upper left corner of the dialog box. The Installer then presents you with a list of options, like this:

```
╔═══════════════════ FileMaker Pro Installer ═══════════════════╗
║                                                                ║
║   ┌──────────────────┐                      ┌──────────────┐   ║
║   │ Custom Install ▼ │                      │  Read Me...  │   ║
║   └──────────────────┘                      └──────────────┘   ║
║   ☐ FileMaker Pro for any Macintosh                 [I]  ▲     ║
║   ☐ FileMaker Pro for this Macintosh only           [I]        ║
║                                                                ║
║   ☐ FileMaker Pro Networking Support                [I]        ║
║   ☐ MacIPX™ System Software                         [I]        ║
║                                                                ║
║   ☐ FileMaker Pro Help                              [I]        ║
║   ☐ FileMaker Pro Graphics Translators             [I]  ▼     ║
║       Disk space available: 55,040K    Approximate disk space needed: OK
║   ┌─ Install Location ──────────────────────┐                 ║
║   │                        ┌──────────────┐  │  ┌──────────┐  ║
║   │      ┌────────┐        │ Select Folder│  │  │   Quit   │  ║
║   │      └────────┘        └──────────────┘  │  └──────────┘  ║
║   │   on the disk "Macintosh HD"  ┌──────────────┐ ┌──────────┐║
║   │                               │ Switch Disk  │ │ Install  │║
║   └───────────────────────────────┴──────────────┴─┴──────────┘║
╚════════════════════════════════════════════════════════════════╝
```

As you can see, you can select only the items you want to install by clicking the checkboxes at the left, instead of having to take them all. As you select various items, the total amount of disk space you need to install them appears to the right and below the list. For a description of each item, click the Info icon at its right.

After selecting the item or items you want to install, click the Install button and follow the directions on the screen to insert the proper disks. If the Installer encounters a problem during the installation, it will display an alert message telling you what's wrong. (See *Troubleshooting* at the end of this chapter for some common problems and solutions.)

Installing more files later

Once you've installed FileMaker Pro, you can run the Installer again later and use the Custom Install option to install the template files, tutorial, examples, dictionaries, translators, or network modules.

Using spelling dictionaries with FileMaker Pro

If you're using another Claris product, such as ClarisWorks or an earlier version of FileMaker Pro, you may have a user dictionary that you've already created. This custom dictionary file is normally named User Dictionary. FileMaker Pro also uses this dictionary when you perform spelling checks. If you don't have an existing User Dictionary file, one will be installed when you install FileMaker Pro. But if you have an existing User Dictionary file, the Installer will leave it alone. (After all, you wouldn't want FileMaker's Installer replacing a User Dictionary you've spent months adding words to.)

TIP

All dictionary files (as well as most other FileMaker Pro resources) are stored inside the Claris Folder in your System Folder. You can create as many user dictionaries as you like and use them for different projects. If you have an existing User Dictionary file and you want the Installer to create a new User Dictionary file when you install FileMaker Pro, rename the User Dictionary file inside the Claris Folder before you begin the installation. During the installation, the Installer program will install a new User Dictionary file. When you run your other Claris program and want to use the user dictionary you created with it, you can use the spelling dictionary options to select the old user dictionary file.

Configuring FileMaker Pro

When you first install it, FileMaker Pro is set to use a certain amount of your Mac's available memory. If you work with very large files or share the file with many other users on a network, FileMaker Pro can slow down when running with the default memory setting. To help maintain FileMaker Pro's peak performance, you can increase the program's memory size.

The minimum memory size you can set for FileMaker Pro depends on which Macintosh and which version of the Mac system software you're using.

Setting the current memory size

Every program needs and automatically asks for a certain amount of your Mac's available memory. However, you can change the amount of memory assigned to FileMaker Pro. You may want to increase the amount of memory the program uses to speed up printing, sorting, or other operations, or you may want to decrease the amount of memory it uses so that you'll have more memory available for other tasks on your Mac.

To change the amount of memory FileMaker Pro uses, quit the program if it's running, and then switch to the Finder. Select the File-Maker Pro icon and press ⌘I to choose the Get Info command. The Mac displays an information window like the one on the right:

Double-click the Preferred size window and type in a larger or smaller number. In this case, you could type a number smaller than the preferred 5002K if you wished, but FileMaker Pro won't run properly with less than 3002K of memory allotted to it. If you increase the preferred memory amount, make sure you don't exceed the amount of memory available for programs on your Mac.

FileMaker Pro Info

FileMaker Pro

Kind: application program
Size: 2.2 MB on disk (2,306,852 bytes used)
Where: Macintosh HD : Applications : FileMaker Pro 3.0 Folder :

Created: Sat, Dec 9, 1995, 12:00 AM
Modified: Tue, Jan 23, 1996, 3:45 PM
Version: FileMaker Pro 3.0v1 (12/6/95) © Claris Corp.

Comments:

Memory Requirements
Suggested size: 5002 K
Minimum size: 3002 K
Preferred size: 5002 K

☐ **Locked**

Note: Memory requirements will decrease by 2,002K if virtual memory is turned on in the Memory control panel.

Switch to the Finder and choose About This Macintosh from the menu to see how much memory is available for programs on your Mac. To make more memory available without buying extra physical memory chips for your Mac, turn on Virtual Memory using the Memory control panel program. See your Mac's user manual for more information.

TIP

Checking the file cache size

FileMaker Pro has a file cache that helps speed up its operation, and part of the memory FileMaker Pro uses is assigned to that cache. With a larger cache, FileMaker Pro stores more of its program files and any open files in your Mac's active memory, so it can perform operations more quickly than it would if it had to read everything from the disk. When you increase the program's current memory size, you also increase its file cache size. To check the size of the file cache at any time, launch FileMaker Pro, choose the Preferences... command on the Edit menu, and then choose the Memory command from the pop-up menu at the top of the Preferences dialog box. You'll see a set of options like this:

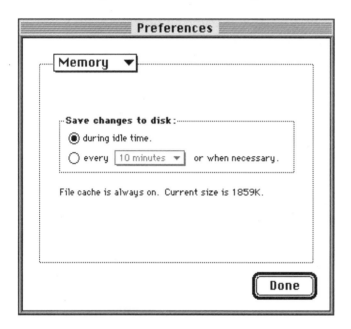

The cache size is shown at the bottom (it's 1859K in this example). For more information about the Preferences... command, see *Setting FileMaker Pro Preferences* on p. 38 in Chapter 3.

Troubleshooting

Now, let's look at some of the alert messages the Installer can display and find out what to do about them.

The Installer says there's not enough room to install FileMaker Pro.
This simply means your disk is too full to hold the files you want to install. In this case, you'll have to put FileMaker Pro on a different disk that has more room, or delete some unneeded files from the current disk to create enough

space for the installation. Click the OK button to put the message away. Then, if you have another hard disk connected to your Mac, click the Switch Disk button in the Installer dialog box and try installing FileMaker Pro there.

The Installer keeps ejecting the disk you've inserted and prompting you to insert the same disk.

As the installation proceeds, the Installer ejects each disk after it copies the files it needs and then prompts you to insert the next one. If you insert what you think is the right disk and the Installer ejects it right away, you haven't inserted the correct disk. All the disks in the installation set must have the exact names the Installer expects them to—it will eject them if they don't. So if you're using a backup set of installation disks, make sure the copy of each installation disk has exactly the same name as the original when you view the disk's icon in the Finder.

The installation fails, and the alert message contains a numbered error.

There are several numbered system-level errors that can stop the installation process. Typically, these occur because the Installer program or the installation script is damaged or because one of the files needed for the installation is missing or damaged. If this happens, you'll need to find another set of FileMaker Pro installation disks to perform the installation. Hopefully this problem has occurred with a backup set, and you can make another set of installation disks by copying the originals.

3 FileMaker Pro Terms and Concepts

- How FileMaker Pro Works
- How FileMaker Pro Manages Files
- FileMaker Pro's Operating Modes
- Using the Help System
- Setting FileMaker Pro Preferences
- FileMaker Pro's Storage Limits

Every database program has its own way of managing information. This chapter looks at FileMaker Pro's basic operating modes, features, and limitations, giving an overall perspective on how the program works. (If you're not familiar with basic database features and concepts, read Chapter 1 first.)

How FileMaker Pro Works

Like other databases, FileMaker Pro organizes data into fields, records, and files.

Making a new file

To create a file, you choose the New… command from the File menu, define the fields for storing your data, and then enter the data. When you define fields, you can choose from several different data types. FileMaker Pro lets you define *text*, *number*, *date*, and *time* fields; *container* fields (which can contain pictures, sounds, or QuickTime movies); *calculation* and *summary* fields (which contain the results of formulas); and *global* fields (which are used to show the same data in every record in a file). See Chapter 4 for more information on defining fields.

NEW FEATURE

Once you create two or more files, you can share information between them using *relationships*. See Chapter 11 for more information about relationships.

Saving your work

Unlike most Mac programs, FileMaker Pro has no Save command. Once you create a file, any changes are saved automatically. (You can control how often the automatic file-saving takes place with the Preferences… command. See *Setting FileMaker Pro Preferences*, later in this chapter.)

Automatic file-saving has its good and bad points. You can't lose work by forgetting to save changes, but you also can't recover from accidental changes by closing the file without saving them. (However, FileMaker Pro does have an Undo command that usually lets you cancel the very last thing you did.)

TIP

To protect yourself against major mistakes, use the Save a Copy As… command on the File menu to make a backup copy of important files on a regular basis. You should always do this anyway in case a file is damaged, but it also protects your data from FileMaker Pro's automatic save feature. If you make some really extensive changes to a file and then decide they were a mistake, you can go back to the last version of the file you saved as a backup.

Arranging data in layouts

When you first define the fields for a file, FileMaker Pro automatically stacks them all on top of one another in one column on the screen. But you can arrange fields to appear on the screen any way you want. Each arrangement of fields is called a *layout*, and you can have as many layouts for a file as you want. All the layouts you've set up for a file appear on a pop-up menu, so you can switch between them easily.

Layouts can be one or several screen "pages" long. Along with field names and data, layouts can include other text or graphics you create. You can create layouts from scratch, or you can choose one of several standard layout arrangements FileMaker Pro offers—such as columnar reports, envelopes, and mailing labels—and have FileMaker Pro automatically place the fields you select on a layout.

Some database programs make it difficult to change the characteristics of fields or layouts once you've defined them, but FileMaker Pro lets you do just about anything you want. When you work with layouts, you can:

- make fields larger or smaller

- add, delete, or rename fields

- change the way data inside any field is formatted (make it boldface, for example)

- change a field's data type (from text to numeric, for example)

- protect fields, so other users can't see the data

- set up special entry options to control the kind of data that can be entered in a field

- add, change, or delete graphics and text on layouts.

All these options make it easier to capture consistent, useful information and to present that information effectively.

Selecting and sorting information

FileMaker Pro's Find mode lets you select, or find, a specific group or subset of a file's records to work with, based on selection criteria you specify. For example, you might choose to work only with the records from California in an address file.

Once you find a group of records in FileMaker Pro, the records in that group, called the *found set*, are the only records you'll see on the screen. If you tell the program to print or export records, it will use only the records in the found set. When you're working with a found set, the unselected records remain in the file, but they're kept out of view and are unaffected by most functions involving multiple records.

IMPORTANT NOTE

The found set concept is crucial to understanding and working with FileMaker Pro. You can always tell whether you're working with a found set or the entire file by looking at the number of records shown on the FileMaker screen. (See *FileMaker Pro's Operating Modes*, p. 27, for more information.)

You can also sort records—within a found set or the entire file—according to the contents of one or more fields. For example, you could sort records alphabetically by the Last Name field in an address file, chronologically by the Date field in a sales order file, or numerically by the Part Number field in an inventory file.

Some database programs limit the number of fields on which you can sort simultaneously, but not FileMaker Pro. So, for example, you could sort an address file by state, and within each state by zip code, and within zip code by company name, and within companies by employee's last name.

For more information on finding and sorting information, see Chapters 7 and 8.

Checking spelling

Using FileMaker Pro's built-in spelling checker, you can check data in an individual record, a found set of records, or in all the records in a file. You can also check the spelling of text typed onto a layout.

The FileMaker Pro spelling checker is exactly like the one in ClarisWorks, so if you have ClarisWorks you already know how to use it. (In fact, if you've added words to a custom user dictionary in ClarisWorks, you can use the same user dictionary to check spelling in FileMaker Pro.)

For more information about checking spelling, see Chapter 8.

Automating FileMaker Pro operations

Most flat-file databases are designed to enable a single person to create files and then work with them. As a result, anyone who wants to work with a file needs to know a lot about using the program. But FileMaker Pro lets you automate its functions with scripts and buttons, so you can create a file that others can use easily without knowing how to use the whole program. That way, order-entry clerks don't have to become database experts just to use a sales-order system you've created with FileMaker Pro.

A *script* stores a whole series of FileMaker Pro commands; to execute all the commands you simply play the script. To play a script, the user just selects it from the Script menu or clicks a button on the screen. Scripts can store commands to select records, change layouts, sort records, import or export data, preview or print records, insert the current date or time, replace data with other data, transfer data to other programs using Apple Events, and much more.

You can create as many scripts for a file as you like. For example, one script might display an order-entry form, while another selects, displays, and prints today's invoices. You can also have a script play other scripts. You can't copy scripts from one file to another, though, because they refer to specific layouts and fields that are unique to each file. For more about using scripts, see Chapter 12.

In FileMaker Pro, a *button* is an object on a layout that can be clicked to issue a command or to execute a script. Buttons make it easy to present a command or script option right on a layout, rather than having it hidden on a menu. You can add as many buttons to a layout as will fit, and you can copy them from one layout to another, or even from one FileMaker Pro file to another. For more about buttons, see Chapter 12.

Along with scripts and buttons, FileMaker Pro has several options to help automate the task of entering data in fields.

- You can set up relationships between fields in two different files so that information like a product's price is automatically displayed in your Invoices file, even though it's actually stored in your Products file.

- You can create lookup fields that copy data from other files into the current file as you create new records (see *Using relational databases and lookups*, below).

- You can set up entry options to automatically enter data such as the current date, user name, or record number in each new record you create.

- You can also create fields that display pop-up menus or lists of data to enter, so users will have only a fixed group of data entry options and it will be impossible for them to make typing errors that result in inconsistent data.

- Finally, you can create calculation or summary fields, which perform calculations on data from other fields and display the result.

For more information about automatic entry options for fields, see Chapter 4. For information about relationships and lookup fields, see Chapter 11. Chapters 4, 15, and 16 cover calculation and summary fields.

Printing reports

Some database programs have completely separate processes for designing entry screens and designing reports. In FileMaker Pro, any layout you have displayed on the screen can also be printed.

In general, what's on your screen is also what your data will look like on paper when you print it. So, to create a printed report that looks different from your data entry layout, you must create a different layout and then make sure it's showing when you print.

**IMPORTANT
NOTE**

There are exceptions to this "what you see is what you get" rule. When you view a label layout on the screen, you see only one label instead of several labels running down and across the screen, as you would on paper. And when you sort and summarize data, summary fields don't always appear on your screen. In each of these cases, you can see what will actually print by going into Preview mode, discussed later in this chapter and in Chapter 10.

Because layouts are for printing as well as for displaying data, the screen you use to design layouts is divided into *parts* that determine which information appears where on paper. On most layouts, the standard parts are a *header*, a *body*, and a *footer*. The header and footer contain information that will appear on each page of a printed report, such as the report name and the date or a page number. The body contains data from records in the file.

To these three standard parts you can add special parts that summarize data from a group of records. In a personnel report, for example, you could create a layout that lists all the company's employees, with summary parts that subtotal the employees by division and show a grand total at the end of the report. For more on using parts in a layout, see Chapter 9.

How FileMaker Pro Manages Files

**NEW
FEATURE**

FileMaker Pro is a relational database, which means you can use it to manage information in more than one file at a time. By creating relationships between files, you can share one file's data with other files.

Using relational databases and lookups

Relational databases allow you to manage data efficiently by storing a piece of data in only one file but using it in any file you like. For example, you might have a Personnel file that contains employee names and addresses. However, you can display the employee name information from the Personnel file in a Salary file.

In relational databases, there is always one *master file*, which is the file you're currently working in, and *related files*, which are the files that actually store the information you want to display. These files are connected to each other with *relationships* that specify how the files relate to one another. A master file can have relationships with as many related files as you like.

Relationships are based on *match fields* in related files. The match field must exist in both files and must be the one used to select the desired record in a related file. For example, when you create a new record in the Invoices file, you type in a customer ID number. If that ID number matches the ID number in a record of the Customers file, the customer name and address data from the corresponding record in the Customers file is displayed in the Invoices file, like this:

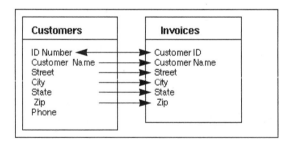

Notice that the match field doesn't have the same name in both files: It doesn't have to. You can create relationships between any two fields regardless of how they're named.

Relational database operations can also be two-way. For example, if you're viewing customer data in the Invoices file and you edit the street address, that change is also made in the Customers file so that the actual stored data is updated as well.

In addition to relational databases, you can also use lookup fields in FileMaker Pro. These are set up with the same relationships you might use in a relational database. But unlike a relational database, a lookup actually copies data from a related file into the master file, rather than simply displaying it.

We'll look closely at relational databases and lookups in Chapter 11.

Sharing files on a network

FileMaker Pro is a *multi-user* program, which means that if your Mac is on a network, FileMaker Pro files stored there can be used by several different users at once. However, all the users must have a copy of the FileMaker Pro program installed on their own Macs.

Unlike most other multi-user programs, FileMaker Pro makes a distinction between the person who originally opens a file (the *host*) and those who open that file afterward (the *guests*). The host controls other users' access to the file. For more information on sharing FileMaker Pro files, see Chapter 14.

Recycling data and file structures

FileMaker Pro offers three ways to reuse data and file structures. You can use the Save a Copy As… command to create copies of a file, with or without the data. A copy of a file without its data—called a *clone*—includes all the field definitions, layouts, and scripts you set up for the original file, so you can use them with new data.

You may also want to use data from another program's file in FileMaker Pro, or use a FileMaker Pro file's data in a different program. FileMaker Pro's Import Records… and Export Records… commands handle these exchanges of data with other programs. For example, a simple telephone list created with a word processor can be saved in a format that FileMaker Pro can import.

You can share FileMaker Pro data with other programs by exporting to a format they can use. FileMaker Pro lets you choose from the most common data formats when you export, so you can share data with most programs on the market.

Using FileMaker Pro's selection features to choose groups of records, you can export only a portion of your data. Similarly, FileMaker Pro's Import Records… command lets you use all or only part of the data from other programs by selecting only the fields whose data you want to import. And while some programs give you no control over the order in which data from other programs is imported, FileMaker Pro lets you determine which imported data goes into which field of a FileMaker Pro file.

You can also import pictures and (if you're running System 7 and have the QuickTime extension installed) QuickTime movies. See Chapter 13 for more information on importing and exporting records, and see *Importing pictures or movies*, on p. 81 in Chapter 5 for more about working with these data types.

FileMaker Pro's Operating Modes

FileMaker Pro has four basic modes of operation: called *Browse, Find, Layout*, and *Preview*. What you can do with your data and what information you see on the screen depends on which mode you're in at the time. So if you want to perform a particular operation and find that you can't, you're probably in the wrong mode. You select each operating mode from the Mode menu at the top of the screen or the mode selector at the bottom of the screen. Here's an overview of what you can do in each mode.

What each mode does

In Browse mode, you can look at records; add, delete, sort, or print them; enter or change data within specific records; add new fields to the file; or change field definitions. The group of records you can see at any given time in Browse mode depends on whether you're viewing the whole file or working with a subset of records chosen in Find mode (a *found set*). (See p. 72 in Chapter 5 for more information.)

You use Find mode to enter search criteria for selecting a particular record or group of records. Each set of criteria you enter is called a *request*. Once the program has found the record(s) that match your request(s), only that record or found set of records is available for viewing, sorting, printing, or exporting. (See Chapter 7 for more information.)

You use Layout mode to change the arrangement or format of fields on the screen, to add new fields to the file or change field definitions, to create or delete layouts, to add graphics or text, and to format printed reports and create summaries of data from all the records in a report. The way information appears on the screen in Browse, Find, or Preview mode depends on which layout you have selected at the time. You can have as many different layouts for a file as you like, and you can name them all so they're easy to distinguish from each other on a menu. (See Chapter 6 for more information.)

Preview mode is for viewing a particular layout as it would appear when printed on paper. The Browse screen usually shows how individual fields will be arranged on paper, but Preview shows exactly how data will print out, including multi-column labels, summary fields, and the margins around data on a page. (See Chapter 10 for more information.)

Each of these modes has its own screen, as you'll see in detail in later chapters. But first let's look at the elements that are common to every FileMaker Pro screen.

Common screen elements

The basic FileMaker Pro screen looks like this:

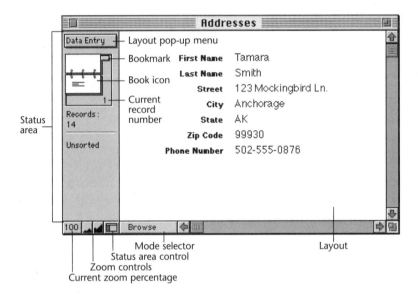

This happens to be a Browse mode screen, but the items identified appear in one form or another in every FileMaker Pro operating mode.

The *status area* on the left side of the screen contains controls you can use to move among records, select layouts, or change the way the layout is displayed. A vertical line separates it from the layout itself, which shows the file's data with the fields arranged the way you want. The specific controls available in the status area vary from one mode to another.

TIP

You can hide the status area from view to display more of a layout by using the status area control.

When you click on the *layout pop-up menu* at the top of the status area, it displays a menu listing every layout that's been created for the file. The menu always shows you the current layout name, and selecting another layout name from the menu switches you to that layout. This menu works the same in all FileMaker Pro modes.

The *book icon* lets you move from one record to another in Browse mode, from one layout to another in Layout mode, from one find request to another in Find mode, or from one page of a printed report to another in Preview mode. You just click on the upper or lower book page to move to the previous or next item.

The *bookmark* is like a scroll box—you can drag it to move quickly to a different record or layout. The bookmark is only visible in Browse and Layout modes. If your file contains more than a couple of dozen records, though, you can't scroll through individual records (or pages) with the bookmark; it will skip some records no matter how little you move it.

The *current record number* below the book icon shows the current record's position within the file or found set in Browse mode, the current request number in Find mode, the current layout number in Layout mode, or the current page number in Preview mode.

You can skip directly to a specific record, request, layout, or page by selecting the current number, typing in a new one, and pressing (Return) or (Enter). This is especially useful in Preview mode when you know exactly which page you want to see, or when you want to browse a particular record.

TIP

The area below the current record number is different in each mode:

- In Browse mode, it shows how many records are in the file, how many records are in the current found set and whether or not the records have been sorted. (If you're currently viewing all of a file's records, the area doesn't show the number found because you're not viewing a found set.)

- In Layout mode the area shows how many layouts are in the file; it also contains a selection of tools for working with layouts.

- In Find mode it shows how many find requests you currently have defined and contains a pop-up menu of operators you can use to find records based on different selection criteria.

- In Preview mode it shows the number of pages in the report you're previewing.

The buttons at the bottom of the status area that look like mountains are *zoom controls*. You click them to magnify or reduce the size of the layout. You can view the layout at 25, 50, 75, 100, 150, 200, or 400 percent of its actual size. Clicking the large mountains increases the magnification, making it easier to see precise field alignments or placements of graphic objects. Clicking the small mountains reduces the current size, so you can see an entire large layout on a small screen. The zoom controls work in all four modes.

The *current zoom percentage* shows the magnification relative to actual size. For example, *100* means 100 percent, or actual size, while *200* means the layout is magnified to twice its actual size.

TIP

Clicking on the current zoom percentage always returns the viewing size to 100 percent.

The *status area control* is a button you can click to hide the status area completely or to display it when it's hidden. When you hide the status area, the layout area expands so you can see more of the layout itself.

The *mode selector* displays a pop-up menu you can use to select Browse, Find, Layout, and Preview modes. (These commands are duplicated on the top of the Mode menu in the menu bar.)

Other than these controls, FileMaker Pro windows also have the usual Macintosh window controls such as scroll bars, scroll boxes, a size box, a zoom box, and a close box.

Using the Help System

**NEW
FEATURE**

FileMaker Pro version 3 comes with a comprehensive online Help system that explains all the operating aspects of the program, including the purpose of individual screen controls, the procedure for performing any operation, the format and purpose of each calculation function, and definitions of technical terms used by the program. All the Help features are always available whenever you're using FileMaker Pro via the 🅿 (or Guide) menu. You can get help in two ways:

1. Use Balloon Help to get brief descriptions of various screen controls and menu commands.

2. Use the Help window for more detailed information on FileMaker Pro operations.

Using Balloon Help

Balloon Help is a standard feature on every Macintosh running System 7.0 or later. To activate it, choose Show Balloons from the Guide menu. Then, when you point to various parts of your screen or to menu or command names, you'll see balloons containing explanatory text, like the following figure:

> Horizontal scroll bar
>
> Shows items not displayed in the window.
>
> To scroll a little, click a scroll arrow. To scroll a window a little at a time, click the gray bar. To scroll to another part of the window, drag the scroll box.

This balloon appears when you point to the horizontal scroll bar in a File-Maker Pro window, for example.

Balloon Help is a good way to get instant descriptions of screen items, but once you know what menus, commands, and screen controls do, the balloons can become annoying. To turn off Balloon Help, choose Hide Balloons from the Guide menu.

Using the Help window

The Help window is essentially an online version of the FileMaker Pro manual, but because it's on your computer, you can locate things in the Help system much more quickly than you can by paging through the printed manual. Display the Help window by choosing Help Topics... from the Guide menu. You'll see a window like this:

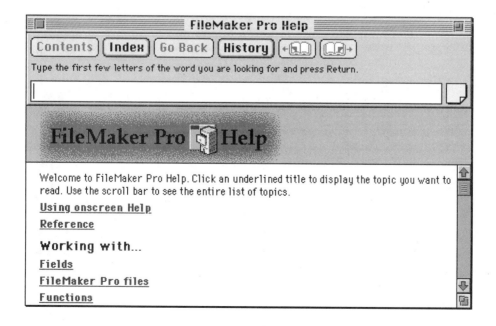

You can also display the Help window by pressing ⌘? or the Help key on a Macintosh extended keyboard.

The Help system in FileMaker Pro is presented by a completely separate program called the Claris Help Viewer. When you first open the Help system, you load the Help Viewer program, and the Help window appears. The Help Viewer program continues to run until you quit FileMaker Pro or quit the Help Viewer. Because of this, you can access the Help window much more quickly once you've opened it by simply choosing Claris Help Viewer from the Finder's Application menu.

The Help window displays a list of boldfaced, underlined topic names. When you click on a topic name, you'll see a list of subtopics beneath it. For example, if you clicked the Fields topic in the window shown above, you would see a list of field subtopics, like this:

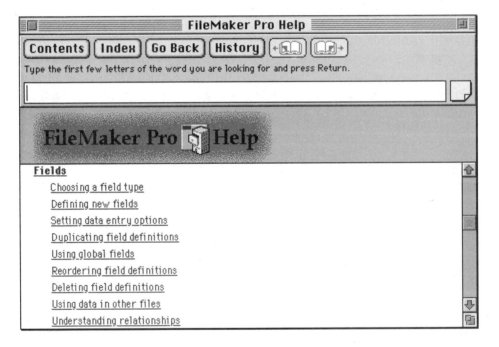

You can then click on any listing to read information on that subtopic. For example, if you clicked on *Setting data entry options* in the window above, you would see a screen like this:

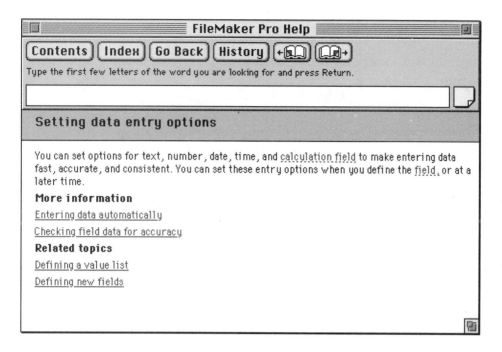

Within the text of any subtopic, you may see terms that have a solid or dotted underline. Click on a term with a solid underline and you'll be taken to another page of text on that topic. Click on a term that has a dotted underline, and you'll see a glossary definition of that term, like this:

calculation field

Calculation field
A field that stores the result of a calculation of values. You can create a formula for the calculation using functions, constants, operators, and information in other fields in the same record.

You can resize the Help window or drag it around the screen, just like a window for any other program. When the window contains more information that it can display at once, you'll see scroll bars you can use to view information that is currently hidden.

The buttons and the search box at the top of the Help window let you navigate through the Help system in various ways.

The Contents button takes you back to the top of the Help system, where you'll see the main topics are listed, as shown on p. 31.

The Index button displays the Help system's index, like this:

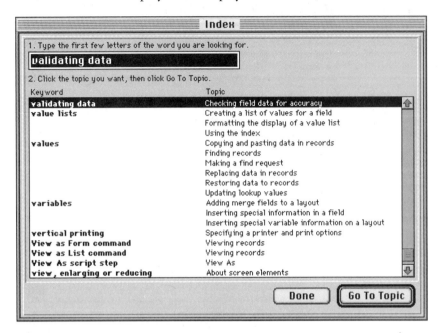

The Help system is indexed by keyword and phrases (shown at the left of the screen), each of which is associated with one or more topics (listed at the right). You can scroll the window up or down to locate a keyword and topic, or you can search for a keyword by typing it into the entry box at the top of the screen and then pressing [Return]. Once you've located and selected the keyword you want, press [Return] or click the Go To Topic button to view Help text about that topic.

TIP

You can also display the index by choosing Index... from the Guide menu.

The Go Back button takes you back to the Help screen you most recently viewed. This is useful when you read about a topic, then move on to a second topic, and then want to return to the first topic.

The History button displays the History window, like this:

In this window, you see the names of every topic you've accessed since you opened the Help window. You can go directly to any of the listed topics by double-clicking on it or by selecting it and clicking the View Topic button. Clicking the Clear button clears the history list.

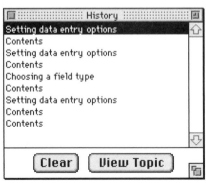

The Previous Topic and Next Topic buttons ⬅📖 📖➡ take you to the previous and next related topic in the Help system. Typically, these are the topics listed under *More information* in a topic window. For example, if we were viewing the topic shown on p. 33, clicking the Next Topic button would display the *Entering data automatically* topic.

The data entry box below the row of buttons in the Help window lets you find a topic quickly by entering a keyword or phrase, based on the list in the Index window. When you type in the first few letters of a keyword or phrase, the Help window automatically suggests the full keyword or phrase. When the keyword or phrase you want to look up is displayed in the entry box, press ⟨Return⟩ to view the topic associated with it.

Finally, the Note Pad tool 📝 lets you take your own notes and attach them to any page of the Help system. Just drag this tool onto the Help system page and release the mouse button, and you'll see a small note page with a blinking insertion point. You can then type the text of your note. The note page expands to accommodate the text as you type.

To stop entering text and return to navigating the Help window itself, just click outside the note. To move the note after you've entered text into it, point to one of its boundaries until the pointer turns into a hand icon, and then drag the pad to its new location. To delete a note, click inside the note and then choose Delete Note from the Edit menu.

Help system commands

The Help system has its own menus and commands. Here's a brief rundown of those commands and how they make it easier for you to use the Help system.

On the File menu, the Print... command prints the currently displayed topic. The Print All Topics... command prints the entire contents of the Help file (you'd better have a lot of paper for this).

On the Edit menu, the Delete Note command deletes a note you've added to a topic when the insertion point is blinking inside that note. The Copy Topic Text... command displays all the text of the current topic in a window, like this:

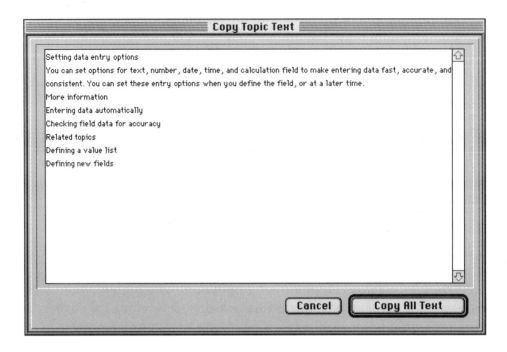

Using this window, you can select all or part of the topic's text and then copy it to the Clipboard by clicking the button in the lower right corner.

The button reads Copy Selected Text when you've selected only a portion of the text in the window.

TIP

By copying portions of Help text into a word processor document, you can create your own customized printed manuals that explain specific FileMaker Pro operations to other users.

IMPORTANT NOTE

You can't use the normal Cut, Copy, and Paste commands on the Edit menu in the Help system.

The Copy Topic as a Picture command copies the current topic as a graphic, rather than as editable text (although why you would want to do this is beyond me).

On the Find menu, the Global Find… command displays a text entry box where you can type any text string and then search for it. Unlike the entry boxes in the

Help or Index window, the Global Find... command searches all the text in the Help system, not just a list of keywords in the Index. When the entry you type is found, the Help window displays the topic where that text is located, and the text itself is highlighted. The Global Find Again command simply searches again for a text string you entered previously.

The Bookmarks menu lets you add an electronic bookmark to any location within the Help system. Once you've found a topic that you'll want to return to, you can create a bookmark at that location. The bookmark name is added to the Bookmarks menu, and when you choose that bookmark name, you're returned to the location it marks.

To set a bookmark:

1. Navigate to the location you want to mark and then choose the Set Bookmark... command. You'll see a dialog box like this:

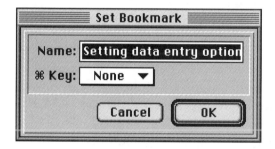

2. Type the name of the bookmark (unless you want to accept the name suggested, which is the same as the topic name itself).

3. If you like, choose a keyboard shortcut to go to the bookmark location: Just choose a number from 0 to 9 from the pop-up menu. (This lets you go to the bookmark location by pressing ⌘ and the number key you define.)

4. Press ⟨Return⟩ or click the OK button. The bookmark name is added to the Bookmarks menu.

The Edit Bookmarks... command lets you edit existing bookmarks in a dialog box like this:

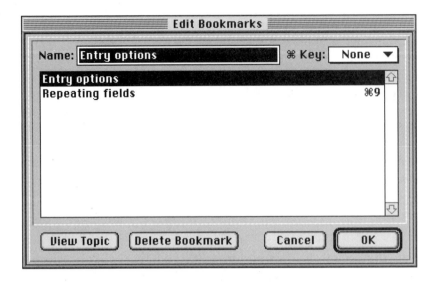

Here, you can rename, delete, or change the keyboard shortcut for any book-mark you've defined. You can also go to a bookmark's location by selecting its name and clicking the View Topic button at the bottom.

Finally, the Help system's View menu lets you determine the behavior of the window itself. The three commands on this menu are all toggles: They're either on (when checked) or off. All three commands are normally checked, or on. To turn a command off, just choose it, and the check mark disappears. The Show Notes command lets you hide any notes you've created in the Help system. Choose this command to remove the check mark from it, and all notes you've created will be hidden. The Animation Effects command causes little zooming lines to appear when you jump from one topic to another, or when a word's def-inition pops up. The FileMaker Pro Help command is just the name of the Help system file that's currently open. If you have other Claris products, you can open their Help files with the same Help Viewer (using the Open… command on the File menu), and their names will be added to the bottom of the View menu.

Setting FileMaker Pro Preferences

The Preferences… command on the Edit menu in FileMaker Pro allows you to change some of the standard operating characteristics of the program and of individual files you work with. These preferences options will be mentioned as appropriate in later chapters, but let's take a quick look at them here.

To set preferences, load FileMaker Pro and choose the Preferences... command from the Edit menu. FileMaker displays the Preferences dialog box:

```
┌──────────────────── Preferences ────────────────────┐
│  ┌─ General    ▼ ─────────────────────────────────┐ │
│  :                                                 : │
│  :   ☐ Enable drag and drop text selection         : │
│  :   ☐ Show templates in New File dialog            : │
│  :  ┌─ User Name ──────────────────────────────┐   : │
│  :  │  ⦿ System: "Charlie"                     │   : │
│  :  │  ○ Custom: [                          ]  │   : │
│  :  └──────────────────────────────────────────┘   : │
│  :   Network protocol: [ <none>     ▼ ]             : │
│  :                                                 : │
│  └─────────────────────────────────────────────────┘ │
│                                    ┌──────────┐       │
│                                    │  Done    │       │
│                                    └──────────┘       │
└──────────────────────────────────────────────────────┘
```

The options that are available depend on which command you choose from the pop-up menu at the top of this dialog box. Whenever you choose the Preferences... command, the General options are automatically selected, as shown above. To set different options, click the checkboxes or radio buttons or choose menu commands as necessary, and then click the Done button or press [Return] to close the Preferences dialog box.

NEW FEATURE

General preferences

The General preferences apply whenever you use FileMaker Pro, no matter which file you're using. Here's what the General options do.

Enable drag and drop text selection lets you use Apple's Drag and Drop technology to move text from one place to another within fields or text boxes in layouts. When you check this box, you can select text and drag it to its new location rather than cutting and pasting it.

Show templates in New File dialog tells FileMaker Pro to display a list of available template files when you choose the New command from the File menu.

When you check this option, choosing the New command from the File menu displays a dialog box like this:

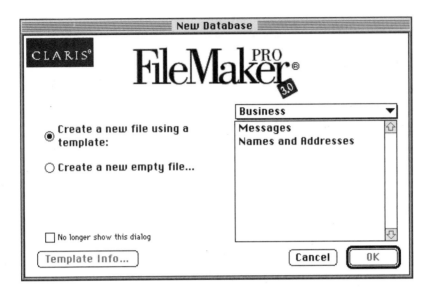

FileMaker Pro comes with a few template files that you can modify and use right away. If you don't check this option, you'll see a standard New File dialog box, as shown on p. 50 in Chapter 4.

The User Name buttons let you tell FileMaker Pro which user name you want it to supply when you share a FileMaker Pro file with others on a network. The user name is important when using FileMaker Pro's access-control features with multi-user files (see Chapter 13). Normally, FileMaker Pro uses the System name (the user name entered in the Sharing Setup control panel's dialog box), but you can enter a custom name in the box and then click the Custom button to have FileMaker Pro use that name instead.

The Network protocol pop-up menu at the bottom lets you set FileMaker Pro to use the kind of network you're working on. You can choose AppleTalk, MacIPX, or TCP/IP as the network options here.

Document preferences

Document preferences apply only to the file you currently have open. When a file is open and you choose Document from the pop-up menu in the Preferences dialog box, the options look like this:

```
┌──────────────── Preferences ────────────────┐
│  ┌─ Document ▼ ┐···························  │
│  ·                                        · │
│  · ☒ Use smart quotes (' ', " ")          · │
│  · When opening "Contacts":               · │
│  ·    ☐ Try default password: [         ] · │
│  ·    ☒ Switch to layout: [Contact Entry ▼]· │
│  ·    ☒ Perform script: [Go to Main Menu ▼]· │
│  · When closing "Contacts":               · │
│  ·    ☐ Perform script: [<unknown>      ▼]· │
│  ·                                        · │
│  ···········································  │
│                              ( Done )        │
└──────────────────────────────────────────────┘
```

If you don't have a file open when you click the Document icon, all these options are dimmed and unavailable. If you have a file open, that file's name is shown after "When opening" in the second line (it's "Contacts" here).

The Use smart quotes option tells FileMaker Pro to use curly apostrophe and quotation marks (' ', " ") instead of the straight ones your Mac normally applies. In the default state this box is checked because the curly characters look better than the straight ones.

If you plan to export data to another program, use straight marks (by unchecking the Use smart quotes option), because the curly ones use different ASCII character codes and won't produce quotation or apostrophe characters on another type of computer. (The curly characters are only recognized as such by Macintosh systems.)

TIP

The three checkboxes under When opening "Contacts" tell FileMaker Pro to perform certain operations each time you open the current file. In the default state, none of these boxes is checked, so FileMaker Pro does nothing special when you open the file. By clicking the checkboxes, you can:

• Submit a default password needed to open the Contacts file. (This keeps you from having to manually enter a password to open the file each time.)

TIP

If you've set a default password to be used when opening a file and it's no longer valid, you'll see a message asking you to enter a different one. If you want to use a different password when opening a file than the default password you've set here, hold down the Option key when opening the file. You'll see a dialog box where you can enter any password you want.

- Have FileMaker Pro switch to a certain layout you've defined (check the box and then choose the layout name from the pop-up menu).

- Perform a script you've defined (check the box and choose the script name from the pop-up menu).

In a file of business contacts, for example, you could use these options to automatically supply the password you need to access the file, switch to a telephone list layout, and run a script that automatically sorts the records by last name.

IMPORTANT NOTE

If the file is being opened by another script, the startup script you set here won't be performed.

The Perform script checkbox under When closing "Contacts" lets you have FileMaker Pro perform a particular script you've defined each time the file is closed. For example, you might have the program perform a script that saves a copy of the file as a backup each time the file is closed.

Layout preferences

NEW FEATURE

Layout preferences let you control the behavior of tools and objects when you're working in FileMaker Pro's Layout mode. The Layout preferences options look like this:

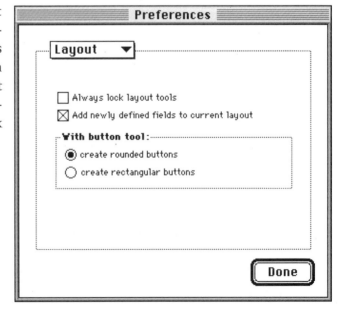

Always lock layout tools tells FileMaker Pro to keep any layout tool selected after you use it. Normally, you must select a layout tool each time you want to use it, and FileMaker Pro returns you to the pointer tool after each use. (See Chapter 6 for more on layout tools.)

Add newly defined fields to current layout tells FileMaker Pro to automatically place any new fields you define on the current layout. This is the default setting. By unchecking the box, you can set FileMaker Pro so that new fields are only added to layouts when you actually place them there. (See Chapter 4 for more about defining fields or Chapter 6 for more about placing them on layouts.)

The button tool options let you determine how buttons will look when you use the button tool to create them on layouts. You can choose between rounded and rectangular buttons by clicking either of the options here.

Memory preferences

The Memory preferences apply whenever you use FileMaker Pro. They look like this:

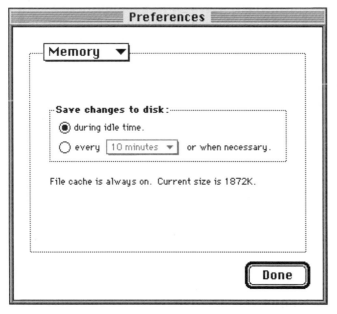

The bottom line shows the current size of the file cache, which is a portion of memory FileMaker Pro uses to temporarily store changes you've made to the file. When the file cache is full, the changes are saved to disk. If a file is set for multi-user operation or you make lots of changes to it frequently, a larger file cache can improve FileMaker Pro's performance. (See *Setting the current memory size* in Chapter 2 for more about enlarging the cache.)

The Save changes to disk buttons let you tell FileMaker Pro when to perform its automatic file-saving operations. The default choice is during idle time, which tells FileMaker Pro to save changes to your file whenever the Mac isn't busy doing something else or whenever the file cache is full. The other option lets you set a specific time interval at which to save changes, although even with this option set, FileMaker Pro will still save any changes automatically when the file cache is full or when you quit the program or close the file.

IMPORTANT NOTE

Don't use the during idle time option when you're working on battery power from a laptop computer. It will run your battery down more quickly.

Modem preferences

NEW FEATURE

The Modem preferences options let you customize FileMaker Pro to work with a particular modem. Modem and Dialing preferences are only used when you're running a script that includes the Dial Phone command. The Modem preferences options look like this:

```
═══════════════ Preferences ═══════════════
  ┌─ Modem      ▼ ─────────────────────────┐

   ┌─Modem Commands─────────────────────┐
    Setup :   │ATQ0V1E1S0=0              │
    Prefix :  │DT                        │
    Hang up : │+++ATH                    │
   └────────────────────────────────────┘

   ┌─Connection─────────────────────────┐
    Output :  │ Modem Port      ▼ │
    Speed :   │ 14400 baud ▼ │
   └────────────────────────────────────┘

            ┌─ Defaults ─┐

                              ┌── Done ──┐
```

Under Modem Commands, you can enter commands to set up your modem for proper operation with FileMaker Pro.

The Setup box is where you enter an initialization string to set up your modem. (The default setup command should work with most modems: If it doesn't, check your modem manual for the proper initialization string.)

The Prefix box is where you enter the command that precedes any telephone numbers you dial. The *DT* shown as the default is the standard Hayes command that sets your modem to dial using standard touch tones.

The Hang up box is where you enter a command to reset your modem when you disconnect. The standard command is shown here.

The Connection area at the bottom lets you choose the communications port where your modem is connected and the speed at which data is sent through your modem. Your modem (whether it's internal or external) should be connected to the Modem port, so the Output option should remain unchanged here. Set the Speed option to the maximum speed your modem will support. For example, if you have a 28,800 baud modem, choose that option from the Speed pop-up menu.

Dialing preferences

The Dialing preferences options let you set FileMaker Pro to dial special prefixes or partial phone numbers to properly connect you with another party at different locations. For example, if you're at your office, you may need FileMaker Pro to dial a 9 for an outside line before it dials the phone number. Or you may want FileMaker Pro to dial only a four-digit extension to reach someone who works in the same building with you. The Dialing preferences options look like this:

NEW
FEATURE

The At location menu lets you choose different locations so you can specify different dialing preferences. For example, your dialing needs may be different at home than at your office. You have four choices here: Office, Home, Road, and Other.

The If text begins with and Replace with boxes are where you enter specific dialing requirements. For example, a database record will show a person's phone number as 305-555-1100, but you may need to dial a 9 before this to get an outside line, or you may need to dial a 1 before the area code, or you may need to omit the area code if the number is in your local dialing area. In the If text begins with box, enter portions of phone numbers you don't need to dial, and in the Replace with box, enter the digits you actually need to dial. FileMaker Pro looks in the If text begins with boxes for the longest entry that matches the phone number in the script being performed, and then dials the digits in the corresponding Replace with box at the right.

Here's an example:

```
If text begins with:          Replace with:
┌──────────────────┐         ┌──────────────────┐
│ 520-273-         │ ----->  │                  │
└──────────────────┘         └──────────────────┘
┌──────────────────┐         ┌──────────────────┐
│ 603              │ ----->  │ 9,1603           │
└──────────────────┘         └──────────────────┘
┌──────────────────┐         ┌──────────────────┐
│                  │ ----->  │                  │
└──────────────────┘         └──────────────────┘
┌──────────────────┐         ┌──────────────────┐
│                  │ ----->  │                  │
└──────────────────┘         └──────────────────┘
```

In this case, two rows of boxes are filled in for two different scenarios. In the first row, all numbers with the area code 520 and the prefix 273 are internal company numbers, so FileMaker Pro needs to ignore the area code and prefix and dial only the last four digits of the number. In the second row, all 603 area code numbers require a 9 to be dialed for an outside line, followed by a 1 before the area code itself.

In the Always append box you enter digits you always want to dial after a phone number, such as a billing code.

FileMaker Pro's Storage Limits

NEW FEATURE

You don't hear much about FileMaker Pro's data storage limits because they're generally a lot higher than the hardware limits imposed by your Mac's memory or disk space. Files can be about 320 megabytes, and a file can have as many fields as will fit on a layout.

Maximum number of fields

Theoretically, you can create as many fields as will fit on one FileMaker Pro layout, which can be up to 110 inches across and 110 inches long. But since layouts are stored entirely in your Mac's memory while you use them, you'll probably run out of memory well before you make a layout that big and fill it with fields. Besides, a layout with more than a couple of dozen fields gets really difficult to manage.

It's better to design several different layouts for different purposes and place a few fields on each layout than it is to try to design one "all-purpose" layout with several dozen fields. When you begin adding so many fields to a file that its original purpose becomes unclear, you should create new files and build a relational database (see Chapter 11).

The amount of data each field can store depends on what type of field it is. For more information, see *Defining Fields* in Chapter 4.

Now that we've covered the basic operating concepts of FileMaker Pro, let's move onto creating files and fields in Chapter 4.

4

Making Files and Defining Fields

- Creating a New File
- Defining Fields
- About Repeating Fields
- Setting Entry Options

Before you can manage data in FileMaker Pro, the data must be stored in a file. In this chapter, we'll learn how to create new files from scratch and define fields for them. We'll cover how to enter data in Chapter 5.

This chapter explains how to create individual files from scratch. For information about relating files to one another, see Chapter 11. For more information about saving copies of existing files or importing and exporting data, see Chapter 13.

IMPORTANT
NOTE

Creating a New File

To create a new file:

1. Double-click on the FileMaker Pro icon in the Finder, and then click the New button in the dialog box that appears (or, if FileMaker Pro is already open, choose New... from the File menu). You'll see a dialog box like this:

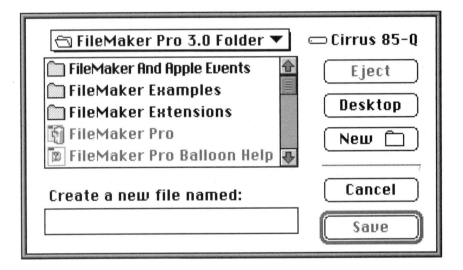

2. Choose a location for the file and type a name, then click the Save button. FileMaker Pro creates the file on your disk and displays the Define Fields dialog box.

Defining Fields

The Define Fields dialog box looks like this:

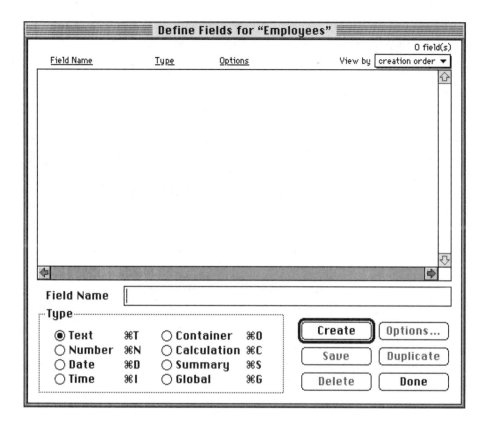

This dialog box is where you create or delete fields, specify or change field names and field data types, and set data entry options for any field.

Before you create fields, think about all the categories of information you'll need to manage your data flexibly. For example, use separate fields for first names and last names, so you'll be able to sort the file on the Last Name field, or use the First Name field's data in the greeting of a form letter.

Here's the basic procedure for creating a field:

1. Type the field name in the Field Name box.

2. Choose the field data type by clicking a button in the Type area.

**IMPORTANT
NOTE**

When you select a field type, that type remains selected. For example, if you create a Number type field and then want to create a Text type field after it, be sure to click the Text button (or press ⌘T) to change the field type.

3. Click the Create button to create the field. The field's name and type appears in the list of fields at the top of the dialog box, like this:

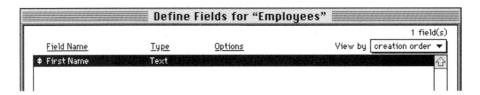

In the upper-right corner, you can see how many fields are in the file. Once a field is created, you can select it in the field list and change its name or type, set its data entry options, delete it, or duplicate it by clicking the Save, Options…, Delete, or Duplicate button in the lower right corner of the dialog box. For example, if you've spent a long time defining a complex calculation field and want to use a similar field elsewhere, you can select the original field in the field list, click the Duplicate button, and then modify the duplicate field's definition rather than defining it from scratch. Or you may want to change a field's type from Text to Number, in which case you'd select the field name in the list, click the Number button in the Type area, and then click the Save button. (For more on the Options… button, see *Setting Entry Options* on p. 64.)

You can also change the order in which fields are shown in the list by clicking the View by pop-up menu in the upper-right corner of the dialog box. You can arrange fields in the list by creation order (the default), name, or type; or you can put them in a custom order by dragging the field names up or down in the list until they're the way you want them.

4. Repeat steps 1 through 3 until you've created all the fields you need to store your data.

5. Click the Done button. The dialog box disappears and you see the Browse mode screen with the fields on it, ready for you to enter data.

Now let's take a closer look at your options when defining fields.

Field names

Field names can be up to 60 characters long. Other than length, there are no absolute restrictions on field names in FileMaker Pro. They can contain any letter, number, or symbol, and they can be more than one word long with spaces between the words. But you shouldn't use certain symbols or words if a field name will later be referenced in a calculation formula. If you do, FileMaker Pro may think that the symbols or words in the field's name are calculating instructions. The symbols and words that FileMaker Pro interprets as calculating instructions are: ,(comma), +, -, *, /, ^, &, =, ≠, >, <, ≤, ≥, (,), ", :, ::, AND, OR, XOR, NOT, and the name of any FileMaker Pro function or operator, such as SUM, AVERAGE, LOG, HOUR, or TODAY.

When you try to define a field with a name that contains calculation operators or function names, FileMaker Pro will display an error message. You can override the warning and use such a field name anyway, but if you do, you won't be able to refer to that field in calculations.

Keep field names as short and descriptive as possible. Field names often appear on layouts, and the longer they are, the more space they use. This is particularly important in columnar layouts, where you may be cramped for space across the screen or a printed page. As a rule, try to keep a field name as short as or shorter than the data it will contain. (Use "Phone" instead of "Phone Number," for example.)

TIP

Field types

As you can see in the field definition dialog box, there are eight different field types you can choose from. The standard setting is Text, because it's the least restrictive type, allowing you to enter letters, numbers, or symbols as data.

Every type of data other than pictures or sounds can be stored in a text field. So why bother with the other field types? There are several reasons:

- To store nonstandard data. To store pictures or sounds, for example, you must create a Container field.

- To restrict the data being entered to a particular type. For example, if you define a Date type field and you try to enter data that isn't a date, FileMaker Pro will alert you like this:

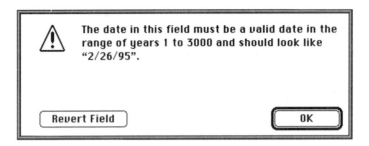

The OK button here retains the data in the field as you entered it; the Revert Field button here deletes your entry. You could enter dates in a text field, but if you do, FileMaker Pro won't alert you if you enter a date in the wrong format or with a missing number.

- To indicate a particular type of data so you can find or sort in a certain way. Text fields are sorted alphabetically and numerically, number fields are *only* sorted numerically, and date and time fields are sorted in chronological order.

- To calculate or summarize information from other fields or records. When you define a calculation or summary field, you must define the calculation you want performed, and the result of that calculation appears in the calculation or summary field. You never type information into a calculation or summary field.

- To produce the right type of data so it can be used in a calculation or summary field. For example, if you want to calculate the contents of the Quantity field by the contents of the Cost field, and the Quantity field has been mistakenly set as a Date type field, the calculation won't come out right (and the data entered into it won't look right either, for that matter).

- To enter the same data automatically into each record of a file. To do this, you create a Global field (see below).

Now that you know why there are different field types, here are the kinds of data each type of field handles:

Text fields can store any combination of letters, numbers, or keyboard symbols, up to 64,000 characters per entry (which amounts to around 20 single-spaced pages of text!). You can use FileMaker Pro's entry options to automatically enter data or to restrict entries in text fields to a certain alphabetic range. (This is explained under *Setting Entry Options*, p. 64.)

Number fields can store letters or numbers in any format, but the data must be all on one line and the maximum limit is 255 characters. Only numeric data can be indexed in number fields, so any text entered in such a field isn't indexed. Further, only the first 124 digits of a number are indexed. If you want to restrict a number field to accept only numeric entries, you can use field entry options to do so. (See *Setting Entry Options*, p. 64.)

When numeric data (such as phone numbers, part numbers, or zip codes) won't need to be calculated, it's best to store it in text fields. Fields set to store numeric data automatically eliminate leading zeroes from zip codes or other numbers.

TIP

Date fields can store only valid dates in either MM/DD/YY or MM-DD-YY format, and you must enter at least the day and month of a date for FileMaker Pro to recognize it as a date. Data in date fields is always displayed on one line.

You can set a date field's format to convert MM/DD/YY entries into a variety of formats, including those with day and month names spelled out (see *Changing Field and Object Formats* on p. 138 in Chapter 6). You can also use FileMaker Pro's entry options to automatically enter the current date when a record is created or modified, or to restrict entries to certain date ranges.

TIP

Time fields can store up to 255 numbers in any format, but the data is all displayed on one line. If you try to enter text, you'll get an alert box like the one above for date formats. The alert box suggests you use HH:MM or HH:MM:SS formats, but FileMaker Pro will allow other numeric entries. For example, you could enter just hours or minutes—it's up to you to enter data consistently. You can use FileMaker Pro's entry options to automatically enter the current time or to restrict entries to certain time ranges.

Container fields can store pictures, sounds, or QuickTime movies. You can store pictures or movies in such a field by pasting them from the Clipboard or by using the Import Movie… or Import Picture… commands on the Import/Export submenu on the File menu. To add a sound to such a field, either paste it from the Clipboard or record it directly using a microphone connected to your Mac.

NEW FEATURE

When you paste in a picture, movie, or sound using QuickTime, FileMaker Pro doesn't paste the data itself—it places a pointer in the field that indicates the location of the real picture, movie, or sound file. If you're pasting a movie or picture, FileMaker Pro also places a still representation of the picture or the movie's first frame in the field. (For more information about storing and playing back QuickTime movies or sounds, see *Importing pictures or movies*, *Playing movies*, and *Recording sounds* on pp. 81–84 in Chapter 5.)

Aside from its QuickTime support, FileMaker Pro also accepts picture data in MacPaint, PICT, GIF, TIFF, and EPS (Encapsulated PostScript) formats for picture fields.

NEW FEATURE

Global fields can contain text, numbers, dates, times, pictures, sounds, or QuickTime movies. When you store information in a global field, it's stored only once in your file, but is displayed in every record in that file. This is useful, for example, when you want to use a company logo on many different layouts in your file (such as form letters), or you want to use a particular number constant in many different calculation fields. When you create a Global field, you're asked to specify the type of field it will be, and you must indicate whether or not the field is a repeating field. (See *About Repeating Fields* on p. 62.) You can't use Find mode to search for data in global fields.

Calculation fields contain formulas that produce results by calculating data from other fields (or constants you enter as part of the formula) from one specific record. Although a calculation field contains a formula, the result of the formula is what you see in the field in Browse or Preview modes. For example, a payroll file might contain a calculation field called Gross Pay that multiplies each record's Hours Worked field by its Hourly Rate field. In this case, each record in the payroll file would represent a different employee's pay, so the Gross Pay field would show a different result in each record, depending on each employee's pay rate and hours worked.

Since calculation fields calculate and display their own data, you can't enter your own information into them. (However, you can select the result displayed in a calculation field when you're in Browse mode so you can copy it to another location, and you can type comparison information into a calculation field when you're in Find mode.)

When you define a calculation field, you must choose the data type of the field (text, number, date, time, or container). The number of characters allowed in the field depends on the format you choose. As to the formulas themselves, you can enter up to 255 characters when creating them. (See *Defining calculation fields* below for more information on building formulas.) Once the formula is defined and a calculation field is created, it calculates its result based on the data in the other fields referenced in the formula. If you change the data in fields referred to in a calculation field's formula, the formula will recalculate and the field will display a new result.

While calculation fields work within one record at a time, *Summary fields* perform calculations on all the records in a file or all the records in a found set. Summary fields are typically used in reports, where you want to calculate a total or an average of values from many records in a file. Summary fields can display up to 255 characters, all of which are displayed on one line. Like calculation fields, summary fields recalculate when you change information in a field being summarized or add new records with new data in a field being summarized. And as with calculation fields, you can't type information into a summary field in Browse mode, but you can select the result shown in a summary field and copy it to another location.

Defining calculation fields

A calculation field contains a formula and displays the result of that formula. The results shown can be numbers, dates, times, text, pictures, movies, or sounds. For example, suppose we have an Invoices file like this:

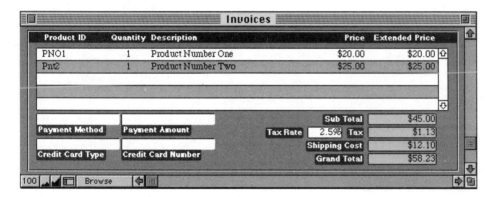

The data in the Extended Price field at the upper right comes from multiplying the contents of the Quantity field by the contents of the Price field. Let's pretend we've created the Quantity and Price fields, but the Extended Price field doesn't exist yet. To define the field:

1. Choose the Define Fields... command from the File menu to display the field definition dialog box.

2. Type *Extended Price* in the Field Name box.

3. Click the Calculation button to set the calculation field type.

4. Click the Create button. FileMaker Pro will display the Specify Calculation dialog box:

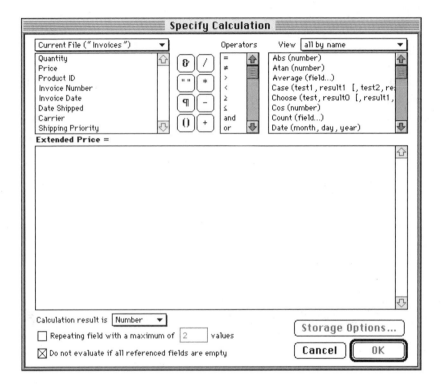

5. Double-click Quantity in the list of fields at the upper left to place it in the formula box below.

6. Click the ⊛ button or type an asterisk to indicate multiplication. The asterisk will appear next to the field name in the formula box.

7. Double-click Price in the fields list to place it in the formula box. The complete formula now looks like this:

Extended Price =
Quantity * Price

8. Select Number as the result's data type from the pop-up menu below the formula box, if necessary, so the computer will calculate a numeric result. (It's already selected in our example.)

9. Click the OK button. The field is created and you're returned to the Field Definition dialog box, where the new field name and definition appear in the list of fields.

You can enter field names and operators in formulas by typing them, if you prefer. If you do, you don't have to leave spaces between the field names and the operators.

TIP

Once you place this field in a layout, FileMaker Pro will automatically multiply the data in the Price and Quantity fields of each record and show the result in the Extended Price field in that record. If there's nothing in the Quantity or Price fields of a particular record, its Extended Price field will contain a zero or it will simply be blank, depending on which option you have set (see below).

Calculation field options

You can create simple calculation fields using the steps outlined above, and if you're familiar with mathematical or statistical functions and operators you can do much more on your own. If you need help understanding FileMaker Pro's operators and functions, Chapter 15 offers detailed descriptions. To finish off our look at calculation fields here, let's look at the options available at the bottom of the Specify Calculation dialog box.

The Calculation result is pop-up menu lets you choose the format of the result that appears in the calculation field. The choices are Number, Text, Date, Time, and Container. The format you choose is important, especially if you plan to use the result in another calculation field formula. For example, if you choose a Text result, you won't be able to use that result in a mathematical calculation elsewhere. (See Chapter 15 for more on this.)

The Repeating field checkbox lets you create a calculated field with several entries per record, to match other repeated fields in the file. For more information on repeated fields, see *About Repeating Fields* on p. 62. Some calculation functions work specifically with repeating fields. For more on these, see *Repeating Field Functions* on p. 375 in Chapter 15.

The Do not evaluate if all referenced fields are empty checkbox is normally checked. It tells FileMaker Pro to overlook the calculation if all the fields referenced in its formula are empty. This way, the calculation field will remain blank rather than show a zero. Also, since the calculation is never made, you save a little bit of computing time when your calculation field has nothing to calculate.

NEW FEATURE

The Storage Options... button lets you determine whether or not the field you're defining is indexed. When you click this button, you see a dialog box like this:

Storage Options for Field "Product ID"

Indexing improves performance for some operations like finds and supports functionality like joins and field value uniqueness at the cost of increased file size and time spent indexing.

Indexing: ○ On
           ● Off   ☒ Automatically turn indexing on if needed

Default language for indexing and sorting text: | English ▼ |

[Cancel] [OK]

Indexing is an internal operation of database programs that allows them to find unique pieces of data much more quickly. Each unique entry in a field is added to the index, along with a pointer that indicates the record or records where it's located. Rather than manually scanning all the records in the file when you search for a piece of data, the database program can consult the field's index and find out where the data is located.

Normally, FileMaker Pro automatically indexes text, number, time, and date fields as needed. (Container and global fields are never indexed.) For example, it indexes match fields used for relational operations or lookups. Using the Storage Options dialog box, you can turn indexing on for any field you create, so an index of that field is always maintained.

When you turn on indexing for several fields in a file, it will speed up data searches, but it will probably slow some FileMaker operations and it will increase the size of the file. Unless there's a particular field you know you want indexed all the time, it's best to leave indexing off for every field and let FileMaker Pro take care of this chore as it sees fit.

The pop-up menu in the Storage Options dialog box lets you choose the language by which text index entries are sorted. Normally, the default language is the same one your Mac is set to use in all its operations, but you can change the language using this menu if you like. This option is not available if you're working with a number, date, time, or container field.

Defining summary fields

To define a summary field, you must specify which field's data you want summarized and the type of summary calculation you want performed. In an accounts receivable file, for example, you might have a separate record for each invoice you send out. Each record contains a Total Due field showing the total from that invoice. A summary field could sum the amounts in the Total Due field for all the invoices in the file to show you how much you're owed altogether.

You can set up summary fields to produce grand totals for every value in the file, and you can also have them calculate subtotals for sorted groups of records. For example, if you sort a file on a Department field, you could produce summary field subtotals for accounting, marketing, production, and sales departments. If you're working with a found set of records, the summary field will only calculate the values from those records.

If you're calculating summaries by a certain field, the file must be sorted on that field for the summary calculation to occur. You must view a file in Preview mode to see summary calculation results.

IMPORTANT NOTE

FileMaker Pro offers several types of summary calculation. Here's how you define a summary field:

1. Choose the Define Fields... command from the File menu.

2. Type in a name for the new field.

3. Click the Summary button.

4. Click the Create button. FileMaker Pro displays the Summary Options dialog box, like this:

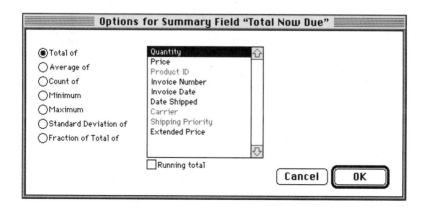

5. Select the name of the field whose values you want summarized from the list of field names in the center. (Fields that can't be summarized, such as text or container fields, are dimmed and unavailable in the list.)

6. Click a button on the left to select the type of summary calculation you want. Depending on the type of calculation you select, the checkbox option below the field list changes. Check the box to select the option for your calculation, if you like. (See Chapter 16 for details about these options.)

7. Click the OK button to finish defining the field.

For more details on creating and using summary fields, see Chapter 16. For information on placing summary fields in reports, see *Using Summary Parts* in Chapter 9.

About Repeating Fields

A repeating field contains more than one piece of data, with each piece of data in a separate row.

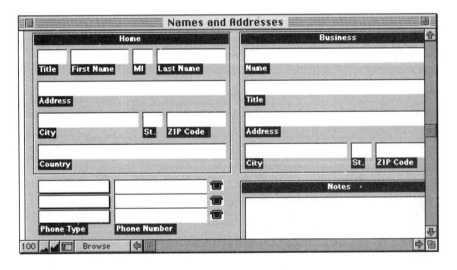

The Phone Type and Phone Number fields in the bottom left corner of this example are repeating fields. One person's address data might include two or three numbers, so the repeating fields here let you list them all in a single record. (Otherwise, you would have to create separate fields with names like Phone Type 1, Phone Type 2, and so on.)

Defining repeating fields

Except for summary fields, all FileMaker Pro field types can be set up as repeating fields. When you define a field as repeating, you must also specify the number of repetitions you want. A field can repeat up to a thousand times in FileMaker Pro.

With calculation and global fields, the option to make the field repeating appears when you first define the field.

- In a calculation field, just check the Repeating field checkbox at the bottom of the Specify Calculation dialog box, as discussed on p. 59, and then specify the number of repetitions you want.

- When you define a global field, you'll see an Options dialog box when you first create the field, like this:

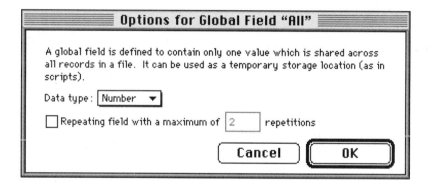

Just click the Repeating field checkbox, and then specify the number of repetitions in the box at the right.

To define a text, number, date, time, or container field as repeating (or to make a calculation or global field repeating after it has already been defined):

1. Double-click on the field's name in the Define Fields dialog box to display the Entry Options dialog box.

2. Click the Repeating field checkbox and then specify the number of repetitions you want.

3. Click the OK button.

Displaying repeating field data

Although defining a repeating field tells FileMaker Pro how many repetitions of data can be stored in a field, you must still indicate how many of those repetitions you want to display on a layout. For example, the repeating field layout shown on p. 62 displays three repetitions of its fields, but there could be many more repetitions defined for those fields. See *The Field Format... command* on p. 147 in Chapter 6 for more information.

Processing repeating field data

Since repeating fields contain more than one instance of data, FileMaker Pro deals with them a little differently than it does other types of fields. Even though each repetition of data is displayed and stored separately, the field is considered to contain the data from all of its repetitions. Here are some repeating field considerations:

• When you search for data, FileMaker Pro searches all the repetitions of data within a field, whether or not they all happen to be showing on a layout.

• When you perform a calculation or summary on a repeating field, all the field's repetitions are included in the calculation or summary.

• When you sort on a repeated field, FileMaker Pro uses only the first repetition's data as the sort key.

~~~~~~

Setting Entry Options

Once you've defined a text, number, date, time, or container field, you can use several options to automatically enter data into a field or to check manual data entries for consistency. All these options are available in the Entry Options dialog box. (Calculation, summary, and global fields have their own Entry Options dialog boxes, as shown in the sections above.) To display the Entry Options dialog box:

1. Choose the Define Fields... command from the File menu.

2. Double-click the name of the field whose options you want to set, or select the field name and click the Options... button. The Entry Options dialog box appears, like this:

Entry Options for Field "Product ID"

Auto Enter ▼

- ⦿ Nothing
- ○ [Creation Date ▼]
- ○ Serial number
  - next value [1]   increment by [1]
- ○ Value from previous record
- ○ Data [   ]
- ○ Calculated value   [Specify...]
- ○ Looked-up value   [Specify...]

☐ Prohibit modification of value

☐ Repeating field with a maximum of [2] repetitions

[Storage Options...]   [Cancel]   [OK]

There are two sets of options available, Auto Enter options and Validation options. You choose which set of options to display with the pop-up menu at the top of the dialog box.

Auto Enter options

The Auto Enter options tell FileMaker Pro to automatically enter a certain kind of data into the field in each record when it's created (or in some cases when it's modified). Depending on the option you choose, you can prohibit users from making changes to automatically entered data or you can allow them to select this data and change it (see below). The default Auto Enter option is Nothing.

The Creation Date pop-up menu displays several options when you click on it, like this:

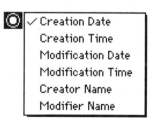

The available options on this menu depend on the data type of the field you've selected. Here, for example, if you were working with a Date type field, only date-oriented options would be available. (None of these options is available for container fields.) Here's a rundown of the various options:

Creation Date is the date on the Mac's internal calendar when the record is created.

Creation Time is the time on the Mac's internal clock when the record is created.

Modification Date is the date when the record was last modified.

Modification Time is the time when the record was last modified.

Creator Name is the name of the person who created the record (that is, the name listed in the Sharing Setup control panel of that person's Mac when the record was created).

Modifier Name is the name of the person who last modified the record (according to information stored on that person's Mac at the time).

The Serial number option lets you have FileMaker Pro enter a number automatically. This is a good way to add serial numbers or invoice numbers to new records as you make them. The next value box lets you set the value to be entered into the next record you create. FileMaker Pro will automatically increase this number each time you enter a new record; you can indicate how much the number increases by in the increment by box.

**IMPORTANT
NOTE**

FileMaker Pro adds a serial number to each new record that's created. As a file is used, sometimes new records are created and then not used, which creates gaps in the serialization sequence. You can always return to the Entry Options dialog box and reset the next value box to eliminate these gaps. If a file's numbers are really screwed up, select the number field in Browse mode, then use the Replace command on the Mode menu to replace all the field's numbers with new serial numbers. (See *Replacing data in several records at once* on p. 78 in Chapter 5.)

The Value from previous record button tells FileMaker Pro to automatically enter the value from this field in the record that was previously accessed.

The Data option lets you enter specific text or a number that you want to appear automatically in this field in every new record you create.

**NEW
FEATURE**

The Calculated value option tells FileMaker Pro to enter a value calculated from a formula you specify. When you select this option, the Specify Calculation dialog box automatically appears (see p. 58), and you can then enter a formula to be calculated. The formula must have a numeric result.

The Looked-up value option tells FileMaker Pro to enter a value looked up from another file. When you choose this option, you must choose a relationship that defines what information will be looked up from which file. If you haven't defined a relationship, you must define one. See Chapter 11 for more information on creating lookups.

Prohibit modification of value prevents the automatically entered data from being changed by anyone using the file. This is a good idea for fields that display a part number, customer number, employee number, or other data that shouldn't be changed.

The Repeating field checkbox is discussed under *About Repeating Fields* on p. 62.

The Storage Options… button lets you change the indexing option for this field. Indexing is discussed under *Calculation field options* on p. 59.

Validation options

The Validation options let you have FileMaker Pro check to make sure the correct type of data is entered in a field. (None of these options is available for container fields.) The options appear when you choose Validation from the pop-up menu at the top of the Entry Options dialog box. They look like this:

The Of type checkbox lets you enforce a data format. The pop-up menu lets you specify that numbers, dates, or times must be entered in a field. FileMaker Pro will display an alert if the proper data format isn't used.

The Not empty checkbox ensures that the field isn't left empty. If someone tries to leave a record without entering some data in this field, FileMaker Pro displays a warning message like this:

This dialog box warning can simply be put away when the user clicks the OK button, and the field will be allowed to remain empty. To prohibit a user from leaving the record with this field blank, you must also check the Strict: Do not allow user to override validation box, discussed on p. 70.

The Unique checkbox helps prevent duplicate data in fields that must be unique. If you're entering data in a Customer file and giving each customer an account number, this option makes sure no two customers are assigned the same number.

The Existing checkbox prevents new, unique data from being entered. If you want this field to only accept data that matches data in the same field of an existing record, choose this option.

The Member of value list checkbox tells FileMaker Pro to validate entries by presenting a list of options. This is handy for eliminating typing errors when a field must contain one of a handful of specific options, because you can give users a list to choose from. To define one or more value lists for this option, choose Define List… from the pop-up menu at the right. You'll see a dialog box like this:

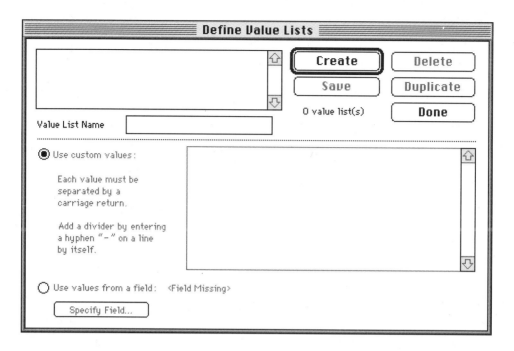

You can create several different validation lists using this dialog box. To create a new list:

1. Type a name for the new list in the Value List Name box, and then click the Create button.

2. In the box below, type in the values you want to offer (press ⌐Return⌐ after each one), and then click the Done button.

You can also specify a different field whose values you want to use as a validation list for the current field by clicking the Use values from a field button and then choosing another field. If you use this method, the value list will contain values from the field you specified.

Having created a value list, you can make it appear in Browse mode as a pop-up menu, list, or set of radio buttons or checkboxes. (See *The Field Format...* *command*, in Chapter 6, to find out how to set this up in Layout mode.) With values displayed in a list or menu, the list will appear on top of the field when you click or tab into it. See p. 74 in Chapter 5 for more information on this.

To edit the values in the list at any time, return to the Entry Options dialog box, choose the Define List... command from the pop-up menu next to the Member of value list option to display the list dialog box once again, select the name of the list you want to edit (if you've defined more than one), and then make the changes you want. You can also use this procedure to specify a different field as the source of the value list.

The In range checkbox lets you specify a range of text, numbers, dates, or times that will be accepted in the field. If users enter a value in this field that isn't within the range you've specified, FileMaker Pro displays a warning. They can still enter data outside the range, but only by overriding the warning by clicking OK.

The Validated by calculation checkbox lets you check a numeric entry for validity by calculating it. When you click the Specify... button, you see the Specify Calculation dialog box, where you can define the calculation formula you wish to use for validation (see p. 58).

The Strict: Do not allow user to override validation checkbox tells FileMaker Pro to prohibit users from ignoring field validation criteria. Unlike the warning shown on p. 68, which alerts users to the problem but allows them to override the warning, this option forces users to comply with the validation requirement. If a user creates a new record and then attempts to view a different record without satisfying this field's validation criteria, FileMaker Pro displays a message identifying the field and requiring the user to fill it in. This is a good idea, for example, when you want to make sure that a number entered in a certain field falls within a particular range when a record is created.

If you're sharing the file on a network, you can also prevent others from changing a field's values by denying them access to that field. See *Controlling Access to Files*, p. 322 in Chapter 14.

The Display custom message if validation fails checkbox lets you display a message of your own composition when a data entry doesn't match the validation requirement you have set. When you check this option, you can then enter the custom message in the box below.

As you can see, FileMaker Pro offers dozens of field definition options you can use to make data entry much simpler and prevent errors.

You can define new fields or change field definitions at any time in FileMaker Pro, whether you're in Browse, Find, Layout, or Preview mode.

As you create files of your own, you can experiment with these options to see just how useful they are. If you have problems when defining calculation or summary fields, see the *Troubleshooting* sections in Chapters 15 and 16. If you have trouble when defining relationships or lookup fields, see Chapter 11.

5 Entering and Changing Information

Once you've created a file and defined fields, you're ready to start entering data. You use FileMaker Pro's Browse mode whenever you want to add, view, change, or delete data or records. You can also add or delete fields or change field definitions in Browse. In this chapter, we'll take a closer look at these activities. (You can also sort records or check your data for spelling errors in Browse—these functions are covered in Chapter 8.)

~~~~~~

The Browse Screen

When you first create a new file, FileMaker Pro automatically arranges fields in a Standard layout like the one below, with the field names to the left. It shows you this layout in Browse mode, with a new, blank record on it and the first field selected, like this:

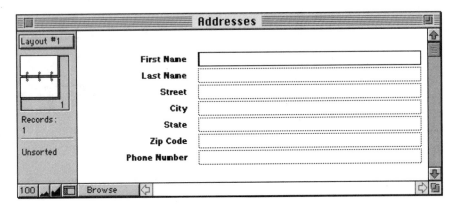

Whenever you select a field to enter information into it, all the fields on the layout are outlined.

Notice that the status area indicates there's one record in the file, and that the file is unsorted. To get to Browse from one of the other modes, choose Browse from the Mode menu or from the mode selector, or press ⌃⌘Ⓑ.

The layout pop-up menu shows this layout name as "Layout #1." FileMaker automatically gives layouts numbers unless you name them otherwise. Since this layout was automatically created, the default name is given. To change the layout name, use the Layout Setup... command in Layout mode. See *Changing layout names, printing order, and margins* on p. 114 in Chapter 6.

The status area also tells you when you're working with a found set of records. *Browsing* a group of records means having that set of records available to work with, whether it's a found set or the entire file.

~~~~~~

Entering Information

There are several ways to enter information into fields in Browse mode:

- You can type data into fields with the keyboard.

- You can select a predefined value with a menu, list, button, or checkbox.

- You can paste data, pictures, or sounds into fields from the Clipboard or with the Paste Special submenu.

- You can have FileMaker Pro automatically replace existing data with new data you enter in a dialog box using the Replace… command.

- You can have FileMaker Pro automatically place data in a field via a lookup.

- You can import a movie or picture into a container field with the Import Picture… or Import Movie… commands.

- You can place a sound in a container field by recording it with a microphone while the field is selected.

Let's look at these options individually.

Entering data from the keyboard

With the file in Browse mode and a field selected, you're ready to type in your data. If you make a mistake typing, use the [Delete] key or other standard editing tools to make the change. To move to the next field, just hit [Tab], or click in any field you want to select.

You can't use [Tab] to move into calculation, summary, or global fields because information is entered into them automatically.

**IMPORTANT
NOTE**

Be sure to use [Tab]—not [Return]—to move to the next field. If you press [Return] in a text field or enter more information than will fit on one line, the field will expand to show another line, covering up whatever's below it, like this:

First Name	
Last Name	
Street	20332 Whispering Sycamore Drive,
City	Apartment 23B
State	

As explained in Chapter 4, number, date, and time fields can only be one line long. Pressing [Return] when you're typing in them just makes the Mac beep.

**IMPORTANT
NOTE**

As soon as you select another field, though, the expanded text field will shrink back to its original size, hiding the data in the expanded area, like this:

First Name	
Last Name	
Street	20332 Whispering Sycamore Drive,
City	
State	

Later, when you're looking through your records, the field will show only as much of its data as the current field size permits. If a field is fairly small but it contains a lot of data, you may not realize you've got a second, hidden line of data in text field. The data is still stored in the field, but you have to select the field to make it visible. (Of course, you can always resize a field so it shows more than one line of data at once — see *Moving Objects in Layouts* on p. 119 in Chapter 6.)

Pressing ⎆Tab⎆ moves you from one field to the next from top to bottom, and from left to right on the layout. Pressing ⎆Shift⎆⎆Tab⎆ moves you from field to field in the opposite direction. If you have the bottom field selected in a new file's layout and you press ⎆Tab⎆, you'll select the top field again. (In some simple database programs, pressing ⎆Tab⎆ in the last field of a record moves you to the next record in the file, but not in FileMaker Pro.)

TIP If the order in which ⎆Tab⎆ moves between fields is inconvenient for what you want to do, you can set your own tab order — see *Changing the Tab Order* on p. 151 in Chapter 6.

Using a list, menu, or button to enter data

As explained in Chapter 4, you can use entry options when defining a field so predefined values are stored for that field. By formatting the field properly in Layout mode, you can cause FileMaker Pro to display those predefined values in several different ways (see *The Field Format... command* on p. 147 in Chapter 6). Once you've defined a value list and formatted the field to display it, the field will show a series of options when you tab into it or select it.

Depending on how you format the field, the predefined field values will appear as a pop-up list, on a menu, or as a set of checkboxes or radio buttons. Here's how to enter the data in each case.

A *pop-up list* looks like this:

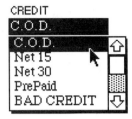

To locate an item on the list, type the first few characters of the data you want to select, and then press the ⎡Return⎤ key to enter it into the field and put the list away.

To select and enter one of the items on a pop-up list quickly, just click on the item you want.

TIP

If you want to enter a value that's not on the list, press the ⎡Esc⎤ key or click in the field again to make the list disappear, then enter the data using the keyboard.

A *pop-up menu* looks like this:

To select an item, drag down the menu to select the item, and then release the mouse button to enter the data and put the menu away. Notice the Other... item at the bottom of this menu. You can add this item to a pop-up list or menu when you want to give users the option to enter data that's not on the list or menu. When you choose this option, you get a dialog box where you can enter any text or value you want. (There's also an Edit... option you can add to a list or menu. When users choose it, they can edit the contents of the field's value list. See p. 148 in Chapter 6.)

A set of *radio buttons* looks like this:

Here, you simply make the choice you want by clicking the appropriate button. With radio buttons, you can click only one button in the set.

A set of *checkboxes* looks like this:

REFERRAL
☐ Newspaper Ad   ☒ Word of Mouth
☐ Radio Ad   ☐ Other
☐ Yellow Pages

You can click in one or more checkboxes. If you do, the data for each checkbox will be entered in the field in the order you selected them, separated by carriage returns.

Copying, cutting, and pasting data in fields

If you need to enter the same information in several records (or in more than one field in the same record), it's faster to copy and paste the information than to type it in each time. To copy or move data from one field to another:

1. Select the field from which you want to copy.

2. Drag the insertion point across all the data in the field, or press ⌘A to choose Select All from the Edit menu.

3. Press ⌘C (to copy) or ⌘X (to cut) the data from the field.

4. Select the field where you want to enter the data, and press ⌘V to paste it there. (If the field is in another record, you'll have to select that record first.)

If you want to enter the same information in the same field in several records in a row (the same postal abbreviation in a State field, for example), there's an even easier shortcut: Select a field and press ⌘'. FileMaker Pro will copy the data from the same field in the last record you worked with and paste it into the current record. If you want to copy this information and then tab to the next field automatically, press Shift ⌘'. (See *Viewing and Selecting Records* below for more on moving from one record to the next.)

The ⌘' shortcut always copies field data from the last record you displayed, which isn't necessarily the previous record in the file. For example, if you made a change in record 2 and are now working in record 8, using ⌘' will copy data from the same field in record 2, not from record 7.

IMPORTANT NOTE

Using the Paste Special submenu

Another way to enter certain kinds of data into a selected field is to use the Paste Special submenu. This submenu includes a collection of commands that appear when you hold down Paste Special on the Edit menu. You can select these commands from the Paste Special submenu, but it's easier to use their keyboard shortcuts. Here are the shortcuts, commands, and what they do:

Keys	Command	Pastes In
⌘I	From Index...	data you select from the index it displays (see below)
⌘'	From Last Record	data from same field of last record selected
⌘-	Current Date	current date
⌘;	Current Time	current time
Shift⌘N	Current User Name	the user name currently set for your Mac (see p. 40 in Chapter 3)

As mentioned in Chapter 3, FileMaker Pro automatically creates an index for each field, containing every unique entry you store in that field. You can use this index to avoid mistakes or inconsistency when entering data you know has been entered in a field before—just display the index, and then paste your entry directly from it.

When you press ⌘Ⓘ (or choose the From Index... command on the Paste Special submenu), the selected field's index is displayed in a box on the screen, like the one to the right:

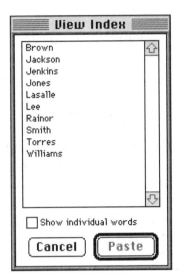

(In this case, the index is of the Last Name field in an address file.) Just double-click on the entry you want or select it with the arrow keys and press Return to paste it into the selected field.

NEW
FEATURE

The Show individual words option at the bottom changes the index list so it breaks up phrases into individual words when a field's index contains phrases. If this entry were checked, for example, the index entry "Los Angeles" would be shown in the window as the two entries, "Los" and "Angeles", on separate lines.

There are six other Paste Special commands that are active only in Layout mode—they're discussed in *Adding special text or symbols* on p. 132 in Chapter 6.

Replacing data in several records at once

Sometimes you'll want to change a field entry in several records at a time. For example, maybe you've changed a part number in your inventory, and you want to change the number where it occurs in every record in your sales order file. FileMaker Pro's Replace... command replaces the contents of a selected field in every record being browsed with whatever new data you specify.

The Replace... command always affects the selected field's data in every record in the current found set. So to replace information in only a certain set of records (those with a particular part number on them, for example), you must first select the records you want to change, so that they're the only ones available on the Browse screen. Otherwise, the replacement will affect every record in your file. Here's the procedure for changing a part number in our hypothetical situation:

1. Use Find mode to select all the records containing the part number you want to change. (See Chapter 7 for more information on selecting records.)

2. Select the field containing the old part number.

3. Type in the new part number.

4. Choose the Replace… command from the Mode menu, or type ⌘=. You'll see a Replace dialog box, like this:

```
┌─────────────────────────────────────────────────┐
│░░░░░░░░░░░░░░░░░░░ Replace ░░░░░░░░░░░░░░░░░░░░░│
├─────────────────────────────────────────────────┤
│                                                 │
│  Permanently replace the contents of the field  │
│  "Item Number" in the 5 records of the current found │
│  set?                                           │
│  ◉ Replace with: "B1200"                        │
│                                                 │
│  ○ Replace with serial numbers:                 │
│      Initial value:  [1              ]          │
│                                                 │
│      Increment by:   [1              ]          │
│                                                 │
│      ☐ Update serial number in Entry Options?   │
│                                                 │
│  ○ Replace with calculated result:  [ Specify… ]│
│                                                 │
│                    ( Replace )  [ Cancel ]      │
└─────────────────────────────────────────────────┘
```

The top button is automatically selected, because FileMaker Pro proposes replacing data in the found set of records with the part number you've typed into the field.

5. Click the Replace button to make the change in every record in the found set.

If you prefer, you can use the Replace… command to replace a field's contents with serial numbers. This is handy when you want to place consecutive numbers in a field such as Record Number or Invoice Number. In this case, you would click the Replace with serial numbers button in the Replace dialog box and then enter starting values and increments in the boxes below it. When you replace a field's contents with serial numbers, you can also update the serial number in that field's entry options. (See *Setting Entry Options* on p. 64 in Chapter 4 for more information on field entry options.)

Finally, you can also replace a field's data with a calculated result. When you choose the Replace with calculated result option, you'll see the Specify Formula dialog box, where you can enter a formula to calculate the result you want as a replacement. See p. 57 in Chapter 4, or Chapter 15, for more information on specifying formulas. Any formula you specify for a replacement must have a numeric result.

Entering data with lookups

You can have FileMaker Pro automatically insert data into a field or fields by looking it up from another file. You'll find detailed information about defining lookups in Chapter 11. For now, it's enough to understand how the procedure works in general and how data is treated in Browse mode when you use this option.

To enter data using a lookup, you use the field's Entry Options dialog box to select a lookup file and define the nature of the lookup. Once you've set up a lookup for a field and typed in the appropriate information in a match field, FileMaker Pro automatically opens the lookup file, locates the record with the same information in the appropriate match field, and then copies data from the source field in the same record into the lookup field in the current file. (For more information on how this works, see Chapter 11.)

A lookup occurs only once, however. If you find it necessary to change the information in a lookup file at a later date, the information that was previously placed into a lookup field in records you've already created may become out of date. For example, suppose you've set up a lookup in a file called Payroll so that entering an employee number tells FileMaker Pro to find that employee number in a file called Employees and transfer data from the Salary field there into the Salary field in the Payroll file. If you change the salary information in the Employees file, the salary information in the Payroll file won't match anymore.

Fortunately, you can tell FileMaker Pro to perform the lookup again at any time, updating any information that may have changed in the lookup file. Here's the procedure:

1. Select the records in which you want to update lookup information by using the Find command, if necessary.

2. Select the match field that normally triggers the lookup whose data you want to update.

3. Choose the Relookup command from the Mode menu. FileMaker displays a warning asking you if you really want to update the data from the lookup file, like this:

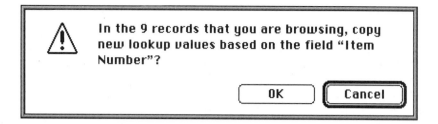

In the 9 records that you are browsing, copy new lookup values based on the field "Item Number"?

OK   Cancel

4. Click the OK button to replace the existing data in the lookup fields affected by this match field with the new information in the lookup file.

You can't undo the Relookup command, so make sure you want to update the data before you do it.

IMPORTANT NOTE

You must select the match field that triggers the lookup before choosing the Relookup command. If your file contains several different match fields that trigger different lookups, and the data in the lookup file has changed in many different fields, you will have to select each different match field, one at a time, and perform the relookup in each of them to update the information.

If you find it necessary to use the Relookup command frequently, consider using a relational database instead, so data updated in the related file will always be updated in the current file.

TIP

Importing pictures or movies

If you're working in a container field, you can copy pictures, movies, or sounds into it using the Cut and Paste commands. You can also import movies or pictures using the Import Picture... and Import Movie... commands on the Import/Export submenu on the File menu. Just select the container field where you want to place the picture or movie, choose the Import/Export command from the File menu and then choose the Import Picture...or Import Movie... command on the submenu. FileMaker Pro will display a directory dialog box where you can select the picture or movie file you want to import.

If you're importing a picture, you'll see a dialog box like the one on the following page:

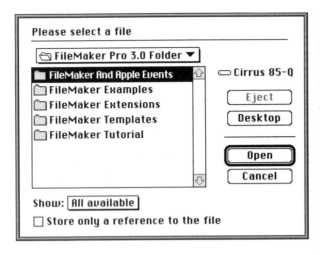

Select a picture file from the list, and click the Open button to import it. The picture will appear in the field you've selected. When you use this method, a copy of the picture is placed in the current field. If you check Store only a reference to the file at the bottom, FileMaker Pro stores only a pointer to the original file: You'll see the file in the field, but it won't actually be stored in the field. Pictures take up lots of disk space, so the Store only a reference to the file option is a good choice if you use lots of pictures and you want to keep the file size small.

If the list in the directory dialog box is long, you can choose a specific picture format from the pop-up menu below the list, and then the list will display only pictures in that format. FileMaker Pro can import pictures in EPSF, GIF, MacPaint, PICT, and TIFF file formats.

If you're importing a movie, you'll see a dialog box like this one:

Here, you have the option to view a preview of the movie. When you click the Show Preview box at the bottom, you see the first frame of any movie you have selected at the left.

To import the movie, just select its name, and click the Open button. The movie will appear in the field you've selected. With movies, FileMaker Pro always stores only a reference to the movie rather than the entire movie file.

Playing movies

When you import a movie into a container field, FileMaker Pro stores a reference to the movie file and the movie's first frame. When you play the movie, FileMaker Pro locates the movie file and plays it, displaying the results in the container field.

To play a movie in Browse mode, click on the movie's field. A set of controls appears below the movie, like this:

Then click the play button (the right-pointing triangle) at the left. When a movie is playing, clicking the play button again stops it. As the movie plays, the slider below it moves to indicate, proportionally, how much of the movie has played. You can also select and drag the slider to jump to any specific frame in the movie. By clicking the two arrows at the right, you can move through the movie forward or backward a frame at a time.

IMPORTANT
NOTE

The movie file must be stored on a disk that's available to FileMaker Pro at the time you click on the movie's representation, or else you won't be able to play it. If the movie isn't available, you'll see a warning message.

Once you've imported (or pasted) a movie or picture into a field, you can remove it by selecting the field and pressing the Delete key or choosing Cut from the Edit menu.

Recording sounds

To record sounds directly into a container field, you must have a microphone connected to your Mac and you must have the Sound control panel program from Macintosh System 7 or later installed in your System Folder. (The Sound control panel is a standard part of System 7 and later versions of the Mac system software.) To use a microphone, you must be using either a Mac with a built-in microphone or one equipped with a microphone port and an external microphone.

Once you have your Mac set up properly for recording sounds, double-click on the empty picture/sound field where you want to place the sound. The Sound Record dialog box will appear, like this:

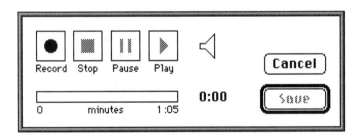

Click the Record button to begin recording the sound. As you record, the elapsed time in seconds will show in the bar below the buttons, so you can see how long your sound is. (Sound takes up a lot of disk space, so every second counts.)

You can stop, pause, or play back the sound you've recorded by clicking the corresponding control buttons. Once you've recorded a sound, you can cut, copy, or paste it from the original field to another field or to the Clipboard or Scrapbook.

Viewing and Selecting Records

Depending on the layout you've selected, FileMaker Pro presents records in Browse mode either individually (one per screen) or as a list. (See Chapter 6 for a complete description of the various types of layouts.) A new file uses only the standard layout FileMaker Pro creates automatically, which shows you one record per screen. (See the example at the beginning of this chapter.) When you use a single-record layout, the record that is currently on the screen is automatically selected.

To move from one record to the next, click the upper or lower pages in the book icon, drag the bookmark to move through the file, or select the record number at the book's lower right corner and type the number of the record you want to view. To view parts of a record that don't fit on the screen, use the window's scroll bars to view other parts of the record.

Once you've created a list or columnar report layout, you can see several records on the screen at once, each in its own row, like this:

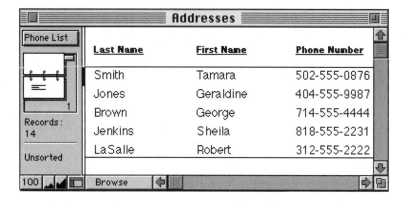

The record that's currently selected is indicated by the black selection bar at the left edge of the layout. (In the example above, the top record on the screen is selected.) You can select any other record on the screen by clicking on it or by using the book icon. You can also scroll the layout window with the scroll bars to view other records below or other fields to the right. (See Chapter 6 for information on creating columnar report layouts.)

Scrolling to view another record in a columnar report layout doesn't select it. You must always click on a record or use the book icon to select a record.

Viewing a found set

If you've used Find mode to select a certain group of records, you'll only be able to view that found set of records on the Browse screen. The status area will tell you if you're browsing a found set by showing you the number of records in the set, like this:

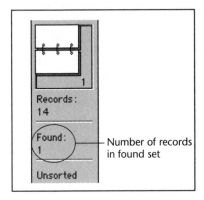

Number of records in found set

To make all records in the file available after you've been working with a found set, choose Find All from the Select menu.

Changing from form view to list view

Normally, a single-record layout like the one at the beginning of this chapter shows one record at a time, and you view different records by clicking the book icon. In a columnar report, like the one on the previous page, you can see several records at a time, and you can view others by using the book icon or scrolling the layout window. However, you can change from single-record to multiple-record views, or vice versa, with one simple command.

To change from a single-record view to a multiple-record view, choose View as List from the Select menu. If you're viewing a single-record layout, you'll now be able to view the file's records as a continuously scrolling list by using the scroll bar on the right of the screen. Remember, though, using the scroll bar this way to bring a record into view doesn't select the record; as with a list layout, you must click on the record itself to make it active for entering or changing data.

To change from a list view to a single record view, choose View as Form from the Select menu. When you do so, the layout will show only one record at a time, rather than a list of records. When you're viewing a columnar or list layout as a form, you must use the book icon to move from one record to the next, and the record currently showing on the screen is automatically selected.

NEW FEATURE

Adding Records

To add new records to a file, choose New Record from the Mode menu or type ⌘N. As soon as you add a new record, the number of records shown in the status area changes. New FileMaker Pro users often think a blank record is just an "entry screen" that will disappear when you close the file. But actually, each new, blank record you create is added to the file, and FileMaker Pro stores every new record you add whether or not you enter data there.

Whenever you add a new record, FileMaker Pro puts it at the end of the file. For example, if you have an alphabetic list of names, you can't just add a record for Bennett between existing records for Baker and Brown. The only way to display records in alphabetical order, if they're not all entered that way in the first place, is to sort the file alphabetically. See Chapter 8 for more on sorting.

To find and eliminate blank records you may have created accidentally, choose the Find All command from the Select menu to display all the file's records, sort the file on any field, and then drag the bookmark all the way up so you're displaying the first record in the file. Since FileMaker Pro sorts blank fields before any data, the blank records will be the first ones in the file. You can then select them one at a time and press ⌘E to delete them. This technique works best if you're working with a columnar report layout, so you can see several records on the screen at once.

TIP

Duplicating records

If you want to add a new record in which many of the fields will contain the same information as the current record, you can duplicate the current record and then modify the fields that contain different data. In a file of business contacts, for example, you may want to enter several records in which the company name and address are the same and only the first and last names and phone numbers are different. It's easier to duplicate one record and just change the names and phone numbers than to retype the same company name and address over and over.

To duplicate a record, make sure the record you want to duplicate is selected on the Browse screen, and then choose the Duplicate Record command from the Mode menu, or press ⌘D. A copy of the record will appear and will be selected on the Browse screen. As with any added record, the duplicate will be added as the last record in the file.

Omitting Records

As explained in Chapter 3, you can work with all the records in a FileMaker Pro file, or you can work with a subset, or found set, of records that you've selected using Find mode. In either case, you can eliminate records from the group you're working with using FileMaker Pro's Omit and Omit Multiple... commands.

Omitting a record doesn't delete it from the file, it simply removes it from the set of records being browsed. If you're working with a found set of records when you omit a record, the Found number shown in the status area will decrease. If you're viewing all the file's records when you omit one, the Found number will appear in the status area, to indicate that you're no longer viewing all the records.

To omit one record:

1. Select the record using the book icon or by scrolling to it and clicking on it.

2. Choose the Omit command from the Select menu or press ⌘M. The record will disappear from the current set of records being browsed.

To omit more than one record:

1. Select the first record in the group you want to omit.

2. Choose the Omit Multiple... command from the Select menu or press ⌘Shift M. FileMaker Pro will display a dialog box like this:

FileMaker Pro

Starting from the current record, omit [1] records.

Cancel   Omit

3. Type the number of records you want omitted.

4. Press Return.

FileMaker Pro will omit the selected record and all records following it until the number of records you've specified have been omitted.

Before omitting multiple records, be sure the records you want to omit are arranged in consecutive order and that the first record you want to omit is selected. Remember, records in an unsorted file are arranged in the order in which they were created, so you may need to sort the records to arrange them properly before omitting them.

IMPORTANT NOTE

If you want to swap groups of records—so the ones in the current found set are hidden and the ones currently hidden become available—choose Find Omitted from the Select menu.

To return to viewing all the records in a file after you've been using the Omit or Omit Multiple commands, choose Find All from the Select menu.

Deleting Records and Data

To remove data from a file, you can delete it from a specific field, delete a single record, or delete a whole group of records.

To delete data from a field, select the data inside the field and press the Delete key. If you delete something by mistake, choose Undo Delete from the Edit menu or press ⌘Z immediately. The Undo command usually undoes the very last thing you did, and it will undo deletions like this.

To delete a record, select the record on the Browse screen, and then choose Delete Record from the Edit menu or press ⌃⌘E. You'll see an alert message asking you to confirm that you want to permanently delete the record, like this:

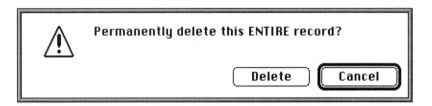

Click the Delete button to confirm the deletion.

IMPORTANT NOTE

Once you delete a record or records from a FileMaker Pro file, there's no way to undo the deletion—it's gone forever unless you have a backup copy of the file.

To delete a group of records, choose Delete All from the Mode menu. You'll be asked to confirm the deletion, and the alert box will show how many records you're about to delete. Click Delete to delete the records.

When you use the Delete All command, you delete every record that's currently available for browsing. If that happens to be every record in the file, you'll delete every record. If it's a subset of the file's records, you'll delete just that subset. The only way to control which records are deleted using the Delete All command is to use Find mode to create a found set that contains only the records you want to delete (see Chapter 7).

Adding or Changing Fields

You always define a few fields when you first create the file, but often you find you need new fields after you've been working with a file for a while, or you may want to change the name, data type, or entry options for an existing field. You can use the Define Fields dialog box at any time to add new fields, delete fields, change field types, or reset field entry options.

The basic procedure for adding fields is the same as when you make a new file— you choose Define Fields… from the File menu and then specify a field name and data type. This process is described in detail in Chapter 4.

When you add a field to an existing file, FileMaker Pro automatically adds the new field to the bottom of the current layout. (That is, unless you've set FileMaker Pro's preferences so this doesn't happen—see *Layout preferences* on p. 42 in Chapter 3.) You probably won't want a new field added to your layouts where FileMaker Pro puts it, and you may not even want it on the current layout at all. To move or eliminate a field from the current layout, use Layout mode (see *Moving Objects in Layouts* on p. 119 in Chapter 6).

IMPORTANT NOTE

The procedures for changing the name, type, and entry options of an existing field are pretty similar:

1. Choose Define Fields… from the File menu to display the Define Fields dialog box.

2. Select the field's name in the list of fields.

3. Make whatever changes you want: Edit the field's name in the Name box, click a new Type button, or click the Options… button to display and change the field's entry options.

4. Click the Save button to change the definition.

    If you've changed the field's type or certain entry options, you'll see an alert box asking you to confirm that you want to make the change, because some changes affect your options for working with the field's data. For example, changing a date field to a text field will mean you can't sort the file chronologically on this field anymore.

5. Click the Done button to close the field definition dialog box.

Changes to field definitions can't be undone with the Undo command. But if you change a definition and then want to go back to the old definition, you can just choose Define Fields… again and reset the field's definition back to the way it was.

Troubleshooting

In this section, we'll look at some common problems you may encounter in viewing, entering, or changing data, and see how to solve them.

Viewing data

The field you want to look at is missing from the Browse window.

If you're viewing a record and you can't find a particular field, you may need to scroll the layout to bring the field into view. If you can't find the field after scrolling to all areas of the layout, the field isn't on the layout you're currently viewing. Look for the field on a different layout.

1. Use the scroll bars at the right and bottom of the Browse window to see if there are more fields on the current layout than can fit on one screen. If scrolling doesn't bring any more fields into view, you'll have to select a different layout to see the field you're looking for.

2. Click on the layout pop-up menu above the book icon and choose another layout. Keep choosing different layouts until you find one that contains the field you want.

Parts of two records appear on the screen at once.

Sometimes, you're viewing records in a single record layout and you can see parts of two records, like this:

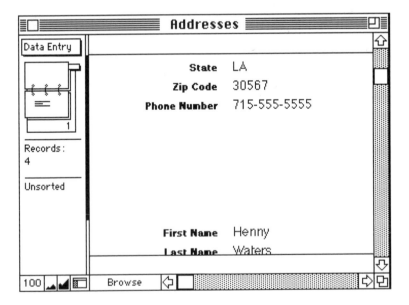

This happens because you have the View As List command selected on the Select menu. Choose View As Form from the Select menu, and FileMaker Pro will only display one record on the screen at a time.

You can't find a record you're looking for.

If you know a certain record is in your file but you don't see it when you browse through the records, it's because you're currently viewing a found set that doesn't contain the record you're looking for. Choose the Find All command from the Select menu to make all the file's records available for browsing, and then you'll be able to locate the record. Also, you can use the Find mode to locate the specific record you're looking for (see Chapter 7).

The Browse screen only shows one label on a multiple-column label layout.

When you view a multiple-column label layout in Browse mode, only one label's information appears on the screen, like this:

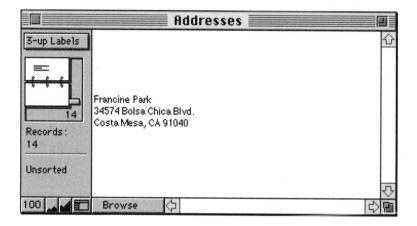

This is just the way FileMaker Pro works. In multicolumn label layouts, it only shows the contents of one label on the Browse screen. To see the labels as they will print on a page, choose Preview from the Mode menu, which displays the labels as they'd appear if printed.

Information appears very slowly in certain fields of the layout when you choose Browse mode.

FileMaker Pro is usually pretty fast, but if the file you're viewing is stored on a network server, if the file contains fields from a file stored on a network server, or if the layout you're viewing contains summary fields, it may take a while for some of the data to appear in fields. If a summary field has to show a total that's calculated from every record in a 5000-record file, for example, it will take a few seconds for FileMaker Pro to calculate and display the result.

A calculation field displays a question mark instead of the result you expect.
This usually happens when the calculation formula can't be performed or when it causes FileMaker Pro to divide by zero. Check the formula itself to make sure the calculation is correct.

Blank records appear in the file.
Remember that when you choose New Record from the Mode menu, FileMaker Pro creates a record and stores it, whether or not you enter any data into it. As a result, it's easy to create blank records and forget they're there. When you come across one, just delete it by pressing ⌘E.

Entering and changing data

FileMaker Pro won't let you select a field or type in it.
If FileMaker Pro won't let you type in a field, it's probably because the field contains a calculation or summary formula. You can't type new data into a calculation or summary field, and you can't tab into such a field. However, you can click on a calculation or summary field and select the data it contains (and then cut or copy it to the Clipboard). You can easily see whether it's a calculation or summary field by choosing the Define Fields… command from the File menu and checking the field's type.

It's also possible that the field's entry options are set to prohibit you from entering data into the field. See *The Field Format… command* on p. 147 in Chapter 6.

A field is blank or dimmed and you can't type in it.
This means either the field has access restrictions or it's in a part of the layout that doesn't permit data entry.

If you're sharing the file over a network and the password you used to open the file doesn't give you access to a particular field, the field will be dimmed or covered up on the layout. Contact the person who manages this file to find out whether you can gain access to the field. (For more on accessing shared files, see Chapter 14.)

Another possibility is that the field is in the layout's header or footer part. If even a tiny portion of a field overlaps into a header or footer part, the field won't be accessible for entering data. Fields must be entirely in the body part of the layout for you to enter data there. (See Chapter 9 for more on parts.)

A set of entry options doesn't appear when you select a field.
If a field has been defined with a list of entry options, but the list doesn't appear when you select the field, it's because the field hasn't been formatted to make the entry options appear. (See *The Field Format… command* in Chapter 6.)

A set of entry options doesn't contain a particular option.

If a selected field displays a set of entry options but the option you want isn't on the list, you either have the wrong value list selected for that field, or you need to edit the value list with the Define Fields... command:

1. Choose Define Fields... from the File menu.

2. Select the name of the field whose options you want to change.

3. Click the Options... button to display the Entry Options dialog box.

4. Choose Validation from the pop-up menu in the upper left corner of the Entry Options dialog box to display the validation options. Look at the pop-up menu next to the Member of value list checkbox. The list name on that menu should be the name of the value list you want to use for this field. If it isn't, choose the name of the correct value list and then skip to step number 8.

5. If the correct value list is showing on the pop-up menu, choose Define value lists... from the pop-up menu next to the Member of value list checkbox in the Entry Options dialog box to display the Define Value Lists dialog box.

6. Select the name of the value list that should be defined for this field.

7. Add the new option you want to appear on the list, then click the Done button.

8. Click the OK button to exit the Entry Options dialog box, and then click the Done button to exit the Define Fields dialog box. The new entry option will now appear when you select this field in Browse mode.

FileMaker Pro tells you a file is missing.

If your file contains fields from a related file or fields that perform lookups from a related file, FileMaker Pro must be able to locate the related file to display that field's data. If the related file has been renamed, moved, or deleted, FileMaker Pro won't be able to find it and will display a message like this:

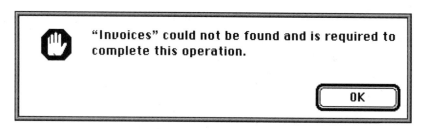

Click the OK button. FileMaker Pro will display a directory dialog box you can use to find and open the related file. If you've moved the file to another folder, you'll be able to locate and open it here.

If you've renamed the file, click the Cancel button in the directory dialog box. You'll need to either rename the file again with its original name or redefine the relationship with that file so it contains the correct file name (see Chapter 11).

FileMaker Pro says the file is damaged.

When you're viewing or changing records, you may see an alert message that says the file is damaged. Such damage also shows up when data from existing records appears and then disappears from the screen in Browse mode. This kind of damage happens most often to files that are shared by many users on a network. You need to correct the damage as soon as possible, because if it gets worse you may not even be able to open the file in the future. To repair the damage:

1. Close the file immediately. If it's a shared file, ask other users to close it, too.

2. Open the file again. FileMaker may display a message saying that the file needs minor repairs and asking whether you want to repair it. Click the OK button to repair the file. This should solve the problem.

If you keep having problems with the file, you'll have to recover it using FileMaker Pro's Recover... command. See *Recovering Damaged Files* on p. 297 in Chapter 13 for more information on this.

FileMaker Pro asks you to insert a disk when you click in a container field.

QuickTime movies and pictures compressed with QuickTime aren't stored directly in a database file, so the disk containing the actual picture or movie file must be available to your Mac when you click in the container field. If the disk isn't available, you'll see a message asking you to insert the necessary disk.

If you click Cancel to put that message away, you'll see another message that says FileMaker Pro can't play the movie, like this:

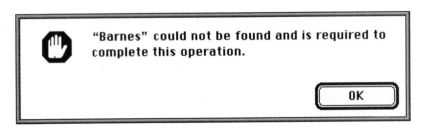

Click the OK button to put the alert away. You'll then see a directory dialog box, where you can navigate to the file and open it.

If you use compressed pictures or movies in your database file, make sure you store the picture or movie file in the same location as your database file. And remember to move all the files when you copy or move your database to a new location.

6 Arranging Information in Layouts

- The Layout Screen
- Using the Layout Tools
- Making New Layouts
- Moving Objects in Layouts
- Using Layout Helpers
- Adding Fields
- Adding or Changing Layout Text
- Using Graphics
- Changing Field and Object Formats
- Changing the Tab Order
- Sliding Objects
- Creating Non-Printing Objects
- Troubleshooting

You use FileMaker Pro's Layout mode to set up the way fields, text, and graphics will appear on the screen and in printouts. You can also use Layout mode to design reports that summarize data from many records, to create onscreen buttons that execute commands when you click them, or to create *portals* that contain a series of fields from a related file.

In this chapter, you'll learn how to:

- create new layouts or delete existing ones

- rearrange fields on a layout

- add text and graphics to a layout

- change field attributes such as text and number formatting or the appearance of automatically entered data

- control the order in which fields are selected when you press ⸢Tab⸥ in Browse mode

- control whether fields slide together to eliminate gaps on layouts when certain fields don't contain data.

We'll discuss summary reports in Chapter 9, and how to make buttons in Chapter 12.

The Layout Screen

To get into Layout mode, choose Layout from the Mode menu or mode selector, or press ⸢⌘L⸥. The screen that appears is like a drafting table where you can design how the screen will look in the other three modes. It shows the field names, sizes, and positions, but not the data they contain. Instead, it treats the fields, text, and graphics on the layout as graphical objects. You can select any object on a layout and move it, resize it, or change its format as you would in a graphics program such as Adobe Illustrator.

In a simple address file, the Layout screen looks like this:

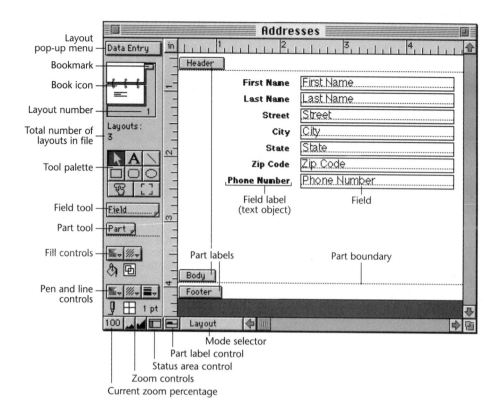

On the right side of the screen, the fields and field names are shown where they will appear in Browse, Find, and Preview modes. Instead of data, the fields contain their own names, underscored by *baselines* (these become important when you move fields—see *Rearranging and resizing objects*, p. 119). The field labels next to the fields are text objects.

FileMaker Pro shows field names inside fields in Layout mode, because field labels can be edited so that they're different from the actual field names. For example, the field called Phone Number could have the label "Phone."

TIP

The layout is also divided into *parts*—a header, body, and footer in this example—which are indicated by *part labels* and separated by dotted *part boundary* lines. (For more on parts, see Chapter 9.)

IMPORTANT NOTE

Notice that the rulers at the top and left sides of the layout don't start at zero. That's because the layout represents a printed page, and the layout normally shows only the part of a page that you can actually print on. The portions of the layout and rulers that don't show (at the left in this case) are the page margins. The page margin sizes are determined by the options you've chosen with the Layout Setup… command. Before you begin rearranging items on a layout, set the margin options the way you want them. (See *Changing layout names, printing order, and margins* on p. 114.)

TIP

To see the right edge of the layout's printable area, scroll to the right and look for the vertical dashed line.

In the status area at the left are the tools you use to select different layouts and change the way they look. The layout pop-up menu lists all the layouts defined for this file and shows the name of the layout you're currently viewing.

TIP

If you don't specifically name each layout you create, FileMaker names them Layout 1, Layout 2, and so on. For information on naming a layout, see *Changing layout names, printing order, and margins* on p. 114.

The number below the book icon shows the number of the current layout. Below that, you see the total number of layouts in the file. There's no limit on the number of layouts you can have for a file.

There are three ways to switch layouts:

- Click on the book icon or drag the bookmark.

- Select the layout number, type a different number, and press Return.

- Use the layout pop-up menu.

Using the Layout Tools

Below the layout pop-up menu are various tools for modifying the look of a layout. Here's how they work.

The tool palette

The tools in the tool palette enable you to add, select, move, resize, or modify text, graphic objects, buttons, and portals on a layout.

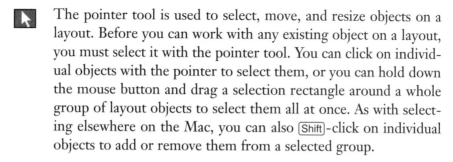

The pointer tool is used to select, move, and resize objects on a layout. Before you can work with any existing object on a layout, you must select it with the pointer tool. You can click on individual objects with the pointer to select them, or you can hold down the mouse button and drag a selection rectangle around a whole group of layout objects to select them all at once. As with selecting elsewhere on the Mac, you can also [Shift]-click on individual objects to add or remove them from a selected group.

The text tool creates or edits field names or other explanatory text on a layout. When you have the text tool selected, the pointer becomes an I-beam. You can click on the layout to create a small text box, and then begin typing the text you want to add. You can also use the text tool to draw text boxes of specific sizes before you begin typing. Once you type text on the layout and click away from it, the text becomes an object which you can then move, delete, reformat, or resize. You can also edit existing text objects (such as field labels) with the text tool—see *Editing and reformatting layout text*, p. 134.

The line tool draws straight lines on a layout. Just point to the place where you want a line to begin or end, and then hold down the mouse button and drag to draw the line. When you release the mouse button, the line will be complete.

You can draw straight lines at any angle you like. To automatically create lines that are straight up and down or straight across the layout, hold down the [Shift] key as you draw the line. To create lines at perfect 45-degree angles, hold down the [Option] key as you draw the line.

TIP

The rectangle, rounded rectangle, and oval tools draw those shapes on a layout. Just hold down the mouse button, drag in any direction to create the shape, and release the mouse button to complete it.

Hold down the [Option] key while you draw to create perfect squares with the rectangle tool or perfect circles with the oval tool.

TIP

See *Creating graphics on a layout*, p. 136, for more details about using the graphical object tools.

The button tool adds buttons to a layout. When you choose this tool, you hold down the mouse button and draw the outline for a button on the layout just as you would draw a rectangle. When you release the mouse button, however, you see the Specify Button dialog box, like this:

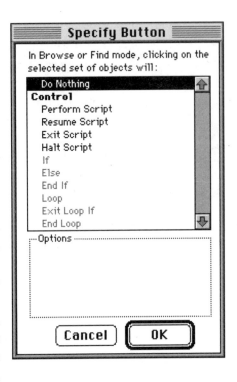

You use this dialog box to define the action that the button will perform when it is clicked in Browse mode. After you define the button's action, you return to the button shape on the layout. The text cursor is blinking there, and you can either type a name for the button or paste a graphic icon onto it from the Clipboard.

IMPORTANT NOTE

Once you type a name for a button and click away from the button, you can't change the button name. The only ways to alter a button name are to paste a new text box on top of the button's existing name (so the original name is covered up) or to delete the button and add a new one with a different name.

The button shown here is used to switch from a data entry layout to a telephone list layout. For complete details about buttons, see Chapter 12.

The portal tool adds portals to a layout. A portal contains one or more fields from a related file. After you choose this tool and draw a portal shape on your layout, you'll see the Portal Setup dialog box, like this:

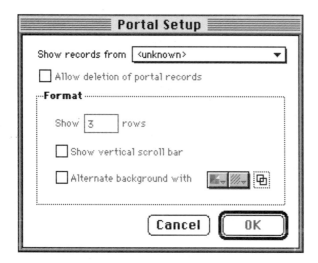

Here, you choose a relationship to specify which field or fields you want to appear in the portal. You can also set options for the number of rows you want displayed for that field or fields, whether or not the portal has a scroll bar and whether or not the rows show an alternating color or pattern background on the layout. A finished portal might look like this:

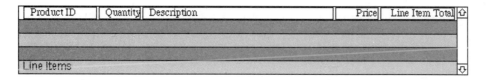

In this case, the portal contains five fields (Product ID, Quantity, Description, Price, and Line Item Total). It has been formatted to show five rows of these fields with a vertical scroll bar, and it has a green fill color for alternating rows. For more information on portals, see Chapter 11.

After you use any tool in the tool palette, the pointer tool is automatically selected again as the default.

- To reselect the last tool you used (instead of the pointer tool), press Enter.

- To lock a tool so it remains selected after you use it, double-click on it when you first choose it.

- If you want FileMaker Pro to always keep the last tool selected (instead of reselecting the pointer each time), choose the Preferences... command from the Edit menu and check the Always lock layout tools box in the Layout preferences (see p. 42 in Chapter 3).

The Field and Part tools

The *Field tool* lets you add fields to the layout. You can't define new fields with this tool—you can only add previously defined fields to a layout. To add a field, select the Field tool and drag it to the place on the layout where you want the field to appear. A list of currently defined fields will appear, and you can then select the name of the field you want to add to your layout. (See *Adding Fields*, p. 130.)

The *Part tool* is for adding new parts to the layout. To add a new part to the layout, just drag the Part tool to where you want the new part to appear, then select the type of part you want from the list that appears. (See Chapter 9 for more about parts.)

The fill, pen, and line controls

These controls allow you to set the pattern, color, and line thickness of objects you're about to draw or of objects that are currently selected on a layout. To use them, point to the control you want and hold down the mouse button. A palette of options will appear, and you can then drag the pointer to the option you want to select.

 The fill controls let you select the fill pattern or color of a selected object. You can set fill colors or patterns for rectangles, ovals, buttons, portals, or fields on a layout. When you click one of these controls, you see a palette of color or pattern options, and you select the option you want. The box next to the paint can below these controls shows the currently selected color or pattern.

 The first two pen controls let you change the color or pattern of a selected line, including lines that make up the boundaries of ovals, rectangles, buttons, or portals. The line control at the far right lets you set the width of the line that borders a selected object on your layout. Clicking this icon displays a selection of line widths. Beneath these controls, the box next to the pen icon shows the current line thickness, color, and pattern; the number to the right of that box indicates the current line thickness in pixels.

To change the line color of a field's border, you must use the Field Borders… command and dialog box (see p. 150).

IMPORTANT NOTE

Try clicking these icons and selecting different patterns, colors, and line thicknesses to see how they work. If you select an object on the layout and then set the controls, they'll affect the selected object. If you set the controls first and then create a graphic using the tool palette, the object will have the color, pattern, and line width you previously selected.

The zoom, status area, mode selector, and part label controls

The zoom and status area controls and the mode selector at the bottom of the Layout screen work the same way as they do in Browse or Preview modes. (See *FileMaker Pro's Operating Modes*, p. 27 in Chapter 3.)

The part label control changes the part labels in the layout from horizontal boxes (as shown at the beginning of this chapter) into vertical boxes, like this:

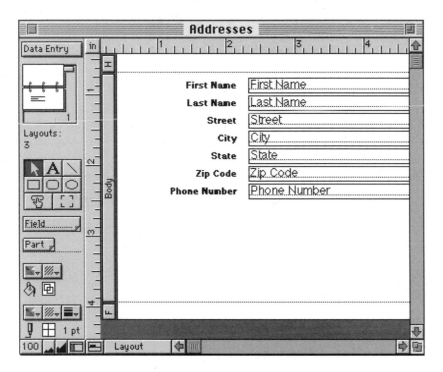

Displaying part labels vertically helps you work with areas at the left edge of a layout that might be covered up by horizontal part labels.

~~~~~~

Making New Layouts

You can add new layouts any time you're working in Layout mode. Here's how:

1. Choose New Layout… from the Mode menu or press ⌘N. You'll see this dialog box:

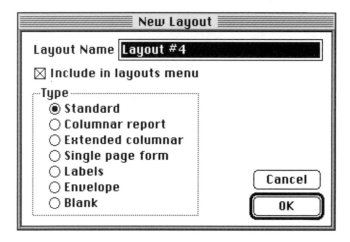

2. FileMaker Pro always gives layouts numbers, but you can type a different name for the layout into the Layout Name box.

TIP   It's a good idea to name every layout so you can tell which is which by their names on the layout pop-up menu.

3. If you don't want the layout's name added to the layout pop-up menu, uncheck the Include in layouts menu option at the top of the dialog box.

4. Click the button for the type of layout you want, and then click the OK button. The new layout will be displayed on the screen.

This is the basic procedure, but it varies slightly depending on which type of layout you choose.

Layout types

Let's look at the types of layouts you can create.

A *Standard layout* is like the one FileMaker Pro automatically creates for a new file. All the fields in the file are stacked on top of each other in a single column on the screen, like the examples shown earlier in this chapter. With a standard layout, the layout form is only as long as it needs to be to make room for all the fields in the file. In our sample file, the body of the layout form is less than 4 inches high, but layouts can be up to 110 inches high.

A *Columnar report layout* lets you choose which fields you want, and then lays the fields out side by side in one row across the screen. This type of layout is best when you want to view or print lots of records on a single screen or page.

When you choose a columnar report layout and click the OK button, FileMaker Pro presents a dialog box like this:

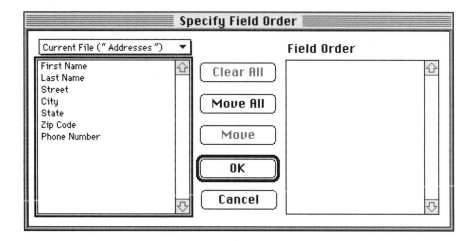

Here you select the fields you want in the layout from the list on the left, clicking the Move button after each one, to create a list in the Field Order box on the right. (You can also double-click field names to move them.) The order in which you move the fields to the Field Order box is the order they'll appear in on the layout, from left to right.

If you make a mistake, you can select a field's name in the Field Order box and click the Move button to remove it from the list. To erase the entire Field Order list, click the Clear All button.

Notice the pop-up menu at the top of this dialog box. Using this menu, you can add fields from a related file to your layout by selecting existing relationships or by specifying new relationships (see Chapter 11).

**IMPORTANT
NOTE**

Once you've selected the fields you want included in the layout and clicked the OK button, FileMaker Pro displays the layout. If we chose the First Name, Last Name, and Phone Number fields from the list above, for example, the layout would look like this:

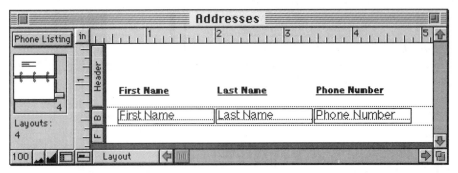

**IMPORTANT
NOTE**

If you've selected more fields than will fit inside the layout's margins in a columnar report, FileMaker Pro will wrap the fields around into a second row.

Choosing the columnar report layout type puts the field names in the header part of the layout, so they'll appear as column headings on every page of a report. The fields themselves are in the body part of the layout. Records will be listed one after the other, running down the screen or page. (The footer in this layout is blank.)

The *Extended columnar layout* is like the columnar report layout, except that FileMaker Pro doesn't create a second row of fields if you've selected too many fields to fit within the layout margins. Instead, the fields stretch across the layout beyond the right margin (up to 110 inches wide), and you have to manually resize fields to fit within the layout margin. An extended columnar layout is handy if you want to see lots of fields on one line, if you have a big screen for your Mac, and if you don't care whether all the fields will fit within the layout's margins for printing.

The *Single page form layout* is like a standard layout, with one record per screen, but with no header or footer. It's automatically made at least one full page high, so there will always be page breaks between records that print out (unless you print with a different page setup than the one the layout was created with). All the fields in the file are automatically laid out in a single column (one on top of the other), but even if there are only two fields in your file, the body of the layout form is a full page high. This type of layout is particularly useful with forms or other full-page documents.

The *Labels* option is for laying out fields for printing onto mailing labels. When you choose this type of layout and click the OK button, FileMaker Pro first needs to know what size labels you'll be printing on. It displays a dialog box like this:

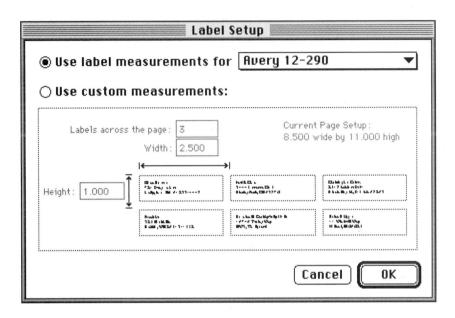

FileMaker Pro assumes you'll be printing your labels on one of a few dozen stock label sizes, so the Use label measurements for button is automatically selected, and you can choose the label stock number from the pop-up menu at the right.

If you don't know the label stock number or are using labels whose number isn't listed on the menu, click the Use custom measurements button, and then enter the label height and width measurements in the boxes below. When you specify a custom measurement, the lower part of the dialog box becomes active, and you can see the current page setup. This page setup is the overall size of the form on which labels are fed through your printer. For example, most label stock for laser printers is 8½ by 11 inch sheets, no matter how many individual labels are on the sheet itself. If the pages that hold your labels are a different size than this, use the Page Setup... command on the File menu to change the page size.

In the label diagram in the lower part of the dialog box, notice that the height and width measurements run from the left edge of one label to the left edge of the next label, rather than indicating the size of one label by itself. Be sure to enter these measurements accurately or FileMaker Pro won't lay out the fields to print properly on each label.

TIP

To change the label measurements, click in the Label size boxes (Width and Height) and type the measurements you want.

Once you've specified the label size, click the OK button. FileMaker Pro displays the Specify Layout Contents dialog box, like this:

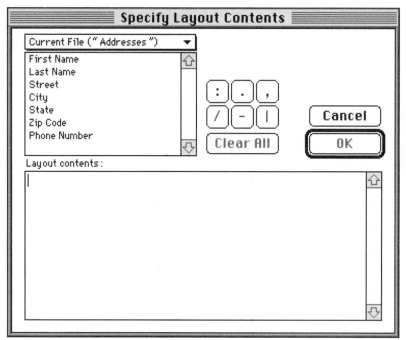

To add fields to the label layout, double-click on the field names you want. Merge field markers appear in the Layout contents box below, as you select them. Merge field markers are different from fields on layouts, because text inserted before or after merge field markers automatically reformats according to the size of data in the merged fields. (With normal fields on other layouts, the data shown in a field is always the size of the field itself.)

Because the Specify Layout Contents dialog box uses merge field markers, you use the Layout contents box to arrange the fields as you want them to appear on the label, and to add punctuation or text as well. For example, you would use spaces to separate merge fields, add carriage returns to put merge fields on different lines in a label, and type colons, periods, commas, spaces, dashes, or slashes between merge markers to punctuate your data. A typical address label might be arranged like this:

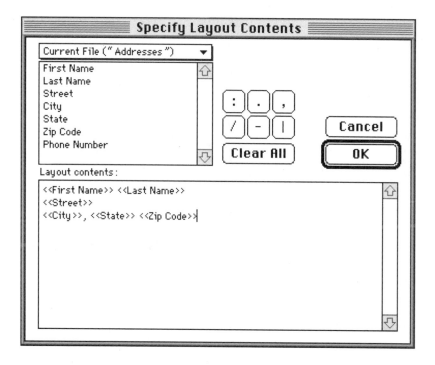

To create this arrangement:

1. Double-click on the First Name field's name to add it to the Layout contents box, press the [Spacebar], and then add the Last Name field.

2. Press [Return] to move to the second line of the address, and add the Street field.

3. Press [Return] to move to the third line of the address, and add the City field.

4. Press [,] and [Spacebar] and then add the State field.

5. Press [Spacebar], and then add the Zip Code field.

You can also click the punctuation character buttons in the Layout contents box instead of typing these characters from your keyboard.

TIP

You can freely edit the information in the Layout contents box, so if you make a mistake and want to add an extra space or carriage return, just click inside the Layout contents box and do it.

When you have the Layout contents box looking the way you want, click the OK button to display the layout itself. A newly created label layout looks like this:

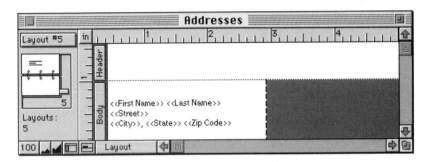

Notice that even though this layout specified three columns of labels on a page, FileMaker Pro only displays fields for one label in Layout mode. If you switch to Browse mode, you'll also only see one label's data at a time. To see 2- or 3-across labels as they will appear when printed, view the layout in Preview mode.

TIP

Normally, labels are printed in order from left to right across the page in the first row, and then down from one row to the next. You may want your labels to print in order down columns rather than across rows. If so, see *Printing data in columns* on p. 117.

An *Envelope layout* arranges fields as if for a label, except the overall size of the layout and the position of the fields on it match a standard business envelope. As with a label layout, FileMaker Pro uses merge field markers in creating envelope layouts. You select the fields you want to include on this layout and arrange along with appropriate punctuation with the Specify Layout Contents dialog box.

TIP

Because of their formatting flexibility when used with text, merge fields are ideal for creating form letters. See *Creating Form Letters* on p. 217 in Chapter 9.

A *Blank layout* is just that: a totally blank form, with header, footer, and body parts sized to fit on your screen. FileMaker Pro doesn't place any fields on the form, so it's up to you to add fields and place them where you want them.

Changing layout names, printing order, and margins

The Layout Setup... command lets you change a layout's name, the order in which data is printed on a page, and the page margins. When you choose Layout Setup... from the Mode menu, FileMaker Pro displays the Layout Setup dialog box, like this:

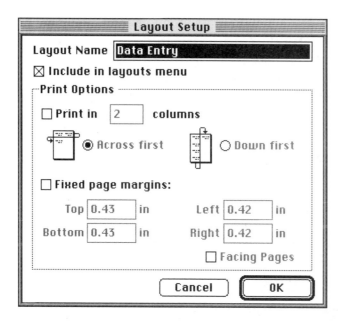

The layout name is selected when you display this dialog box, and you can type a new one. You can also choose whether the name is included in the layout pop-up menu by clicking the option below the Layout Name box.

To change the way records are printed on each page, click the Print in *<number>* columns option and then specify the number of columns you want printed. Once you've done this, you can specify whether you want data printed in order across the rows or down the columns.

If you're working with a layout that already prints in two or more columns, such as a labels layout, the Print in *<number>* columns option is already checked when you display this dialog box.

IMPORTANT NOTE

For more information about displaying data in columns, see *Printing data in columns* on p. 117.

You can also set specific page margins for your layout. Normally, FileMaker Pro sets the minimum top, bottom, left, and right margins for a layout. The position of data on a layout relative to the margin is determined by where you've placed fields or other objects on the layout screen. (For example, you set a 1-inch left margin by aligning objects below the 1-inch mark on the horizontal ruler at the top of the layout screen.) However, you can force FileMaker Pro to set larger margins by clicking the Fixed Page Margins option and then typing in the values you want in the appropriate margin boxes.

NEW FEATURE

You can also lay out pages so the left and right margins alternate, as in books. For example, you might want a 1-inch outside margin (between the printing and the outside edge of the paper), and a 1¼-inch inside margin (between the printing and the center of a bound book). On left-hand book pages, the outside margin is the left margin, and the inside margin is the right margin, but on right-hand pages, the margin settings are reversed. By checking the Facing Pages option, you can have FileMaker Pro alternate the left and right margin settings appropriately, so the outside and inside margins are always the right size.

Changing the layout pop-up menu

To determine how layout names appear on the layout pop-up menu, choose Set Layout Order... from the Mode menu. FileMaker Pro displays a dialog box like this:

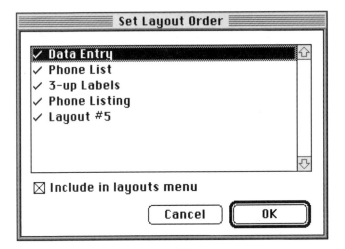

To reorder the layouts on the menu, just select a layout name and drag it up or down on the list.

To add or delete a layout name from the layout pop-up menu, select the name and check or uncheck the Include in layouts menu option. When you're done, click the OK button or press ⌐Return⌐.

TIP

You can divide groups of layouts from one another on the layout pop-up menu by creating one or more new, blank layouts, naming them "———————" or "=============," and then dragging these layout names between groups you want to separate in the Set Layout Order dialog box. These special "layout names" will then act as visual dividers between groups of other names on the pop-up menu.

Printing data in columns

When you set up a label layout, you determine the number of labels that will print across a page by choosing a label stock number or specifying label measurements. This way, you can print columns of labels, with each label representing one record's data. But you may want to arrange blocks of data from other types of layouts in columns as well, without setting up label dimensions. For example, here is a database of names and addresses where the records are arranged in columns on the page:

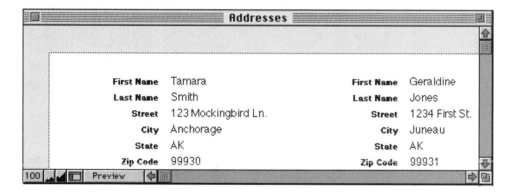

This layout began as a Standard-type layout, but it was set to print the data in columns. To set this type of columnar display:

1. Choose the Layout Setup… command.

2. Click the Print in columns checkbox and specify how many columns will appear on the layout.

3. Click the appropriate button to indicate whether records are to be laid out across the page in rows or down the page in columns.

Once you've specified a column layout, the layout changes to show the width of one column with the fields in it, like this:

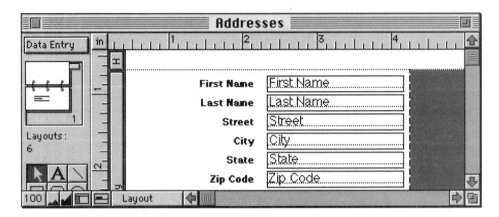

Notice that there's only one set of fields in this layout. That's all you'll see in Browse or Find mode; but when you print or use Preview mode, the records will appear in columns, as in the sample on the previous page.

Duplicating layouts

Sometimes it's faster to duplicate an existing layout and modify the copy than it is to create a whole new layout from scratch. This is particularly true if you want to reuse a lot of fields, graphics, or text objects in a custom layout.

To duplicate a layout:

1. Display the layout you want to duplicate by selecting it from the layout pop-up menu.

2. Choose Duplicate Layout from the Mode menu. The layout is copied, and the copy is displayed on the screen, ready for you to modify. You can tell it's a copy because the word *copy* is added to the layout's name on the layout pop-up menu.

Deleting layouts

As you use FileMaker Pro, you'll end up creating lots of new layouts for different purposes. After a while, your layout pop-up menu will get pretty cluttered with layouts that you no longer use. To reduce clutter and save file storage space, delete any layouts you know you won't need anymore.

To delete a layout:

1. Select the layout you want to delete from the layout pop-up menu.

2. Choose Delete Layout from the Mode menu. FileMaker Pro shows an alert asking you to confirm that you want the layout deleted.

3. Click the Delete button.

You can't undo a layout deletion, so be sure you really want to get rid of a layout before you delete it. If you've referred to a layout with a script or button and then you delete the layout, the script or button won't work properly anymore. See Chapter 12 for more on this.

IMPORTANT NOTE

Moving Objects in Layouts

Now let's see how to use Layout mode's tools to change the arrangement of fields on a layout.

Rearranging and resizing objects

Basically, you can move fields, field names, graphics, or text objects anywhere on the layout by selecting them and dragging them. To move a field, for example:

1. Put the pointer on the field and hold down the mouse button. The baseline beneath the field name will extend from the edges of the field to the edges of the layout, and portions of the vertical and horizontal ruler that show the field's height and width will be highlighted, like this:

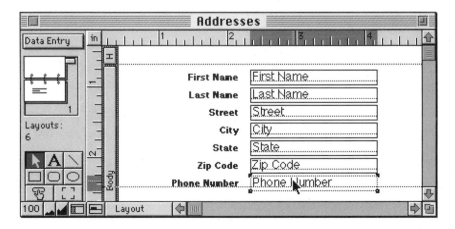

2. Drag the field to a new location and release the mouse button. When you release the mouse button, the extended baselines and ruler highlights disappear but the field remains selected. You need to click on another part of the layout to deselect it.

IMPORTANT NOTE

Fields are separate from field labels: Each is a separate object, and you must Shift-click to select them both if you want to move them both at the same time.

When you move a field, the baseline helps you line a field up exactly with other fields on the same line. For example, if you wanted to move the Zip Code field onto the same line as the State field in the layout above, you would just need to make sure the extended baseline from the Zip Code field lined up with the baseline of the State field.

You move other objects on a layout in the same way, but only fields have baselines that help to line fields up with one another.

IMPORTANT NOTE

In addition to dragging objects, you can also nudge them a little at a time by pressing the arrow keys on your keyboard. However, the freedom you have in moving objects this way depends on whether or not you have the AutoGrid turned on. (See *Using the AutoGrid and changing the ruler settings* on p. 122.) You can also constrain an object's movement to straight horizontal or vertical lines by holding down the Shift key as you drag it.

TIP

Use the zoom controls to magnify the screen when moving items on a layout. It's a lot easier to line up fields precisely if they're magnified. Once you've moved an item into place, reduce the layout to normal size to see how it looks.

To resize an object, first select it by clicking on it. A set of selection handles appears on its corners to show it's selected, like this:

You can now drag any of the four handles to make the object larger or smaller.

TIP

To make any oval or rectangle object into a perfect circle or square, select the object, hold down the Option key, and then drag one of the object's selection handles in any direction.

If you make a text object so small that there isn't enough room for text to fit on one line, the object's text will wrap around onto a second line, like this:

This is
layout text.

(Date, time, and summary fields are exceptions to this data-wrapping rule: no matter how small or large a date, time, or summary field, its data will only appear on one line. If the field isn't wide enough to show all the data, you simply won't see all the data in Browse or Preview mode.)

Don't make text objects any bigger than they need to be to contain their text. If you do, the text object may overlap a field or another item on the layout and make it difficult to select the item underneath.

IMPORTANT NOTE

Aligning objects automatically

The Align and Set Alignment... commands on the Arrange menu tell FileMaker Pro to automatically align selected objects. These commands save a lot of work when you want several fields or other objects to line up. To align objects automatically:

1. Select the objects you want to align with each other.

2. Choose Set Alignment... from the Arrange menu. The Set Alignment dialog box appears, like this:

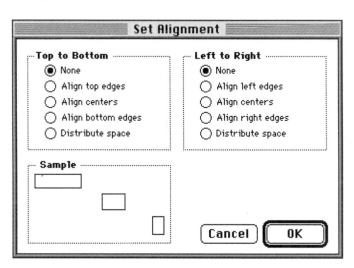

3. Select the types of Top to Bottom and Left to Right alignment you want by clicking the corresponding buttons. As you click each alignment button, the shapes in the sample move to show how the objects will be aligned. (The Distribute space option evens out the spaces between objects you're aligning.)

4. When you see the alignment you want, click the OK button. The selected objects will be aligned the way you've specified.

Once you've specified an alignment option in the Alignment dialog box, you can select other objects on the layout and align them with each other the same way, by choosing the Align command.

Using the AutoGrid and changing the ruler settings

FileMaker Pro has an invisible grid that underlies every layout. When you select AutoGrid on the Arrange menu a check mark appears next to its name. Thereafter every new object you add to a layout or every object you move on a layout will automatically be aligned to the nearest grid point. Objects that are already on the layout don't move, but if they were automatically placed by FileMaker Pro as part of a predefined layout or the first layout for a file, they're on grid points already.

IMPORTANT NOTE

The AutoGrid is on by default when you work in Layout mode. Choose AutoGrid from the Arrange menu to remove the check mark next to this command when you want to turn it off.

The spacing of the grid points is determined with the Set Rulers... command. To change the grid size:

1. Choose Set Rulers... from the Mode menu. The Set Rulers dialog box appears, like this:

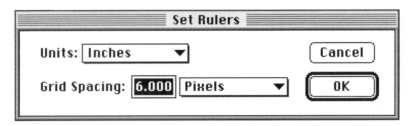

2. Type a measurement in the Grid Spacing box for the distance you want between grid points, and choose pixels, centimeters, or inches from the pop-up menu.

3. Click the OK button.

To change the unit of measurement shown on the rulers you see in Layout mode, choose the Set Rulers... command and then choose a unit of measurement (pixels, centimeters, or inches) from the Units pop-up menu.

When you have the AutoGrid on, pressing the arrow keys on your keyboard nudges a selected object one grid-spacing increment, rather than one pixel, at a time.

IMPORTANT NOTE

Using Layout Helpers

We've seen how you can use alignment options and the AutoGrid to assist you in arranging objects on layouts, but FileMaker Pro has lots of other layout helpers you can use, and they're all available from the Show menu. Let's take a look.

The Size window

Choosing the Size command from the Show menu displays the Size window, like this:

Size	
←	2.333 in
↑	2.264 in
→	4.181 in
↓	2.486 in
↔	1.847 in
↕	0.222 in

This window shows the dimensions and current location of a selected object or group of objects on the layout. The Size window to the left shows the position and dimensions of the Phone Number field on our sample address list layout. The unit of measurement in the Size window (inches, in this case) is the unit you've set with the Set Rulers... command.

The four measurements in the upper part of the Size window show the field's distance from the left, top, right and bottom edges of the layout. The two lower measurements are the field's width and height. The Size window will also show the position of the pointer when you hold down the mouse button, and the dimensions of any shape you draw as you draw it.

The numbers in the Size window change as you drag a selected object around the layout, so you can see precisely where something is at any moment. But you can also use the Size window to move or resize an object to an exact specification by typing the desired position or dimension directly into the appropriate

box in the Size window. For example, if you know you want a field to be exactly
2.35 inches high:

1. Select the field whose height you want to change and then display the Size
   window, if it's not already showing.

2. Double-click in the height-measurement box of the Size window to select
   the number in it.

3. Type *2.35* in the box.

4. Hit ⌈Return⌉. The field will become 2.35 inches high.

TIP

If you type in a measurement number and then change your mind, just click outside the Size window before pressing ⌈Return⌉. The measurement will revert to
whatever it was before you changed it.

Page margins

It sometimes helps to be able to see the page margins on a layout, so that you
know exactly where items are in relation to the edge of your paper. The Page
Margins command on the Show menu in Layout mode changes the layout so
these margins are showing, like this:

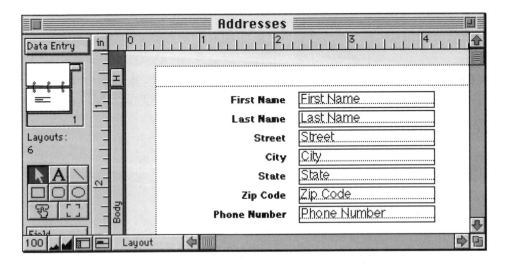

For users of older versions of FileMaker Pro, this command replaces the Non-printable area command on the Show submenu.

Text rulers

When you choose Text Ruler from the Show menu, you'll see a ruler like this in Layout mode:

The text ruler appears at the top of the layout, and it contains lots of controls that make formatting and arranging text more convenient. Here's what the ruler controls do:

 · The font pop-up menu lets you choose a font for the text you're working with.

 The size pop-up menu lets you change the size of text you're working with.

 The style buttons let you set (from left to right) bold, italic, or underlined styles for the text you're working with.

 The alignment buttons let you align text within a field or text object. The buttons set (from left to right) left, centered, right, and justified alignments.

 The tab buttons let you specify tabs when you're working inside a text object. These buttons let you set (from left to right), left, center, and right-aligned tab stops and decimal tab stops. (Decimal tab stops align a column of numbers on their decimal points.)

When you define a text object and have the text ruler showing, a small tab ruler appears in place of the normal text ruler, like this:

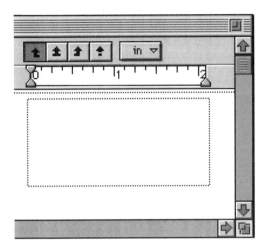

To set a tab stop, click the button corresponding to the type of tab you want to set, and then click below the ruler mark where you want the tab stop set. The tab stop marker appears in the ruler, like this:

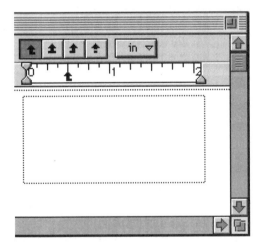

To delete a tab stop you have set, just drag the tab stop marker off the ruler.

TIP

You can specify font, size, style, alignment, and tab settings, as well as line spacing and paragraph indent options, with the Text... command on the Format menu (see p. 140).

The units pop-up menu lets you set the unit of measurement displayed on the text ruler.

All in all, the text ruler controls make it much easier to format layout text precisely in FileMaker Pro.

Graphic rulers

Graphic rulers can be displayed along the top and left sides of the layout, as shown on p. 101. To make these appear, choose Graphic Rulers from the Show menu. When the rulers are showing, a dotted line appears in each ruler and moves as you move the pointer, to show its position on the screen relative to the measurements on the rulers.

The default measurement scale for rulers in FileMaker Pro is inches, but you can change the scale to centimeters or pixels using the Set Rulers... command, as described above.

Ruler Lines

Choosing the Ruler Lines command from the Show menu displays a grid of lines extending from measurements on the rulers, like this:

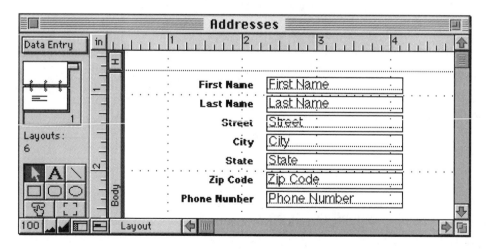

These lines appear whether or not the rulers themselves are showing, and correspond to the unit of measurement selected with the Set Rulers... command. (In the sample above, the unit of measurement is inches, so ruler lines appear every inch.)

T-Squares

T-Squares are a pair of guides that you can position anywhere on the screen and use to align objects. When you choose T-Squares from the Show menu, the guides appear on the layout, as shown here:

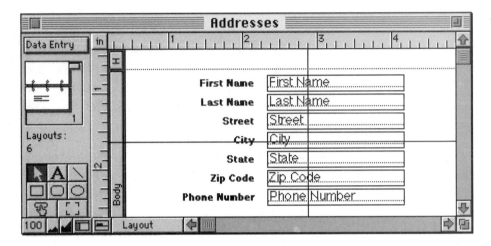

You can move either guide line by dragging it with the pointer. Then, when you move an object's edge up near one of the guides, the object will snap into alignment with the guide as if it were magnetized.

Buttons

The Buttons command tells FileMaker to show a heavy gray border around any object you've defined as a button on the layout. This makes it easy to tell a button from a normal graphic object. See Chapter 12 for more on buttons.

Sample Data

The Sample Data command simply displays sample data in the fields on the layout—usually the data stored in the first record of your file. Sample data is helpful when you're laying out files that don't yet contain anything, or if you don't want to bother switching to Browse mode to see how a field will look with data in it.

Text and field boundaries

The Text Boundaries command displays boundary lines around any text objects you have on your layout, so you can see exactly how big each object is, like this:

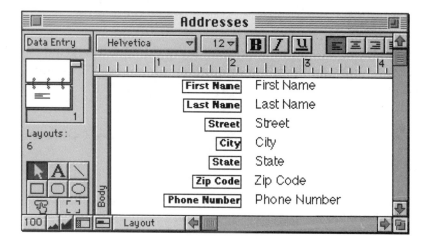

In this case, you see the boundaries around the text objects used as field names in the layout.

The Field Boundaries command displays border lines around fields on a layout, so you can see exactly how big they are. This command is chosen by default when you're in Layout mode, as you can see in many of the previous examples in this chapter (although it's turned off in the example immediately above).

Sliding objects

The Sliding Objects command displays arrows on objects you've formatted so that they'll fill in gaps in the layout when it's printed. The arrows appear at the edges of fields and show the direction in which the fields are set to slide, like this:

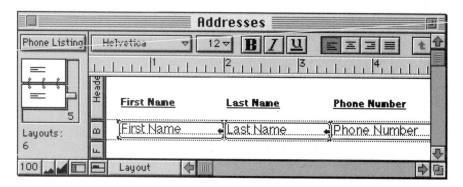

In this case, the First Name and Last Name fields are set to slide to the left. For more on setting sliding objects, see p. 154 later in this chapter.

Non-printing objects

The Non-Printing Objects command displays a heavy gray border around any objects on the layout that are set to not print. For more about non-printing objects, see *Creating Non-Printing Objects*, p. 157.

Adding Fields

You can add a field to a layout any time you're in Layout mode. To do this, use the field tool.

IMPORTANT NOTE

You can also add fields inside text boxes in a layout by pasting in merge fields with the Paste Special submenu (see p. 132 below).

1. Click on the field tool at the left of the Layout screen.

2. Drag the field tool to where you want the new field to appear. FileMaker Pro will display the Specify Field dialog box, listing all the fields currently defined for the file, like this:

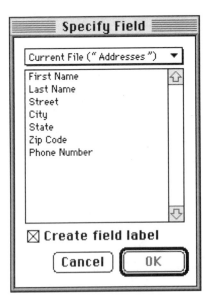

3. Double-click on the name of the field you want to add, or select the name and click the OK button.

The Create field label checkbox tells FileMaker Pro to also add the field's name as a text object to the left of the new field. Uncheck this box if you just want to add the field itself without the label.

The pop-up menu at the top of the Specify Field dialog box lets you add fields from related files or specify new relationships. See Chapter 11 for more information.

If you want to define a new field when you're working with a layout, use the Define fields… command on the File menu just as you would in Browse mode (see Chapter 4 for details).

TIP

Adding or Changing Layout Text

Layout text is text that stays the same no matter which record(s) you're viewing or printing. This can include the names of fields or buttons or titles for whole layouts or areas of layouts.

You can use layout text for more than just titles, captions, and headings. For example, you might create a form letter layout where the letter itself is composed almost entirely of layout text. Along with the layout text, you could add merge fields where you want the form letter to contain names, addresses, or other information from specific records in your file. You can use the text tool in the tool palette to edit field names or to add text anywhere else in a layout.

Adding layout text

To add layout text:

1. Click on the text tool in the tool palette.

2. Draw a text box about the size you'll need to accommodate your text.

3. Type the text.

4. Click away from the text.

Once you click away from a string of text you've typed, the text becomes a distinct object. If you choose the pointer tool and click on the text, FileMaker Pro places a set of handles around the object, like this:

This is layout text.

Since the text is an object, you can select it and move it or resize it just as you would a field or graphic object. However, you can still select the text itself with the text tool and edit it or change the formatting of individual characters inside the object.

IMPORTANT NOTE

If the text box you draw isn't wide enough to contain your text, the text will wrap around within the box. To unwrap the text so it's all on one line again, select the text box and drag one of its handles to make it wider.

Adding special text or symbols

There are several special symbols that FileMaker Pro understands as instructions for inserting certain types of data (dates, times, page numbers, or other information). In Layout mode, you often add these symbols to headers and footers, but you can put them anywhere you like. The Paste Special… command on the Edit menu displays a submenu containing 11 different commands, 9 of which are active when you're working in Layout mode.

The Current Date command pastes the current date (as maintained by your Mac's internal calendar) onto the layout at the cursor position.

The Current Time command pastes the current time (as maintained by your Mac's internal clock) onto the layout at the cursor position.

The Current User Name command pastes the current user name from your Mac onto the layout at the cursor position. The user name is either the name specified with the Sharing Setup control panel or a custom user name you entered in the Preferences command's dialog box. (See *General preferences* on p. 39 in Chapter 3 for more information.)

The Date Symbol command pastes two slash marks (//) into the layout at the cursor position. These marks tell FileMaker Pro to insert the current date at this position whenever you view the layout in Browse or Preview mode or when you print records with the layout. (You can also type two slash marks to indicate you want the date inserted, rather than pasting this symbol.)

The Time Symbol command pastes two colons (::) into the layout at the cursor position. These marks tell FileMaker Pro to insert the current time at this position whenever you view the layout in Browse or Preview mode or when you print records with the layout. (You can type two colons from the keyboard to achieve the same effect.)

The User Name Symbol command pastes two vertical lines (| |) onto the layout. This symbol tells FileMaker Pro to insert the current user name at this position whenever you view the layout in Browse or Preview mode or when you print records with the layout. (You can type vertical bars from the keyboard to achieve the same effect.)

The Page Number command inserts two number or pound symbols (##) into the layout at the cursor position. These marks tell FileMaker Pro to insert the current page number at this position whenever you view the layout in Browse or Preview mode or when you print records with the layout. When you print from the layout, the Print dialog box has a Number pages from box where you can specify the starting page number to be used. (You can type the number symbols as well.)

The Record Number command inserts two "at" signs (@@) into the layout at the cursor position. These marks tell FileMaker Pro to insert the current record number at this position whenever you view the layout in Browse or Preview mode or when you print records with the layout. When calculating record numbers, FileMaker Pro counts only the records in the current found set, and numbers them consecutively from one. (You can type these signs from the keyboard instead, if you prefer.)

IMPORTANT NOTE

FileMaker Pro treats the //, ::, | |, ##, and @@ symbols as commands, so be careful about using these double symbols or you'll get strange results. For example, if you include two slashes as part of a World Wide Web address, such as http://www.myorg.com, you'll end up with the current date between "http:" and "www.myorg.com" when you print or preview the layout.

The Merge Field... command displays the Specify Field dialog box, where you can choose a merge field to insert into a text box on your layout. (If you paste a merge field without having clicked inside a text box first, the merge field is pasted into a text box of its own. When you add a merge field, FileMaker Pro inserts a merge field marker, like this:

<<Zip Code>>

You can also add merge fields to a layout by typing the field's name inside double less-than (<<) (⟨Shift⟩⟨,⟩) and greater-than (>>) (⟨Shift⟩⟨.⟩) symbols when you're inside a text box. Just make sure the field name is correct.

The merge field's data will appear in the layout when you view it in Browse or Preview mode, but not in Find mode. FileMaker displays a merge field's data in these modes, but you don't have the option to display the field's name as well. Also, merge fields are collapsed on a layout when they don't contain any data.

As a result, merge fields are handy when you want to merge data into a line of text in a form letter or other layout in which the field's data will be surrounded by text or other objects. When data is displayed in a merge field, the field shows only as much of its data as the field's size permits.

Editing and reformatting layout text

Even though layout text becomes an object once you've entered it, you can still edit it or reformat it later using the text tool. To edit or reformat layout text:

1. Click on the text tool.

2. Click on the place within any layout text where you want to begin editing. FileMaker Pro shows the borders of the text box and puts the insertion point where you clicked, like this:

> This is layout text.

Once the insertion point is blinking inside the text box, you can use standard Mac editing techniques to make the changes you want. To reformat the text inside a text object, just drag the insertion point across the characters or words you want to select, and then choose formatting options from the Format menu or text ruler. You can even double-click on a word to select it inside a text object, just as you can in most other text-editing situations.

To format data in a merge field, you must select the entire text object. For information about formatting all the text inside a text object, button, portal, or field at once, see *Changing Field and Object Formats* on p. 138.

Using Graphics

There are three ways to add graphics to a layout:

- Use the tool palette's line, oval, and polygon tools to draw graphic objects on a layout and set the fill, line pattern, and line width controls as desired.

- Copy graphics to a layout from the Clipboard.

- Import graphics directly from disk files into layouts or fields using the Import Picture... command. (See *Importing pictures or movies* on p. 81 in Chapter 5 for more information on this.)

FileMaker Pro gives you lots of flexibility for creating graphics or adding them to a layout. Here's an example:

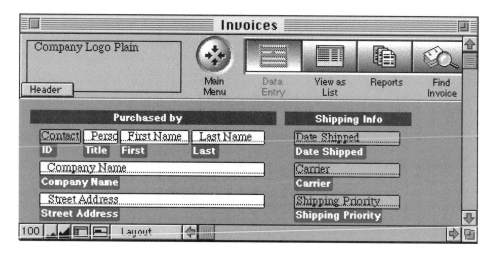

In this layout, the gray backgrounds and bars behind field names are all individual graphic objects. The text inside the field label bars has been colored white and placed on top of the gray background, along with the fields that show the customer and shipping information. There are five buttons at the top of the layout that contain graphics that were turned into buttons.

Let's take a closer look at how graphics like this are created. (For more on turning a graphic into a button, see Chapter 12.)

Creating graphics on a layout

To create a graphic, you use the graphic tools in FileMaker Pro's tool palette. For example, to create a gray bar like one of those above:

1. Click on the rectangle tool in the toolbox.

2. Point to the place where you want to start drawing on the layout.

3. Hold down the mouse button and drag diagonally to create the rectangle.

4. Release the mouse button when the rectangle is the size and shape you want.

   Once you release the mouse button, the graphic object is selected and there are handles around it. You can then drag the object itself to move it or drag one of its handles to resize it.

5. With the rectangle selected, choose one of the gray fill colors using the fill control.

To create a line or an oval or rounded rectangle, you follow the same procedure with the corresponding tool selected.

Copying graphics to a layout

To copy a graphic from the Clipboard:

1. Copy the graphic to the Clipboard from its original location (the Scrapbook or another program).

2. Click where you want the graphic to appear on the layout.

3. Press ⌘V to paste the graphic there. The graphic will appear and will be selected. You can then click on it and drag it to another location or resize it by dragging one of its handles.

IMPORTANT NOTE

If there isn't enough room on the layout to paste a graphic where you indicate, FileMaker Pro will display a message, giving you the opportunity to have it automatically increase the size of the layout to accommodate the image.

Managing graphics in layers

You can create and manage graphics in several different layers in FileMaker Pro, just as you can in most drawing programs. In fact, any layout object, whether it's a field, text object, or graphic, can be overlaid on another one.

In the layout shown on p. 135, for example, the Purchased by text object is overlaid on a dark gray box, which itself is overlaid on a lighter gray background.

To place one object on top of another, just drag it there. To rearrange layers, select the object you want to move, and then use the commands on the Arrange menu, as follows:

Bring to Front puts the selected object in the top layer, so it covers up everything beneath it.

Bring Forward moves a selected object one layer forward, placing it in front of the object it was directly underneath.

Send to Back puts the selected object in the bottom layer, underneath any other objects.

Send Backward moves the selected object one layer deeper, placing it under the object it used to be on top of.

Managing objects in groups

When you create complex arrangements of fields, text objects, and graphics, you may want to move them all as a group. You can always Shift-click or drag a selection rectangle to select several objects at once, but the Group command on the Arrange menu ties several objects together so they're always selected and moved as one object.

To group several objects together:

1. Choose the pointer tool from the toolbox.

2. Shift-click on every object you want to include in the group, like this:

3. Choose the Group command from the Arrange menu. FileMaker Pro will remove the handles from the individual objects and put handles around the entire group instead, like this:

■ **First Name**■
Last Name
Street
City
State
Zip Code
■ **Phone Number** ■
■   ■

From now on, all these items are selected as a unit. To break up a group so the items in it can be individually selected again, just select it and choose Ungroup from the Arrange menu.

Locking objects

Having carefully positioned items on a layout, you may want to lock them in place so they can't be moved. (It's easy to accidentally move an item, especially if it's close to another one you want to work with and you select it by mistake.)

To lock an item, just select it and choose Lock from the Arrange menu. The handles around the object will become dimmed, and you won't be able to move or resize it anymore.

To unlock an item, just select it and choose Unlock from the Arrange menu.

Changing Field and Object Formats

Every field, text object, portal, or button you create on a layout can be individually formatted using the options on FileMaker Pro's Format menu or text ruler. The attributes you can set include font, size, style, text color, alignment, and line spacing for fields or text objects, and border and fill patterns for fields or portals.

The options in this section affect whole objects, not portions of them. For information about formatting individual characters, words, or phrases of text inside text objects, see *Editing and reformatting layout text* on p. 134.

IMPORTANT
NOTE

The Format menu contains several options you can use to format text or data in fields or other layout objects.

For information about the Field Format..., Field Borders..., and Sliding/ Printing... commands, see *The Field Format... command* (p. 140–145), The *Field Borders... command* (p. 150), *Sliding Objects* (p. 154), and *Creating Non-Printing Objects* (p. 157).

IMPORTANT
NOTE

Setting format attributes

Here's the basic procedure for setting text and data formats:

1. Select the field(s) or object(s) you want to format. (Remember, you can (Shift)-click or drag a selection box around several items to select more than one at a time.)

2. Choose the attribute you want to apply from the Format menu or click one of the controls in the text ruler.

3. If you're choosing options from the Format menu, choose the specific format setting—a font size, for example—from the submenu or dialog box that appears.

As with other layout tools and commands, you must select the object you want to reformat before choosing the format option.

If you don't have an object selected when you choose a format option, that option will become the default and will apply to every object you add onto a layout from then on, until you reset it.

IMPORTANT
NOTE

The Font, Size, Style, Align Text, Line Spacing, and Text Color commands all display submenus with lists of options to choose from.

The Text ..., Number..., Date..., Time..., Graphic..., Portal..., and Button commands each display a dialog box that lets you set a whole group of formatting options at once, including all the attributes you can select with the commands listed above. Once you select an object, any inappropriate commands for that type of object will be dimmed on the Format menu. Let's take a closer look at these commands.

Formatting text fields

When you have a text field or text object selected and you choose the Text...
command, you'll see a dialog box like this:

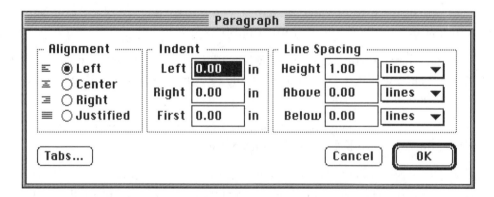

Here, you can select font, size, color, and style options all at once. The Sample
area shows how the text will look with the currently selected formatting options.
If you click the Paragraph... button in the lower left corner, you'll see the
Paragraph dialog box, like this:

Just click the alignment option you want at the left. Then type in the numeric
values you want for indents and line spacing; in the Indent area, the First value
controls the indentation of the first line in a paragraph. The Line Spacing area

lets you set the amount of line space between lines in a paragraph (Height), as well as the amount of spacing before (Above) and after (Below) the paragraph. Using the pop-up menus in the Line Spacing area, you can change the unit of measurement for measuring line spacing from lines to inches, pixels, or centimeters.

The Tabs... button in the lower left corner of the Paragraph dialog box produces the Tabs dialog box, where you can set tab stops for any text object you're working on.

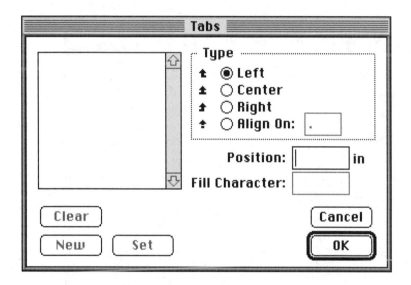

To set a tab stop, choose the type of tab you want in the Type area, type its position in the Position box, and then click the Set button. The tab stop setting will appear in the list at the left. You can set as many tab stops as you like this way. Click the OK button to exit the Tabs dialog box when you're finished.

Tab stops only apply to text objects, not to fields. The position settings you specify apply to the tab ruler that appears above a selected text object, not to the text ruler. (See p. 126 for an example of the tab ruler.) For example, a *.25″* tab stop will always be set ¼ inch from the left edge of a text object, no matter where that object is on the layout.

IMPORTANT NOTE

If you like, you can specify a fill character by typing it into the Fill Character box. For example, if you want the space between one tab stop and the next to be filled with dashes, you would type a dash character (–) in the Fill Character box.

To change a tab stop setting, select the setting in the list, type the new position setting, choose a new type, or type a new fill character, and then click the Set button.

To delete a tab stop from the list, select it and click the Clear button.

Formatting number fields

When you have a number field selected and you choose Number…, the dialog box looks like this:

```
┌─────────────────────────────────────────────────────────────┐
│          Number Format for "Quantity"                       │
│                                                             │
│  ◉ Leave data formatted as entered                          │
│  ○ Format as Boolean                                        │
│      Show non-zeroes as : [Yes]    Show zeroes as : [No]    │
│  ○ Format as decimal                                        │
│      □ Fixed number of decimal digits : [2]                 │
│      □ Use notation : [Currency (leading) ▼]  Currency symbol : [$] │
│      □ Do not display number if zero                        │
│   ┌ Separators ──────────────┐   ┌ Negative ──────────┐    │
│   │ Decimal separator : [   ] │   │ Format as : [-1234 ▼] │    │
│   │  □ Use thousands separator : [   ] │ □ Use color : [▼] ▨ │  │
│   └──────────────────────────┘   └────────────────────┘    │
│   ┌ Sample ──────────────────┐   ┌──────────────────┐      │
│   │ -6543.9871               │   │  Text Format...  │      │
│   │                          │   ├──────────────────┤      │
│   │                          │   │ Cancel    ║ OK ║ │      │
│   └──────────────────────────┘   └──────────────────┘      │
└─────────────────────────────────────────────────────────────┘
```

Using the radio buttons at the left, you can tell FileMaker Pro to leave numbers as they are entered (as you might with decimal fractions), to automatically format them according to your specifications (as with dollar amounts), or to display them as Boolean values such as Yes and No or True and False (for survey data, perhaps).

If you choose the Format as Boolean option in the Number Format dialog box, FileMaker Pro will display zeroes as No and any other number as Yes. If you'd rather use another pair of terms, like False and True, you can type them into the Show non-zeroes as and Show zeroes as boxes.

Clicking the Format as decimal button allows you to activate any of the options in the box below it. You can have FileMaker Pro automatically add a fixed number of decimal digits to a number, use percentage or currency notations, use a custom currency symbol, hide zero-value numbers, use a decimal separator (you can specify the separator character), add commas (or another character you specify) to separate thousands, or choose the format and color of text for negative values.

The Text Format... button displays the Text Format dialog box (as shown on p. 140) so you can set the font, size, style, alignment, and color of the number's text. You can't set paragraph formats or tabs from inside this dialog box when you display it from the Number Format dialog box, however, because number fields can't contain paragraphs and don't use tabs.

Formatting date fields

If you have a date field selected when you choose Date... from the Format menu, the Date Format dialog box appears, like this:

Here, you can have FileMaker Pro leave dates formatted as entered or choose one of over a dozen specific date formats from the pop-up menu next to the Format as button. With any of the predefined formats, you can specify the character that separates months, days, and years.

If you don't see a date format you like on the Format as pop-up menu, click the Custom button and use its options to design your own date format.

You can also use the Date Format dialog box to add leading zeroes to month and day numbers.

The Sample area shows the format your dates will have with the options currently selected. The Text Format... button displays the Text Format dialog box, so you can apply font, size, style, and color options to your date field.

Formatting time fields

If you've selected a time field and you choose the Time... command, you'll see the Time Format dialog box:

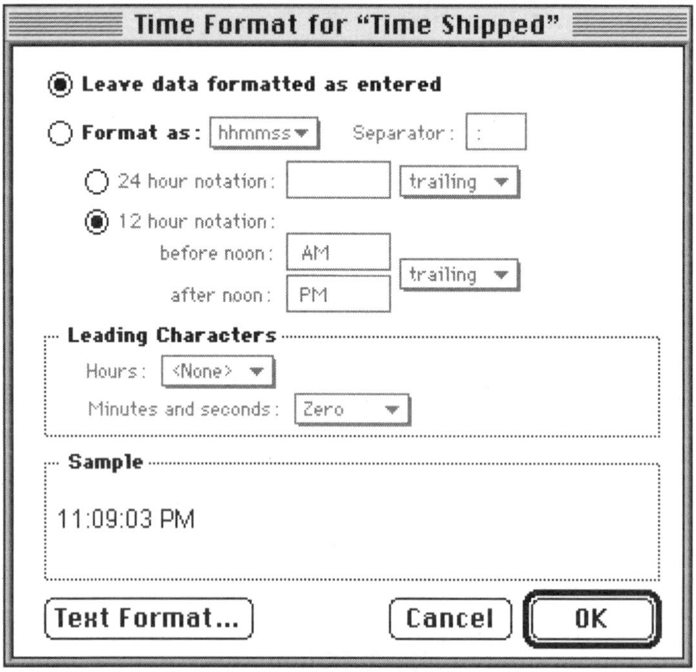

In this box, you can have FileMaker Pro leave times formatted as they're entered or have it automatically format them in one of several standard formats shown on the pop-up menu next to the Format as button. You can choose the character that separates hours, minutes, and seconds; select either 24- or 12-hour time; specify the suffixes used with times; and choose leading characters (such as zeroes) before hours, minutes, and seconds. The effects of the options you select are shown in the Sample area.

As in other dialog boxes, the Text Format... button displays the Text Format dialog box.

Formatting graphic fields

If you have a container field selected when you choose the Graphic... command from the Format menu, you'll see the Graphic Format dialog box, like this:

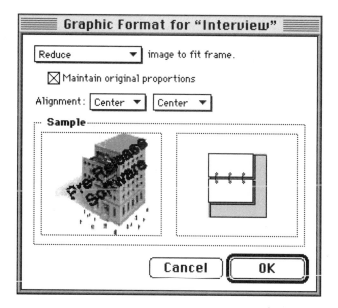

The pop-up menu at the top tells FileMaker Pro to resize the picture to fit the frame (the field's outline). The choices are Reduce, Enlarge, Crop, and Reduce or Enlarge as necessary. The Sample area shows how pictures that are larger than the field (on the left) and smaller than the field (on the right) will look with each of these options set. The Maintain original proportions checkbox tells FileMaker Pro to resize the picture without changing its proportions. The Alignment pop-up menus handle horizontal and vertical alignment. The left-hand menu handles horizontal alignment (left, center, right) within the field, and the right-hand menu takes care of vertical alignment (top, center, bottom).

Formatting portals

When you have a portal selected and you choose the Portal… command from the Format menu, you see the Portal Setup dialog box, like this:

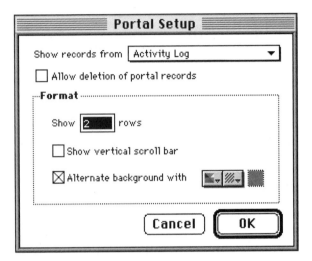

**IMPORTANT
NOTE**

Portals are used to display records from related files in the current file. See Chapter 12 for more information about how to work with related files.

The pop-up menu at the top of the Portal Setup dialog box lets you choose a relationship to determine the related file whose records the portal is set to display. You can choose among existing relationships on this menu, or you can define a new relationship if you like.

The Allow deletion of portal records checkbox lets you set whether users can delete a record in a portal and have that deletion reflected in the related file. Remember, a relationship is set up so you can display a related file's records in the current file. With this option set, users can delete the record shown in a portal, which also deletes it in the related file.

The Show box determines how many rows are displayed inside the portal. Each record in a portal occupies one row, so a portal set up to show three rows would show three records from the related file.

The Show vertical scroll bar checkbox adds a scroll bar to a portal so the user can scroll it to view other records from the related file that aren't currently in view.

The Alternate background with option lets you choose a fill color or pattern for alternating rows in the portal.

Formatting buttons

When you have a button selected on a layout and you choose the Button... command from the Format menu, you see the Specify Button dialog box, as described on p. 104. Use this command to change the definition of a button or to change the button name. For more information about buttons, see Chapter 12.

The Field Format... command

As discussed in Chapter 4, you can define a database field so it has certain Auto Enter or Validation options (see *Setting Entry Options* on p. 64 in Chapter 4). The Field Format... command on the Format menu lets you control which of these data-entry options appears, and how it appears, when you work with the field in Browse mode. When you choose this command, FileMaker Pro displays a dialog box like this one:

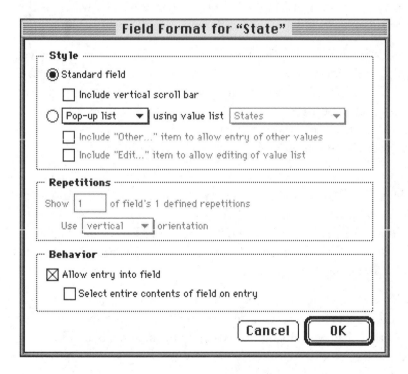

The options you have available in this dialog box depend on whether you used any special entry options when you defined the field originally, and if so which ones.

In the Style area at the top of this dialog box, you can choose either Standard field or an option that uses the field's value list. If you didn't create a list of values for the field when you defined it, only the Standard field option is available.

In a standard field, you enter data by typing it or pasting it in from the Clipboard. If you know the field will contain several lines of data and you want to be able to scroll down the field, checking the Include vertical scroll bar checkbox adds a scroll bar to the field, like the Notes field shown here:

FIRST NAME	LAST NAME	TITLE	PHONE	
Dennis	Smith	Marketing Associate	617-555-9876	
Faye	Johnson	Benefits Administrator	518-555-2211	
NOTES:	Willing to assist in shipping assignments during heavy workload.			⬆ ⬇

TIP When you define a field that is several lines high, it's best to give it a scroll bar with this option. Without a scroll bar, pressing the up or down arrow keys is the only way you can move up or down to see different lines of text.

If a field has a predefined value list, the second button in the Style area is active, and you can use it to decide which value list you want the field to use and how that list appears. The left-hand pop-up menu lets you choose the type of display for the field: a pop-up list, pop-up menu, radio buttons, or checkbox. You use the right-hand pop-up menu to select a particular value list to be used for the field. (You can define several different value lists for a field. See p. 69 in Chapter 4.)

When you check the Include "Other..." item to allow entry of other values checkbox, FileMaker Pro adds an Other... choice to the list of entry options for the field you're working with. Then, when you choose Other... from the list of options displayed for the field in Browse mode, FileMaker Pro displays a dialog box where you can enter whatever text or data you want, instead of having to choose one of the predefined values.

The Include "Edit..." item to allow editing of value list checkbox adds an Edit... option to the value list. When you choose this option from the list in Browse mode, FileMaker Pro displays a dialog box where you can actually add items to the field's value list, like this:

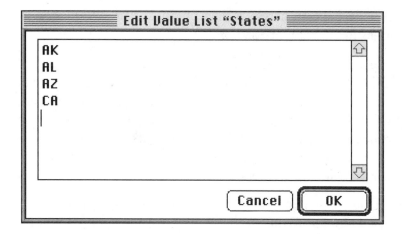

Try the various value list display options to see how they look. For more information on how each of these formatting choices looks and how it affects data entry, see *Using a list, menu, or button to enter data* on pp. 74–76 in Chapter 5.

If the field you've selected was defined as a repeating field, the Repetitions area lets you specify how many of the field's repetitions should show on the layout and how they're arranged. The box initially shows the number of repetitions that are defined for the field. To display all the defined repetitions, leave this number as shown. However, you don't have to show all of the field's repetitions if you don't want to; you can display fewer repetitions than are defined by entering a lower number in the box.

The Use *<option>* orientation pop-up menu tells FileMaker Pro whether to display repeating fields vertically or horizontally. On an address form that shows alternate phone numbers, for example, you'd want each item ordered to appear on its own row, so you'd choose the vertical orientation to display them like this:

The Phone Number field shown here is a repeating field that is formatted to show three repetitions in a vertical orientation.

The Behavior area controls what happens in the field when it is selected. The Allow entry into field checkbox lets you allow or prevent user entries into this field. It's a good idea to deselect this option when the field's data is automatically entered and you don't want anyone changing it. The Select entire contents of field on entry checkbox tells FileMaker to select all of a field's contents when the field is selected. With this option set, you can be sure that existing information in a field will be deleted when the user enters something new.

IMPORTANT NOTE

The options you set with the Field Format… command apply to whatever field you have selected at the time. If you have no fields selected when you choose options with this command, they become the default settings for all fields you add to layouts from that point on.

The Field Borders… command

The Field Borders… command lets you display and format field boundaries and baselines. When you choose this command, FileMaker Pro displays a dialog box like this:

```
╔══════════ Field Borders for "Shipping Priority" ══════════╗
║                                                            ║
║  ┌─ Field Borders ──────────┐  ┌─ Sample ──────────────┐  ║
║  │  ☐ Top      ☐ Left       │  │                       │  ║
║  │  ☐ Bottom   ☐ Right      │  │                       │  ║
║  │     ☐ Text baselines     │  │      -2189.123        │  ║
║  │     ☐ Between repeating  │  │                       │  ║
║  │        values            │  │                       │  ║
║  │  [ Borders  ▼] format:   │  │                       │  ║
║  │                          │  └───────────────────────┘  ║
║  │    [◣▾][▨▾][▤▾]  ⊞       │     ( Cancel )  (  OK  )    ║
║  └──────────────────────────┘                             ║
╚════════════════════════════════════════════════════════════╝
```

You use the checkboxes in the Field Borders area to choose which borders to display and whether to show text baselines and lines between repeating fields.

The format pop-up menu below the checkboxes allows you to set the colors, fill patterns, and line widths for borders and baselines. You can also use the Fill option on this pop-up menu to fill in the field itself with a color and pattern, as a background for the field's data. You just choose the element you want to change (borders, baselines, or fill) from the pop-up menu, and then set its attributes using the color, fill pattern, and line-width pop-up menus below. (These work the same way as the controls in the tool palette on the Layout screen.)

Experiment with these formatting options to see how you can enhance the appearance of fields in your layouts. The Sample area shows the effect of your choices.

As with the other formatting commands, the Field Borders settings apply to whatever field is selected on the layout at the time. If no field is selected, they will apply to every field you add to any layout in the file from that point on, until you reset them.

IMPORTANT NOTE

Changing the Tab Order

When you work with a layout in the Browse mode, you can move from one field to the next by pressing the ⌜Tab⌝ key. The order in which fields are selected, called the *tab order*, is important for efficient data entry.

FileMaker Pro sets the tab order according to the position of fields on a layout. Starting from the field closest to the top, the sequence runs from left to right and then down the screen. But this may not match the order in which you want to move from field to field when entering data. To set it up the way you want, use the Set Tab Order… command on the Mode menu in Layout mode.

When you choose the Set Tab Order… command, FileMaker Pro displays the current tab order on the layout along with a dialog box like this:

The Set Tab Order dialog box assumes you want to edit the current tab order, so the Edit tab order button is selected. The Create new tab order button erases the existing tab order and lets you create a new one from scratch. The Revert To Default button restores FileMaker Pro's standard left-to-right, top-to-bottom tab order, erasing the current one.

When you have the Set Tab Order dialog box displayed, numbered arrows pointing to each field show the current tab order on the layout, like this:

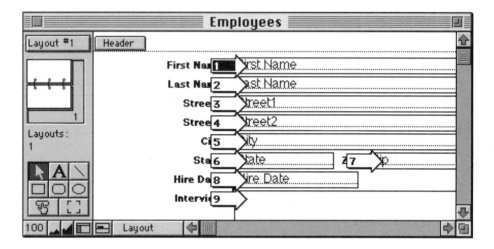

Just drag the Set Tab Order dialog box out of the way if it's covering up any of the arrows.

To change one field's position in the tab order, click inside its arrow and type in a new number. FileMaker Pro will exchange tab numbers between this field and whatever field formerly had the number you typed in, but the swap doesn't take place until you click inside another arrow. When you're finished setting up the new tab order, hit Return or click the OK button.

To change every field's tab order on your layout, click the Create new tab order button in the Set Tab Order dialog box, and then click on the fields in your layout in the order in which you want tabs set.

Changing the tab order in repeating fields

If your layout contains repeating fields, you can set the tab order so that pressing ⌜Tab⌟ moves you either to the adjacent field or to the next occurrence of the repeating field you're already in. Here's an example:

Item No.	Quantity	Item Description	Price
Item Numb	Quantity	Item description	Price

In this order form layout, there are four repeating fields. To set the tab order so that pressing ⌜Tab⌟ moves the selection from Item No. to Quantity to Item Description and then to Price, before returning to the Item No. field in the second row, you would click once in each of the field spaces in the desired tab order, like this:

Item No.	Quantity	Item Description	Price
Item Numb	Quantity	Item description	Price
Click 1	Click 2	Click 3	Click 4
Click 5			

After these mouse clicks, the tab order would be this:

Item No.	Quantity	Item Description	Price
1	2	3 em description	4 Price
5			

Notice that the remaining repeating field spaces don't have tab order numbers, because we didn't click in each of them. To set the tab order for all of them, you must click in each space.

If, on the other hand, you wanted the selection to advance down, from the Item No. field in the first row to the Item No. in the second, you could simply double-click in the Item No. field in the top row, and FileMaker Pro would automatically set the tab order to move down that field for all of its displayed repetitions, like this:

If you have a layout with dozens of fields and field repetitions, it's easy to get the tab order screwed up. If you do, you can always click the Cancel button in the Tab Order dialog box to return to the order in effect when you began. Or you can click the Revert To Default button to switch back to the original tab order dictated by the sequence in which fields were added to the layout.

Sliding Objects

Since the length of the data in a given field may vary from record to record, you have to make the field large enough on the layout to display the longest data the field contains. This can create big gaps between pieces of data or other layout objects that are supposed to appear close together. For example, suppose you lay out the fields for an address directory like this:

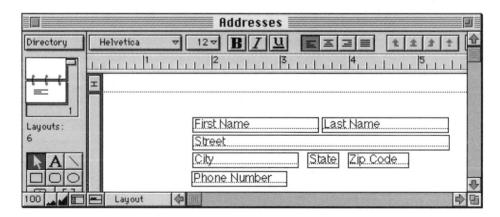

The data in these fields will look like this in Preview mode:

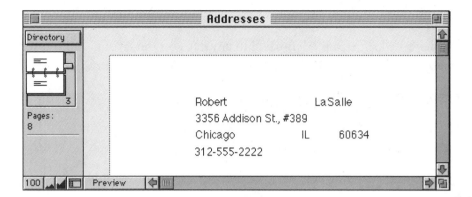

As you can see, there's a huge gap separating the first name from the last name, and there are also gaps between the city, state, and zip code data.

Fortunately, FileMaker Pro's Sliding/Printing… command lets you select objects on a layout and make them slide to the left or up when records are printed to fill in gaps created by missing data or short entries.

The Sliding/Printing… command only changes the way data appears when it's printed or displayed in Preview mode—it doesn't affect the way data appears in Browse mode.

**IMPORTANT
NOTE**

To see how this works, let's make the objects in this directory layout slide.

1. Switch to Layout mode if you're not already in it.

2. Select the fields you want to slide by ⸤Shift⸣-clicking on them. (In this case, we'd select all of the fields except Street and Phone Number.)

3. Choose Sliding/Printing… from the Format menu. FileMaker Pro displays the dialog box as shown below:

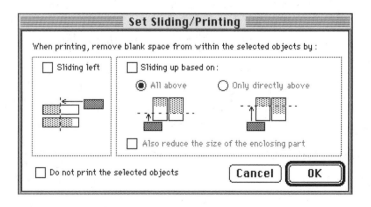

4. Click the Sliding left checkbox, and then click the OK button.

Now the fields will slide to the left to fill in any gaps on the layout. You can see this effect in Preview mode. Here's how it looks:

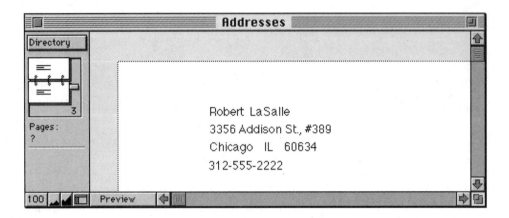

Notice that even though it's the Last Name, State, and Zip Code fields that actually slide left, we had to select the First Name and City fields as well. That's because you have to select the fields or objects *on both sides* of a gap when you slide objects.

The Sliding/Printing dialog box also lets you slide objects up to eliminate gaps caused by missing data. If the street address was missing from the example above, we could check the Sliding up based on checkbox to eliminate the blank space. Notice, though, that there are two options when you slide objects up: All above or Only directly above.

The All above option slides an object up only as far as the next lowest item on the layout, even if that item isn't directly above the object that's sliding. The Only directly above option, on the other hand, slides an object up as far as it can go, even if that means the sliding object moves higher than others to its right or left on the layout. (The example shown in the preceding dialog box helps you picture the difference.)

Finally, the Also reduce the size of the enclosing part checkbox tells FileMaker Pro to make an entire part (header, body, footer) of the layout shorter if sliding objects up creates enough space to make that possible.

Sliding works for text objects and graphics as well as for fields.

Viewing sliding objects

As discussed above, you can see how the Sliding/Printing... options affect the arrangement of data by looking at the data in Preview mode. You can also see how objects will slide by choosing the Sliding Objects command from the Show menu in Layout mode.

Creating Non-Printing Objects

You can also use the Sliding/Printing... command to create non-printing objects on a layout. For example, you might want to include a field on a layout, so that you can enter data into it in Browse or use it to select records in Find mode, but not have the field appear when you print. Or you might make a button non-printing, so that data entry operators can use it, but not have it show up on a printed record.

To make an object non-printing:

1. Select the object you don't want to print.

2. Choose Sliding/Printing... from the Format menu.

3. Check the Do not print the selected objects checkbox at the bottom.

4. Click the OK button.

To make the object print out again, just select it and uncheck the same checkbox in the Slide Objects dialog box.

Troubleshooting

In this section, we'll look at some common problems you may have as you work with layouts and see how to resolve them.

The wrong fields are showing on the layout.

If the wrong fields are showing on a layout, you're probably looking at the wrong layout. Click the book icon (in Layout mode only) or use the layout pop-up menu to look at other layouts until you find the one you want. If you're sure you're using the right layout try scrolling the layout window—the fields you want may be off the screen.

Fields don't show all the information in them in Browse mode.

If a field isn't large enough to contain all its information when you switch to Browse mode, it might look like this:

Department [Accountin]

When this happens, either widen the field or choose a smaller font size to use the existing space better.

Fields, field labels, or other objects don't line up.

To line up fields or other objects precisely, zoom the layout to twice its normal size (or bigger) by clicking the zoom control at the lower left corner of the screen. Once the layout is magnified, it's much easier to see whether things do or don't line up. Remember, if you turn the AutoGrid off, you can nudge any selected object one pixel at a time to the left, right, up, or down by pressing the arrow keys on the keyboard.

If you're adding a bunch of new fields to a layout and you want them all to line up automatically, choose AutoGrid from the Arrange menu before you add them. To align a group of fields after you've added them, select all the fields and then choose an alignment option with the Set Alignment… command on the Arrange menu.

A text object wraps around onto two lines.

Unless there's a carriage return in the text itself, this just means the text object isn't wide enough to display all its text on one line. To fix this, select the object and drag one of its right handles until all the text fits on one line.

A graphic or text object covers up a field or another object.

When you're creating graphics or moving them around, you may end up with a graphic covering up a field or text object. To reveal the covered object, select the one on top of it and choose Send To Back from the Arrange menu.

Lots of objects are so close together that you can't select the one you want.

This happens when you have a complex layout with lots of text and graphic objects close to each other. Click the zoom control in the lower left corner of the screen to make everything on the layout bigger. And then you should be able to select the item you want.

Part labels are in the way, and you can't drag objects underneath them.

If part labels are shown horizontally (which is the default), they cover up the lower left corner of the part they identify. Click the part label control in the lower left corner of the screen to make the part labels vertical, and move them off the layout. (See *The zoom, status area, mode selector, and part label controls,* p. 107.)

Fields, text, or objects that are added to layouts always appear in strange colors, fonts, patterns, or line widths.

When you first add fields and objects to a layout, their attributes are determined by the defaults set in the Format menu and with the status area controls. To reset the default for any of these attributes, click on a blank part of the layout so nothing is selected, then set the new default using the appropriate commands or status area controls.

You want to set a number, date, or time format for a field, but these commands aren't available on the Format menu.

This means you have a text or container field selected, or you're working with a calculation field whose result is set to text. The Number…, Date…, or Time… commands on the Format menu are only available when you have a number, date, or time field selected.

7 Finding Information

Once you have a lot of data in a file, you can use FileMaker Pro's Find mode to locate specific pieces of information, to find records with missing or improper data, or to separate a group of records from the others in the file. First, you enter *find criteria* that tells FileMaker Pro what data to search for and what field to look in, and then it finds the records that contain that data and switches to Browse mode to display them. In this chapter, we'll see how to use Find mode to select records.

Creating a Find Request

Suppose you have an address file, and you want to find all the people named *Jones*. To do this, you create a *find request* and enter criteria in specific fields to find the records you want.

1. Choose Find from the Mode menu. FileMaker Pro displays the Find screen.

2. Type *Jones* into the Last Name field, like this:

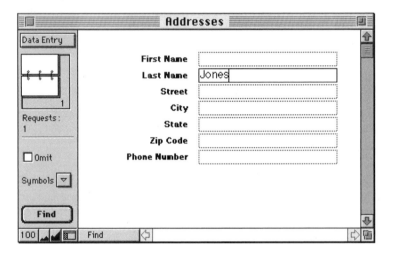

3. Press Return, click the Find button, or choose Perform Find from the Select menu. FileMaker Pro finds the records that contain "Jones" in the Last Name field and displays them in Browse mode, like this:

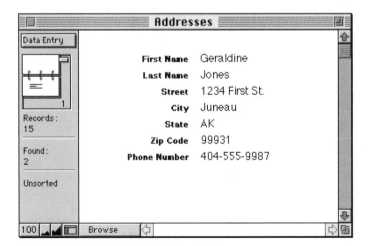

In this case, FileMaker Pro has found two records in which the Last Name field contains the criteria "Jones," so the status area shows this below the total number of records in the file.

You can also use the Paste Special submenu on the Edit menu to enter find criteria into fields. For example, to paste a value from a field's index into a field on the Find screen, select the field, choose the From Index… command from the Paste Special submenu on the Edit menu, and then double-click on the index value you want to enter into the field.

TIP

For this request, you only entered a single find criterion. You could search more specifically by using criteria in two or more fields. For example, you could enter *Jones* in the Last Name field, *Geraldine* in the First Name field, and *Juneau* in the City field, and FileMaker Pro would only display the records where information in all three fields matched those criteria.

Once you've found a group of records, most things you do in Browse mode apply only to the current found set, not to the entire file. The only records available to scroll through or select with the book icon are those in the found set. Only the found set will print, sort, or show up in Preview mode when you select these commands.

To switch from working with a found set to working with all the records in the file, choose Find All from the Select menu.

However, while most operations only apply to the found set, Find always searches the entire file's records. So if you use Find mode while you're already working with a found set, you'll be searching the whole file (not just the found set), and whatever records FileMaker Pro finds will replace the old found set.

What Find finds

In the example above, FileMaker Pro found records where the data exactly matched the criteria you entered. But FileMaker Pro actually selects all records whose search fields contain a string of characters that *begins* with the search criteria. In the example above, FileMaker Pro would have matched "Jones" with any records where the Last Name field contained anything beginning with "Jones," such as "Jonesby" and "Jonesson."

It would also select records where the Last Name field started with something else, but *contained* a name that started with "Jones," such as "Van Jonesson." It would *not* select records where the letters in "Jones" were split between two words or embedded in another name, like "J. Onesly" or "Ojoneso."

TIP

To have FileMaker Pro look for exact matches for the criteria you enter, you must use the *exact match* symbol. (See *Finding ranges, exact matches, or duplicates*, p. 166.) To find text that's embedded in a longer word, you must use the literal text symbol. (See *Finding literal text*, p. 169.)

Reusing or modifying a find request

Each time you choose the Find command from the Select menu, FileMaker Pro displays empty fields on the screen so you can enter criteria in them. In some cases, though, you'll want to use the same request you used previously.

To recall your last find request, choose Modify Last Find from the Select menu. FileMaker Pro will display the last request you entered, and you can then click the Find button, choose Perform Find from the Select menu, or press [Return] to search for records with that request again.

Modify Find also comes in handy when you've created a complex find request and want to modify it slightly to select a slightly different group of records.

The Find Screen

Now that you've seen what Find mode does and how to make a basic Find request, let's take a closer look at the Find screen itself, and the options it offers:

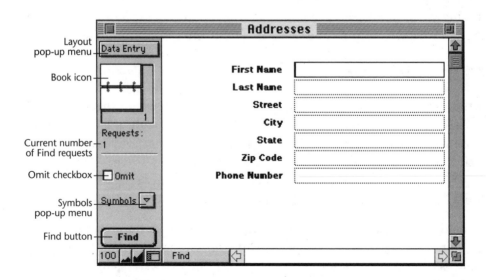

When you choose Find mode, you'll see the same layout displayed previously. As in other FileMaker Pro modes, the layout pop-up menu appears in the screen's upper left corner, and you can choose any layout for the Find screen by selecting it from the pop-up menu.

The book icon lets you display all the different Find requests you've entered. If you've created more than one request, clicking the pages in the book lets you see different requests. The total number of requests is shown below the book icon. (See *Creating Multiple Find Requests*, p. 169.)

The Omit checkbox lets you reverse a Find request, essentially telling FileMaker Pro to find all records *except* those matching the current request. For example, suppose you're sending out a flyer about a sale on snow blowers, and you want to include all your customers except those living in Phoenix. To do this, just type *Phoenix* in the City field, click the Omit checkbox, and then press Return to issue the request.

The Symbols pop-up menu contains symbols (or *operators*) that let you refine a find request by selecting specific ranges, specifying an exact match, or looking for other specific types of data. (See *Refining a Find Request*, below.)

Finally, the Find button is the one you click when you've finished creating your request(s) and are ready to have FileMaker Pro search the file and display the selected records. You can also press Return to select this button, or you can choose Perform Find from the Select menu.

Refining a Find Request

Typing individual words, names, or numbers into fields is a good basic way to find information, but sometimes you'll need to be more specific. The Symbols pop-up menu and the Omit checkbox enable you to refine your requests. First, let's look at the symbols you can use to refine a request.

The Symbols pop-up menu

When you click on the Symbols pop-up menu, you'll see a collection of symbols that make Find requests more specific, like this:

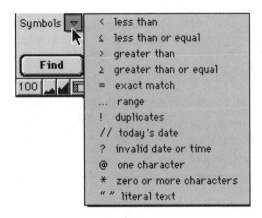

After you select a symbol, it appears in the field you currently have selected on the Find screen. You can also type these symbols from the keyboard to enter them into fields. Let's see how these operators are used to refine various requests.

Finding ranges, exact matches, or duplicates

The first seven symbols on the pop-up menu let you specify ranges, exact matches, or duplicates of data. Let's look at a few examples.

Suppose you know you have records for people named Johnson living in both the Los Angeles area and in the San Francisco area, and you only want to find the Johnsons who live in the San Francisco area. You know the zip codes for San Francisco begin at 94000, so you could use the *greater than or equal symbol* (≥) to tell FileMaker Pro to match only numbers above a certain value. In this case, you would enter *Johnson* for the Last Name field's criteria, and *≥94000* as the Zip Code field's criteria. FileMaker Pro would then find only the records where the Last Name field contained "Johnson" (or names beginning with "Johnson") and the Zip Code field contained values greater than or equal to 94000. The other symbols you use when you know the upper or lower limit of a range you want are *greater than* (>), *less than* (<), and *less than or equal* (≤).

With the *exact match symbol* (=), you can avoid having FileMaker Pro find records containing data that simply begins with the criteria you specified. Remember,

FileMaker Pro usually finds all records where a string of characters in the search field begins with or contains the search criterion. To have FileMaker Pro select only records where the Last Name field contains exactly "Jones" you use the exact match operator (=). In this case, the Last Name field of the Find request looks like this:

Last Name |=Jones |

You can also use the exact match operator to find records in which the search field is empty. Just type the exact match operator into a field by itself, and FileMaker Pro will select all records where that field is blank.

TIP

The *range symbol* (…) lets you locate records where the field's number, time, or date falls within two limits. Rather than specifying only an upper or lower limit, you specify both. For example, suppose you want to find orders for the month of May. You could use the range symbol to enter a date range like this:

Order Date: | 5/1/92…5/31/92 |

Notice that the range specified includes the first and last days of May. When you use the range symbol, FileMaker Pro includes the limiting values in the range, rather than finding only values that fall between those limits.

You can specify the range operator by typing three periods or two periods or by entering the ellipsis character (Option ;) from the keyboard.

TIP

Finding duplicate data

The *duplicates operator* (!) finds all records where the field contains data that is duplicated in that field in another record. In other words, this symbol finds all records in which the data in that field isn't unique. For example, suppose an address file contained five records in all—three records had "NY" in the State field, one record had "CA" in the State field, and the fifth record had "IL" in the State field. A find request with the ! symbol in the State field would find only the records containing NY, because that value isn't unique in the file, while the CA and IL values are unique. If the file had three NY records and two CA records, this Find request would find all five records, because none of the records would contain a unique value in the State field.

The duplicates operator is useful when you want to find every record where a field's data is the same in more than one record. For example, in an order-entry file, you might want to find all the orders from repeat customers. By searching the Customer Name field for duplicates, you could locate all the orders where the same customer names appear.

TIP

Using the Omit checkbox, you could easily locate all the records where the entry in a field *is* unique. Just use the duplicates symbol and then click the Omit checkbox, and FileMaker Pro will find every record except those where data is duplicated in a field.

Finding the current date

The *today's date operator* (//) tells FileMaker Pro to find all records where the field contains the current date (according to your Mac's internal calendar). As with the duplicates operator, you need only enter this operator by itself in a date field (or a calculation field with a date result) to perform the find operation. This operator is handy when your file has an auto-entry field that places the current date into each record and you want to find all the records that were created on today's date. For example, to produce a report showing all of today's orders from an accounting system, you would put the // operator in the Order Date field to find only those records.

Finding invalid dates or times

The *invalid date or time operator* (?) finds entries in date or time fields (or calculation fields with date or time results) that aren't in proper date or time formats. As mentioned in Chapter 5, FileMaker Pro warns you when you're about to enter the wrong type of data in a date or time field, but you can override the warning and enter it anyway. You can also import data from another file that doesn't match the correct date or time format. By using the invalid date or time operator, you can quickly find date or time data that won't compute. (See *Field types*, on p. 53 in Chapter 4 for more on valid date and time formats.)

Using wildcards

The *one character* (@) and *zero or more characters* (*) operators are wildcards that you combine with strings of text to restrict searches to specific variations of that text.

The one character operator tells FileMaker Pro to match any character in this position in a text string. For example, to find people with the first names Red or Rod, you would type *R@d* in the First Name field.

The zero or more characters operator tells FileMaker Pro to match entries with any number of characters (or none) in this position in a text string. This is handy when you're searching for a variety of entries that may be of different lengths. For example, to find all the records with street names that begin with "Br" and end with "e" (such as "Bruce," "Bryce," and "Brandywine"), you would type *Br*e* in the Street field.

If you type the zero or more characters operator (*) by itself in a field, you'll find all records where the field is not empty.

TIP

Finding literal text

The *literal text operator* ("") allows you to find characters within a string of text or symbols that can't normally be found. If you simply enter text into a field, FileMaker Pro will only select records where that field contains the text at the beginning of a word. By using the literal text symbol, however, you tell FileMaker Pro to search for the text wherever it occurs in the field.

For example, suppose you had an inventory file with part numbers that contained mixed letters and numbers, such as "AA001," "AB023," and "AC021," where the second letter in the part number designated a particular group of items. To select records containing only the C group, you would use the literal text symbol to search for the letter *C* in the item number field by typing *"C"* there—FileMaker Pro would find all the records with item numbers containing a *C*.

FileMaker can't search for some symbols, such as #, $, or &, when you type them in by themselves, but if you enclose these symbols inside the literal text operator (""), you can search for them.

TIP

Creating Multiple Find Requests

The options described above enable you to be very specific when making a find request. But sometimes you'll need to find groups of records that match one set of criteria or another, without necessarily matching all the criteria. For example, suppose you wanted to find all the Joneses living in Los Angeles, New Orleans, or Phoenix, but not those living elsewhere. You couldn't perform this search with a single find request:

- If you looked for Joneses only, FileMaker Pro would find them regardless of which city they were in.

- You also couldn't enter the three city names in the City field on one find request, because then FileMaker Pro would look for records where all three city names appeared in that field in the same record (and it wouldn't find any records like that).

Fortunately, FileMaker Pro lets you create as many different requests as you like and then search for records using them all at the same time. To find the geographically scattered Joneses in the example above, you have to create three requests, one for the Joneses in each specific city:

1. Choose Find from the Mode menu.

2. Type in the criteria for the first request (Joneses in Los Angeles), like this:

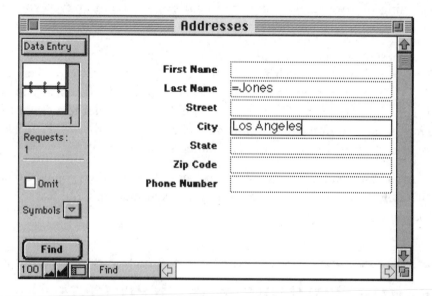

3. Choose the New Request command from the Mode menu or press ⌘N. FileMaker Pro displays a new, blank request screen, and the status area indicates there are now two requests.

4. Type in the criteria for the second request (Joneses in New Orleans), like this:

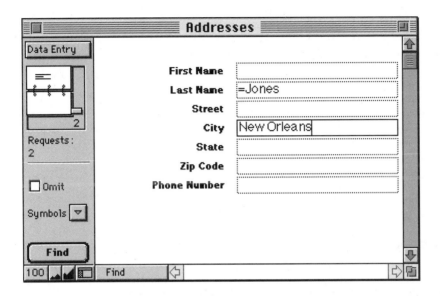

Notice that there are now two requests showing in the status area.

5. Choose New Request from the Mode menu. FileMaker Pro displays another blank request and the status area indicates there are now three requests.

6. Type in the criteria for the third request (Joneses in Phoenix), and click the Find button. FileMaker Pro searches the file and selects all records where "Jones" is in the Last Name field and the City field contains "Los Angeles," "New Orleans," or "Phoenix."

If, during the process of creating multiple requests, you create a request you don't want to use, you can get rid of it by displaying that request and choosing Delete Request ([⌘][E]) from the Mode menu.

Duplicating requests

New Request is the standard command for creating an additional request. But if you need to enter several requests in which most of the criteria are the same, it's easier to make copies of a single request using the Mode menu's Duplicate Request command ([⌘][D]). For example, to create the requests described above, you could fill in one request to find Joneses in Los Angeles, then make a copy using Duplicate Request, change the City field criterion to "New Orleans," choose Duplicate Request again and change the City field's criterion to "Phoenix."

Another reason to use the Duplicate Request command is that you must duplicate most of the criteria in each request to search properly. For example, you couldn't create one request for Joneses in Los Angeles and a second request where the city is New Orleans and the Last Name field is blank and expect FileMaker Pro to find the Joneses in New Orleans. Because "New Orleans" is the only criterion in the second request, FileMaker Pro will find all records where the City field contains "New Orleans," whether there's a Jones living there or not.

This is a very simple example of using multiple requests, but by using operators and the Omit checkbox with multiple requests, you can be extremely specific about which records you want FileMaker Pro to select.

Now let's look at some different kinds of Find requests.

Find Examples

Here are some quick examples of requests you'd use to find information in various ways.

Finding using more than one criterion.
In a personnel file, for example, finding all employees in the marketing department with salaries greater than $30,000 a year. To do this, create a single request and enter *Marketing* in the Department field and *>30000* in the Salary field.

Finding everything except one criterion.
In an address file, for example, finding all records except those in New York. To do this, create one request, entering *NY* in the State field and check the Omit box. Alternatively, try finding all New York records and then using the Find Omitted command on the Select menu—it's sometimes faster that way.

Finding one criterion or another.
In an accounts payable file, for example, finding all records where the customer's name is either "Acme Freight" or "Ajax Trucking." To do this, create two

requests, entering *Acme Freight* in the Customer Name field of one and *Ajax Trucking* in that field of the other.

Finding some criteria but not others.
In an address file, for example, finding everyone in New York or California named Jones except for the Joneses in Los Angeles or Buffalo. To do this, make four requests:

• One request with *Jones* in the Last Name field and *NY* in the State field

• One with *Jones* in the Last Name field and *CA* in the State field

• One with *Buffalo* in the City field and the Omit box checked

• One with *Los Angeles* in the City field and the Omit box checked

Finding empty fields.
The fastest way to find records that aren't complete is to search for empty fields. Just type the exact match operator (=) in the fields you suspect are empty. FileMaker Pro considers number fields empty if they contain text, and it considers text fields empty if they contain punctuation marks without any letters.

Finding Boolean values.
Boolean values are usually Yes, No, True, False, or 1 or 0. To find all records where the Boolean value is Yes, enter *y* or *t*. To find false values, enter *n* or *f*.

Finding dates.
Enter the find criteria as *MM/DD/YY* or *MM/DD/YYYY* (or any variations of either format that uses another symbol to separate months, days, and years, such as *MM-YY-DD*). FileMaker Pro will find matching records no matter how the date is formatted for display in those records. For example, a search for *7/9/96* would find "July 9, 1996" as well as "07/09/96" and "7/9/1996." When you search for a date in a text field, however, you must match the date's exact format, because FileMaker Pro doesn't know it's a date.

Finding numbers.
Numbers in numeric fields can be formatted as percentages, decimals, or currency, but FileMaker Pro will search for the value of the number, not the format. So, when you enter *2.35*, for example, FileMaker will find "$2.35," "2.35," and "235%."

Copying Data from Found Records

If you're finding records to transfer their data to another program, you can copy all the data in a found set by displaying one of the found set's records in Browse mode with no fields selected and then pressing ⌘ Option C. FileMaker Pro will place the data from the found set on the Clipboard, where it can be pasted into another program such as a spreadsheet.

FileMaker Pro puts the data on the Clipboard in tab-delimited format, so data in each field is separated by a tab and each record is separated by a carriage return. This is the format most spreadsheet programs and other database programs use. If the records in a found set include picture, sound, or movie data, this data won't be copied.

Troubleshooting

FileMaker Pro's Find function is fairly straightforward, but there are a few problems you may run into when using it. We'll look at some of them in this section.

The field where you need to enter a criterion isn't on the screen.
You need to either scroll the layout to bring the field into view or switch to a different layout. For example, if your layout is a telephone list that only shows first and last names and phone numbers, it won't contain street, city, state, or zip code fields, and you won't be able to find records based on street, city, state or zip code criteria.

To quickly see which fields are on each layout, choose different layouts with the layout pop-up menu and scan them visually, or choose Access Privileges from the File menu and then choose Overview… from the submenu. (See *Setting a group's access privileges*, p. 328 in Chapter 14, for more information on the Overview… command.)

You can't enter criteria into a field.
You can't enter find criteria into summary fields because this information is produced by FileMaker Pro from data in other records. You can't enter find criteria into a global field, because that field's data is the same in every record. However, you can enter find criteria into calculation fields.

An alert message says there are no valid criteria in a request.
FileMaker Pro won't search for certain kinds of information, and it won't perform a find operation if you haven't entered any criteria into any fields in a layout. In these cases, you'll see an alert message like this:

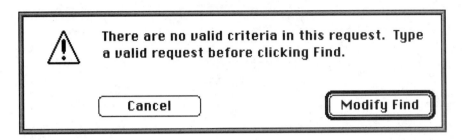

If you click the Cancel button, you'll be returned to the Browse screen. Click Modify Find to select Find mode and then enter find criteria.

FileMaker Pro won't search when a field only contains the symbols #, $, %, ^, &, {, }, [, or]; any of the range operators; or the literal text operator, and it will display the alert message if you enter these as criteria. If you use symbols in fields and you want to find them later, use the literal text operator to find them. For example, to find all the companies with an ampersand "&" in their name, type *"&"* in the Company Name field.

FileMaker Pro won't find information embedded in the middle of a word or number.
If you want to enter several words in a field and then find records based on one of those words, either make sure there's at least one space between each word or else use the literal text operator when you create the find request.

In a personnel file, for example, the Interests field might contain "hiking, skiing, golf." FileMaker Pro will be able to find "skiing" with a normal find request if there's at least one space before it. However, if the entry in the field is "hiking,skiing,golf," you'll have to enter the criteria as *"skiing"* for FileMaker Pro to find it.

When asked to find a range of dates or times, FileMaker Pro selects an incomplete group of records.
FileMaker Pro can't search chronologically if fields aren't defined for date and time data types. Use the invalid date or time operator (?) to see if data is entered in fields improperly in certain records, or use the Define Fields... command to see if the fields you're searching in are defined correctly.

8 Sorting Records and Checking Spelling

- Sorting Records
- Checking Spelling
- Installing Dictionaries
- Maintaining Reliable Data
- Troubleshooting

In this chapter, we'll look at FileMaker Pro's record-sorting function and at its data-checking features, which help you maintain accurate, reliable information.

Sorting Records

As discussed earlier, FileMaker Pro stores records in the order they're added to the file: The first record you enter stays at the beginning of the file, and each new record gets added to the end. But you can use FileMaker Pro's Sort... command to make records appear in a different order, based on the data in one or more fields.

For example, you might sort address records alphabetically by last name to print a telephone directory, or sort products by part classification in an inventory file. And before you can produce sub-summaries in printed reports, you have to sort records into the groups being summarized. (See *Using Summary Parts* in Chapter 9, p. 211.)

Using the Sort... command

You can sort records whenever you're in Browse or Preview mode. If you've selected a group of records with the Find command, FileMaker Pro will sort only the records in that found set. Here's the basic procedure:

1. Choose Sort... from the Mode menu or press ⌘S. The Sort Records dialog box appears, as shown here:

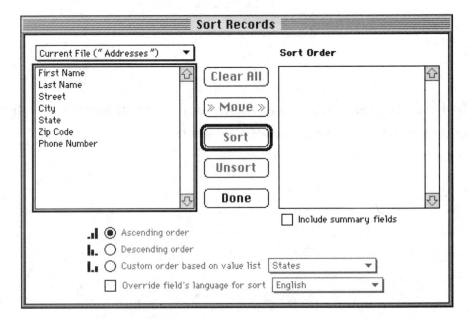

2. In the list of fields at the left, double-click on the name of the field on whose data you want to sort. Its name will appear in the Sort Order list at the right, like this:

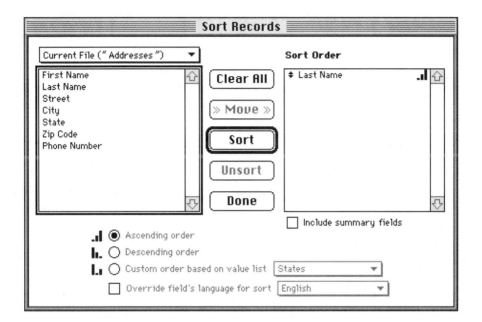

The icon next to the field name in the Sort Order list shows that the field's data will be sorted in ascending order (see the next section for alternative sort orders). Notice that the Sort button only becomes darkened after you've selected a field to sort on.

3. Press [Return] or click the Sort button. FileMaker Pro will display a window showing the progress of the sort operation, and the records will be sorted. The status area will show that the records are sorted, like this:

Once you sort records, they stay that way until you resort them, unsort them, add a record, or switch to a different found set of records with the Find, Find All, Omit, or Omit Multiple commands.

If you add a record to a sorted found set, the status area will report that the file is now *Semi-sorted*, indicating that the records are still mostly sorted but that by adding a new record you have disturbed the sort order somewhat.

Now, let's look at the other features of the Sort Records dialog box.

The Sort Records dialog box

At the upper left corner of the dialog box, the pop-up menu lets you choose related files and sort the file on those fields. This menu is used only when you are working with a relational database and you're displaying fields from one or more related files in your current file. For example, if your file displays the related Customer Number field from the Customers file, you can choose the Customers file relationship from the pop-up menu. When you do, the fields in the Customers file will appear in the list below, and you can then include the Customer Number field in your sort order.

The buttons between the field list box and the Sort Order box let you manage the sort order. The Clear All button clears the Sort Order box so you can specify a new sort order. The Move button moves fields into and out of the Sort Order box. To move a field into the Sort Order box, select its name in the field list and click the Move button. To take a field out of the Sort Order box, select its name in the Sort Order box and click Move.

TIP

You can also double-click on field names to move them between the field list and the Sort Order box.

The Sort button sorts the current selection of records in the order shown in the Sort Order box. The Unsort button returns the records to their original order in the file. The Done button puts the dialog box away.

If you've defined summary fields for your file, those field names are usually dimmed in the Field List box so you can't select them for sorting. Below the Sort Order box, the Include summary fields checkbox lets you include summary fields so you can sort on them, as well. When you sort on a summary field, though, you must also sort on at least one other non-summary field (see *Sorting on a summary field*, on p. 182).

The radio buttons at the bottom of the dialog box let you control the sort order for each field you select to sort on. You can set a different sort order for each of the fields in the Sort Order box, and the button that's selected at the time you move a field name to the Sort Order box determines the sort order for that field. To change a field's sort order after it's in the Sort Order box, select the field and then click the radio button for the order you want.

The Ascending order button is the default selection. Any field moved into the Sort Order box while it's selected will be sorted from lowest to highest numerically, from *A* to *Z* alphabetically, and from earliest to latest chronologically. The Descending order button sorts data in the opposite order.

The Custom order based on value list button sorts records according to a value list. When this button is selected, you can choose a value list name from the pop-up menu to the right (if you've defined one or more value lists for your file), or you can define a new value list that determines the sort order (see *Validation options* on p. 67 in Chapter 4 for more information).

When you sort on a value list, FileMaker Pro sorts records based on the order in which items appear on the value list, rather than in alphabetical, numerical, or chronological order. For example, suppose you had a file of sales prospects and you set up a field called Sales Priority with the following predefined value list:

Hot

Warm

Cool

If you used the Custom order based on value list option to sort on the Sales Priority field, records would be sorted according to the list, with Hot prospects first, Warm prospects second, and Cool prospects last.

The Override field's language for sort checkbox at the bottom of the Sort Records dialog box lets you choose an alternate language by which to sort. If you don't choose this option, FileMaker uses the default language for your computer system. When you check this box, the pop-up menu becomes active, and you can choose from among two dozen different languages on which to sort.

Sorting on several fields

You can sort on several fields at once. In fact, you can include every field in the file in the Sort Order box (except summary fields—see below). If your Sort Order box contains, from top to bottom, State, City, and Last Name fields, the records will be sorted by state, within each state by city, and within each city by last name.

You can select either ascending, descending, or custom sort order separately for each of the fields you sort on. For example, you could sort first by State in custom order, then by City in descending order, and finally by Last Name in ascending order, if you wanted to.

Sorting on a summary field

Summary fields appear in the Sort Records dialog box's field list, but they're dimmed unless you choose to include them among your sorting options. To include a summary field, check the Include summary fields checkbox in the Sort Records dialog box.

When you add a summary field to the sort order, you'll see two special icons on either side of it. In this Sort Order box, for example, the Total Price field is a summary field:

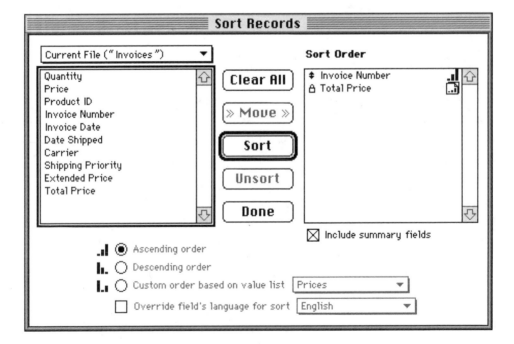

The padlock icon at the left indicates that the field can't be moved in the Sort Order list. You can drag the other fields up and down to change the sort order, but a summary field must always be last. The page icon reminds you that summaries only appear when a layout is viewed in Preview mode or printed.

FileMaker Pro won't sort records on a summary field alone; you must also include at least one non-summary field in the Sort Order box. Also, you can only sort on one summary field at a time.

IMPORTANT NOTE

If you sort on a certain field to produce sub-summaries in a report, and simultaneously sort on the summary field itself, the records will be sorted into groups by the non-summary field, and the groups themselves will be sorted by their summary field data. Here's an example: Suppose you have a personnel file that contains a Salary field, and a summary field called Total Salaries that shows the sum of the Salary field's contents from all the records selected.

In the layout below, the Total Salaries field is in a sub-summary part that appears when the file is sorted on the Department field. (This way, each department's records are grouped together, with the total salaries for that department following the group.) With records sorted on the Department field alone, the departments appear in alphabetical order, like this:

First Name	Last Name	Department	Salary
John	Jones	Accounting	$24,500.00
Oscar	Banuelos	Accounting	$27,500.00
		Total Department Salaries	$52,000.00
Andrew	Graves	Admin.	$18,000.00
		Total Department Salaries	$18,000.00
Fritz	Frangler	Manufacturing	$21,600.00
		Total Department Salaries	$21,600.00
Wilma	Wang	Marketing	$33,100.00
Susan	Pearson	Marketing	$21,750.00
Buster	Sessions	Marketing	$42,500.00
		Total Department Salaries	$97,350.00
		Total Company Salaries	$188,950.00

If we also sort on the Total Salaries summary field, in ascending order, the departments will appear in the order of their total salaries, like this:

First Name	Last Name	Department	Salary
Andrew	Graves	Admin.	$18,000.00
		Total Department Salaries	$18,000.00
Fritz	Frangler	Manufacturing	$21,600.00
		Total Department Salaries	$21,600.00
John	Jones	Accounting	$24,500.00
Oscar	Banuelos	Accounting	$27,500.00
		Total Department Salaries	$52,000.00
Wilma	Wang	Marketing	$33,100.00
Susan	Pearson	Marketing	$21,750.00
Buster	Sessions	Marketing	$42,500.00
		Total Department Salaries	$97,350.00
		Total Company Salaries	$188,950.00

So while it was necessary to sort by the Department field to group each department's records together, sorting by departmental summary rearranged the groups of records in order of increasing total salaries, overriding their prior alphabetic sorting by department name.

Saving the sort order

The sort order you specify remains in the Sort Records dialog box until you select a new one. If you regularly use certain specific sort orders, you can create scripts to store them (see Chapter 12).

Try experimenting with different sort orders to see how sorting can work for you.

~~~~~~

Checking Spelling

Inaccurate spelling of text entries can make it hard to select or use data. A spelling mistake in an address can make a letter undeliverable, and it can make it hard to select the record containing the mistake using Find mode. After all, if you're looking for records with "San Francisco" in the City field, but in one record the entry is spelled "Sam Francesco," you won't find that record.

FileMaker Pro's built-in spelling checker lets you easily search for and correct such spelling problems.

How spell-checking works

FileMaker Pro can check the spelling of data in a selected field, record, or found set of records in Browse mode, or it can check layout text in Layout mode. You decide what part of a file to check by choosing the appropriate command from the Spelling submenu on the Edit menu. Then FileMaker Pro compares the words in the selected item with the words in the dictionary file(s) it has open.

IMPORTANT NOTE

Normally, dictionary files are copied into the Claris folder inside the System Folder when you install FileMaker Pro. If you didn't install the dictionaries, see p. 14 in Chapter 2.

FileMaker Pro's Main Dictionary can't be edited—it's stored in a special compressed format. (Claris offers main dictionaries in several languages. If you buy one, you can substitute it for FileMaker Pro's standard English Main Dictionary—see *Installing Dictionaries*, p. 189.)

The User Dictionary is meant to be changed—you can add whatever words you want to it, or remove words from it. You can have several different user dictionaries, but FileMaker Pro will only use one of them at a time. FileMaker Pro can also use dictionaries from other Claris products, such as ClarisWorks. (See *Editing user dictionaries* on p. 190.)

Running a spelling check

Here's how to check the spelling of all the records you're currently viewing in Browse mode.

1. Choose Spelling from the Edit menu, and hold the mouse button down. FileMaker Pro displays a submenu like this:

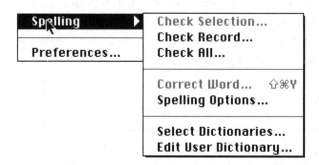

2. Choose Check All... from the submenu. FileMaker Pro automatically begins checking data in all fields of the found set of records. When it finds a questionable spelling, it displays the Spelling window, like this:

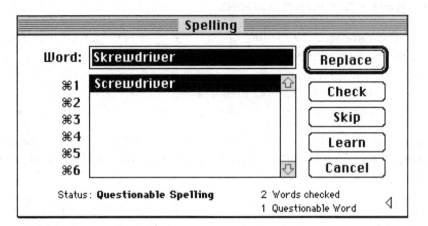

In this case, the word *Skrewdriver* has been found questionable, as indicated by the message in the Status area. Let's look at the Spelling window now as we consider our options for dealing with this questionable word.

The Word box shows the questionable word. If you want to correct its spelling, you can type your correction into this box, or you can select one of the alternates listed below it. After you choose an option for each word, you'll see the next questionable word after it as FileMaker Pro moves through each field and record in the found set. When all questionable words have been found, the Replace button at the upper right of the Spelling window says Done, and you click it to put the window away.

The list below the Word box contains suggested alternate spellings from the dictionaries FileMaker Pro is using to check the file. You can double-click on an alternate, select it, and click the Replace button, or press the ⌘-number combination next to an alternate to replace the questionable word.

The Status area at the bottom shows the status of the current word, how many words have been checked, and how many have been found questionable. Clicking the triangle icon in the lower right corner displays a text box that shows the questionable word in context with the words that surround it, like this:

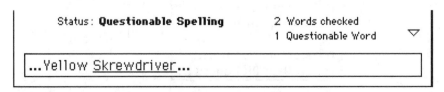

At the right side of the dialog box, the Replace button replaces the questionable word, with either the alternate you've selected or with the spelling you've entered in the Word box. The replacement word is placed in the field or layout where the original was, and the data or layout text around it is automatically reformatted to accommodate the new word.

The Check button checks the spelling of any word you've entered in the Word box. Use this when you type in a correction and you want FileMaker Pro to check the spelling of the word you've typed.

The Skip button tells FileMaker Pro to ignore this word and continue checking. Once you skip a questionable word, FileMaker Pro will skip over all future occurrences of that word during the current round of spell-checking. In future rounds, though, FileMaker Pro will question the word again.

The Learn button adds the questionable word to your currently installed user dictionary. Once the word has been added, FileMaker Pro won't question it again.

The Cancel button ends the spelling check, puts the Spelling window away, and returns you to the Layout or Browse screen you were using before.

Checking individual records, selections, or layouts

The example above showed how to check all the records in the found set. To check an individual record, display the record in Browse mode, and then choose Check Record… from the Spelling submenu. If you're in Layout mode, this command name changes to Check Layout…, and you choose it to check the spelling of all text objects on the current layout.

To check specific data within a record, display the record in Browse mode, select the text you want to check, then choose the Check Selection… command from the Spelling submenu.

Looking up a word in FileMaker Pro's dictionaries

Even if you're not checking the spelling of a found set, record, or layout, you can use FileMaker Pro's dictionaries to look up the spelling of any word you type, without affecting the contents of the current layout or record.

1. Choose Check Record… or Check Layout… (whichever appears on your Spelling submenu) to display the Spelling window.

2. Type the word whose spelling you want to check in the Word box.

3. Click the Check button. If the word is spelled wrong, FileMaker Pro will suggest alternates. If the spelling is correct, the status area will say *Correct Spelling.*

4. Click the Done button to put the Spelling window away.

Checking spelling as you type

You can also have FileMaker Pro automatically check your spelling as you type onto layouts or into records. Here's how:

1. Choose the Spelling Options... command from the Spelling submenu. FileMaker Pro displays a dialog box like this:

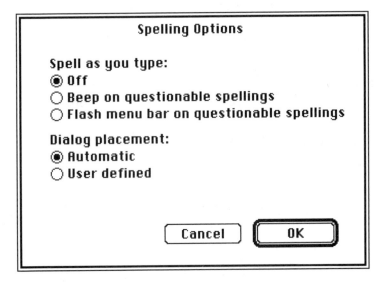

2. Click one of the Spell as you type buttons to have FileMaker Pro beep or flash the menu bar whenever you type a questionable word.

3. Click the OK button.

From now on, FileMaker Pro will check each word as you type it in, and will let you know when you type one it doesn't recognize.

After you've been alerted about a questionable spelling, you can choose Correct Word... from the Spelling submenu to see suggested alternate spellings, replace the word with a correct spelling, or skip over it and continue with your work.

The Correct Word… command is only active if you've just typed a misspelled word and haven't yet pressed the ⌊Tab⌋, ⌊Return⌋, or ⌊Enter⌋ key to move to another field. Once you move to another field, the Correct Word… command is dimmed again.

The Dialog placement buttons at the bottom of the Spelling Options dialog box let you decide where the Spelling dialog box appears on the screen when you check a selection. The Automatic button tells FileMaker Pro to decide where to put the dialog box. If you click the User defined button, the Spelling dialog box will always open at the place where you last dragged it on the screen.

Installing Dictionaries

Ordinarily, FileMaker Pro uses one main dictionary and one user dictionary when it runs a spelling check. If you have more than one of either type of dictionary, you can choose which one FileMaker Pro uses on a particular check with the Select Dictionaries… command.

You can also use this command to remove installed dictionaries. FileMaker Pro will continue to use whatever dictionaries you've installed until you remove them or install different ones.

To install a dictionary:

1. Choose Select Dictionaries… from the Spelling submenu. FileMaker Pro displays a directory dialog box like this one:

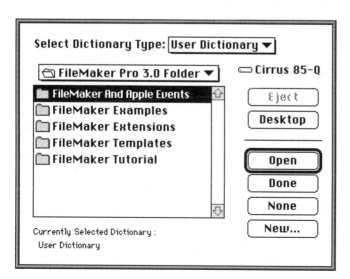

2. Choose either Main Dictionary or User Dictionary from the pop-up menu at the top of the dialog box to indicate the type of dictionary you want to install.

3. Navigate to the location of the dictionary file you want to install and select the dictionary name. The Open button at the left changes to Select.

4. Click the Select button. FileMaker Pro will install the dictionary and put the dialog box away.

Installing a user or main dictionary will automatically remove any dictionary of the same type that's in use. The status area at the bottom of the dialog box shows the name of the user dictionary that's currently selected.

To remove a current dictionary without replacing it with another one, just choose the Main Dictionary or User Dictionary command from the pop-up menu at the top of the dialog box (depending on the type of dictionary you want to remove), and then click the None button at the right.

You can also create new user dictionaries by clicking the New... button at the bottom of this dialog box. FileMaker Pro will display another dialog box where you can name the new dictionary file and choose a location to store it. Once you've done so, click the Save button and FileMaker Pro will automatically install it as the current user dictionary.

To add words to a new user dictionary, you can either click the Learn button in the Spelling window to add a questionable word to the dictionary (see p. 187, or you can use the editing features described next.

Editing user dictionaries

You can add or remove words in the current user dictionary at any time. For adding or removing individual words, the simplest method is to type the words. Here's the procedure:

1. Open the user dictionary you want to edit, using the Select Dictionaries... command described in the previous section.

2. Choose Edit User Dictionary... from the Spelling submenu. FileMaker Pro displays a dialog box, as shown here:

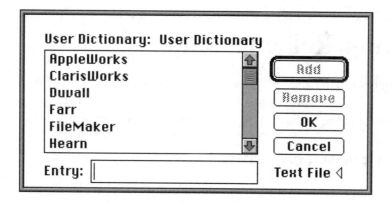

To add a word, type the new word in the Entry box and click the Add button or press (Return). To remove a word, select it from the list of words and click the Remove button.

To edit a word in a user dictionary, you must remove the existing version and then add the new one.

If you want to add a lot of words to a dictionary at once, you can import a text file into the current user dictionary. The file must be in ASCII text format.

1. Click the triangle icon next to Text File in the lower right corner of the dialog box. FileMaker Pro will display two buttons: Import... and Export....

2. Click the Import... button to display a directory dialog box where you can navigate to the text file you want to import.

3. After you navigate to the text file you want to import, select it and click the Open button. The words in the text file will be added to your user dictionary.

Exporting user dictionaries

You can also export the words in a user dictionary as a text file. Just click the Export... button that appears when you click the Text File triangle icon, specify a name and location for your file in the directory dialog box that appears, and then click the Save button to save it.

Maintaining Reliable Data

Spell-checking your files isn't the only way to keep your data "clean" and reliable. In this section, we'll look at various FileMaker Pro features that can help you maintain consistent data and avoid duplicate entries in your files.

Maintaining consistent data

Consistent data is one of the most important requirements for a useful database file. Because of the way FileMaker Pro finds, sorts, and indexes information, you may not be able to select all the records you want if your data entries are inconsistent. For example, if you have a file that tracks deductible expenses and you refer to donations as both "donations" and "contributions," you won't be able to select all the records of such transactions by searching only for "donations."

To help avoid this problem, select the Member of value list validation option when you define fields that should hold only specific entries. For example, in an accounting file where you have 20 different expense account categories, you can create a list of those categories to select from during data entry. Choosing options from a list or menu avoids the possibility of typing errors or memory lapses that might cause a category name to be entered incorrectly (see *Validation options* on p. 67 in Chapter 4 for more information).

TIP

To further eliminate ambiguous categorizations of data, check the predefined value list itself to make sure each category or item is distinct. For example, if a list of accounting categories contains both "Donation" and "Contribution," users might select one category in some records and the other category in other records, even though both categories indicate the same type of expense.

In other situations, you may want to define a field so that FileMaker Pro will automatically enter data into it, so that it will accept only a particular data format or range, or so that it won't accept an entry that isn't unique. The procedures for setting up all these options are described under *Setting Entry Options*, p. 64 in Chapter 4, and *The Field Format... command* on p. 147 in Chapter 6.

Checking indexes

One way to check the consistency of entries in a given field is to examine its index. Since every unique entry in a field appears in the field's index, you can quickly spot inconsistent entries by scanning it.

Suppose, for example, you want to check the City field of an address file. To display that field's index:

1. Select the City field in Browse mode.

2. Press ⌘I. FileMaker Pro displays the index in a window, like this:

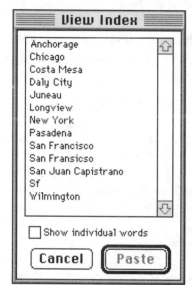

As you can see, FileMaker Pro indexes every group of words entered in a field, and the entries are shown in alphabetical order. You can see that the City field in at least one record has "San Francisco" misspelled as "San Fransicso," and at least one other record has "Sf" instead of a city name.

To display multiple-word names in fields as single words in the index, click the Show individual words checkbox in the View Index dialog box.

TIP

Once you've spotted inconsistencies like this in a field's index, use the Find command to locate the records with the inconsistent data and replace it with correct data. To find records easily, select the field you're searching on in Find mode, press ⌘I to display the field's index, and then double-click on the incorrect index entry to paste it into the find request. Once the incorrect records are found, you can use ⌘I again to paste in the correct data. (See p. 77 in Chapter 5 for details.)

Checking for duplicates

When you enter a lot of data into a file, it's possible to enter the same information twice and end up with duplicate records. In a customer file, for example, one customer's address might be entered two or three times. That means you're likely to print extra labels, extra form letters, or extras of anything else you print from the customer list. If the customer's address changes, you may only find and update one record, leaving the old address in another record and leading to confusion or inaccurate mailings later. To avoid this, use FileMaker Pro's Find command to look for duplicate entries in critical fields.

To search for duplicate customer records, for example:

1. Display a layout that contains a Customer Name or Company Name field.

2. Choose Find from the Mode menu.

3. Type *!* in the Customer Name or Company Name field and press (Return). FileMaker Pro will find and display all the records that have duplicate entries in this field. If there are two "Smith Trucking" entries in this field in different records, for example, FileMaker Pro will display both records. You can then delete the duplicate.

IMPORTANT NOTE

When you're looking for duplications in more than one field at a time, it's best to sort the file on those fields, choose a columnar layout, and then visually scan the file. When you ask FileMaker Pro to search for duplicates on more than one field, the process takes forever.

TIP

Use the Unique validation option when defining fields that should contain unique information to help prevent duplicate data from being entered in your files. See p. 68 in Chapter 4.

Troubleshooting

FileMaker Pro's sorting and spelling features are pretty simple to use, but that doesn't mean everything they do will make sense to you at first. In this section, we'll look at some common problems you might run into while using them.

A file you've sorted becomes unsorted again when you use the Find or Find All commands.

That's just the way it is with FileMaker Pro. Whenever you use the Find or Find All commands, any sort order that was in effect before is tossed out and the records are returned to their original, unsorted order in the file. If you have a particular sort order and found set you want to be able to restore quickly, record them in a script (see Chapter 12).

You sorted a file on more than one field and you didn't get the sort order you expected.

There are several possibilities in this case:

1. First, check the Sort Records dialog box to make sure the correct sort order is set. The Sort Records dialog box always stores the last sort order you set.

If you simply click the Sort button in this dialog box without checking the Sort Order list, you could end up sorting the file in an order you no longer want.

2. As mentioned earlier in this chapter, a sort on a summary field will override a sort on a non-summary field. For example, if you sort expense records by employees' last names to summarize each employee's expenses, the records will be grouped by employee last name in alphabetical order. But if you also sort them by the field that summarizes expenses, they'll still be grouped by employee last name, but the groups will appear in order of each employee's total expenses.

3. If all else fails, simplify a sort. If you try sorting a file on five or six fields, it will become difficult to tell just how it's sorted. So simplify the Sort Order list and sort again, or clear the Sort Order list completely and start over, sorting on just one or two fields.

The Spell as you type options don't work when you turn them on.

When you use the Spelling Options... command on the Spelling submenu to select one of the two Spell as you type options, that option should become active immediately. If it doesn't work right away, close the file, quit FileMaker Pro, restart your Mac, and then reopen the file. The Spell as you type option should work normally.

9 Designing Reports

- Layout Parts Defined
- Adding and Changing Parts
- Placing Objects in Parts
- Using Headers and Footers
- Using Summary Parts
- Creating Form Letters
- Troubleshooting

FileMaker Pro's Layout mode lets you arrange fields, text, and graphics so you can view your data in various ways on the screen. And since the arrangement of data you see on the screen in a layout is what appears on paper when you print from a database, you also use layouts to design printed reports, form letters, and many other documents.

Every FileMaker Pro layout is divided into *parts*, which are horizontal slices of a screen or page, like layers in a cake. Different parts handle layout objects differently, so you place fields, text, or graphics in different parts according to how you want the items to appear in a report.

For example, depending on what part you put it in, a field in a report may appear once for each record, once for each sorted group of records, once per page, or once in the entire report; it may display one record's data or summarize data from many records.

You can add as many parts to a layout as you like, and change their sizes or delete them as necessary. In this chapter, we'll see what the different parts do and how to use them to create reports.

Layout Parts Defined

The different parts in a layout are only visible when you're in Layout mode. There, parts are divided from one another by horizontal dotted lines, and each part is labeled. As mentioned above, you can add or remove parts from layouts, and you can make parts larger or smaller to accommodate as much information as you like or to eliminate empty space on a layout.

Standard layout parts

The three most commonly used parts are the *header*, the *body*, and the *footer*. FileMaker Pro automatically adds these parts to new standard layouts. (New label layouts start out with a header and a body but no footer.)

Like all parts, the header, body, and footer are identified with labels and are separated from each other by dashed boundary lines. For example, here's a columnar report layout whose parts contain fields, text, and graphics:

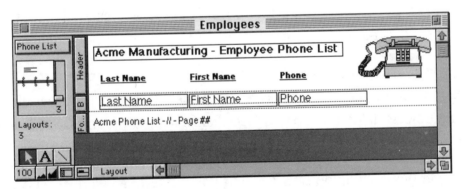

In this example as elsewhere in this chapter, the part labels are shown vertically. Below the header label, the *B* is the body part label and the *Fo...* is the footer part label. To display more of a vertical part label, you must resize the part to

IMPORTANT NOTE

make it taller. You can switch from vertical to horizontal part labels by clicking the part label control at the bottom of the window (see p. 107 in Chapter 6).

The header and footer contain information that will print once on each page of a report. The header at the top of this example contains a title for the report, the names of the fields that will make up the columns of data, and a graphic. The footer in this example contains the title of the report along with special symbols that tell FileMaker Pro to insert the current date (the // symbol) and page number (the ## symbol) when the report is printed or previewed.

Headers and footers appear in Browse mode as well. When a header contains a date or time symbol, the current date or time appears in Browse mode. Page number symbols are only converted to actual page numbers when the report is previewed or printed.

IMPORTANT NOTE

You can only have one header and one footer in a layout, although either of these can contain several lines of text or data and can be as tall as the current page setup permits. You can add fields to headers or footers, but they'll show data from only one record.

- If you include a field in a header, it will display data from the first record on that page of the report.

- If you put a field in a footer, it will display data from the last record on that page of the report.

The body part of a layout contains the fields that show data from the records you're working with. The fields and objects in the body of a layout are repeated once for each record included in the report, as many times as will fit on a page using the current page setup. If FileMaker Pro comes to the bottom of a page and there isn't room for another record's data, a new page will begin and that data will be printed at the top of it.

All layouts automatically contain a body, but you can delete the body if you don't want to show individual records in a report. If you wanted to make a report that shows only summary totals, for example, you could create a columnar report that contains summary parts and then delete the body from the layout.

TIP

Here's how the above layout looks when the report is shown in Preview mode:

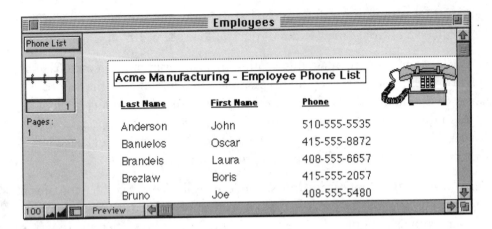

As you can see, the employee first and last names and phone numbers are repeated down the page because these fields were included in the body, while the field names and report title are shown only at the top of the page, because these items were in the header. The footer at the bottom of the page looks like this:

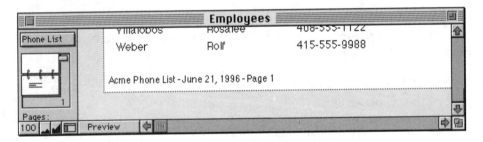

Notice that the date and page number symbols that were included in the footer have now been converted to the current date and page number. For more on putting dates and page numbers in headers and footers, see *Using Headers and Footers*, on p. 208, below.

Other layout parts

There are five other types of parts you can add to a layout besides the three basic ones described above.

A *title header* is a header that prints only on the first page of a report, in place of the normal header for that page. Like a header, this part appears at the top of the page and usually contains the report date, title, the company name, other text, or graphic objects. You can only have one title header per layout, and it will only show up in Preview mode or in printouts.

To make a cover page for a FileMaker Pro report, create a title header that's a full page high and then add the text for the title of the report to it.

A *leading grand summary* is a part that typically contains either summary or regular fields, along with text labels identifying those fields. A leading grand summary always appears between the header and the body. If a leading grand summary part contains a summary field, it will show summary data from all the records in the body of the report. (See *Adding summary parts*, on p. 214, below.) If this part contains a regular field, it will show the data that's in that field in the first record in the report. You can only have one leading grand summary per layout.

A *sub-summary* contains a summary field that summarizes only the data from certain groups of records. When you create a sub-summary part, you also choose the field on which records in the report must be sorted in order to produce proper summary calculations. (See *Adding summary parts*, p. 214.) If the records aren't sorted on the specified field, the sub-summary part won't appear in the report.

Sub-summary parts can appear either above or below the body of a layout. You can have as many sub-summary parts in a layout as you like. Like title headers and title footers, however, sub-summaries don't show up in Browse or Find modes—only in Preview mode and in printouts.

A *trailing grand summary* is like a leading grand summary except that it appears after the body and any sub-summary parts. When a trailing grand summary contains a regular field, the field shows the data from the last record in the group selected for the current report. You can only have one trailing grand summary per layout.

A *title footer* is like a title header except that it prints at the bottom of the first page instead of the top. You might use a title footer to add end notes or a one-page appendix to a report. You can only have one title footer part per layout.

Adding and Changing Parts

To add a part to a layout, use the part tool on the Layout screen or choose the Part Setup... command from the Mode menu.

Using the part tool

To use the part tool:

1. Drag the part tool from the status area onto the layout, to the position—
    above or below another part—where you want the new part to appear.

    The part tool's upper edge determines the part's position on the layout.

2. Release the mouse button and the Part Definition dialog box will appear,
    like this:

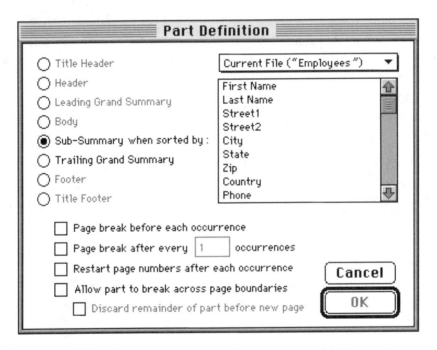

Depending on where you've placed the part tool and which parts are already
on the layout, some of the part type options may be dimmed. For example, if
there's already a footer on the layout, you won't be able to add another one.

3. Click the button for the type of part you want to add. If you choose a sub-
    summary part, the list of fields on the right will become darkened (as they
    are in the example above) and you'll have to select a field on which to sort
    the records for the sub-summary.

4. Click the checkboxes to select whichever of the available options you want. Which options are available depends on which part you choose. Here's what the options do:

Page break before each occurrence tells FileMaker Pro to start a new page before printing a sub-summary or trailing grand summary.

Page break after every *<number>* occurrences tells FileMaker Pro to start a new page after printing a leading grand summary, a trailing grand summary, or a certain number of sub-summary parts. (When you choose this option, you type in a number to specify the number of occurrences.)

Restart page numbers after each occurrence lets you start page numbering over again at 1 after you print a title header, title footer, leading grand summary, or sub-summary part.

Allow part to break across page boundaries tells FileMaker Pro to break up the information in a leading grand summary, sub-summary, or trailing grand summary between two pages if there isn't enough room for all the information in the part on one page. When you check this option, the Discard remainder of part before new page option becomes active. If you check the box, FileMaker Pro will discard leftover portions of a part when the part is broken between pages, rather than printing the remainder at the top of the following page.

5. Click the OK button when you're done. The part will be added to the layout. For example, if we added a title header to the columnar phone list layout shown earlier, it would look like this:

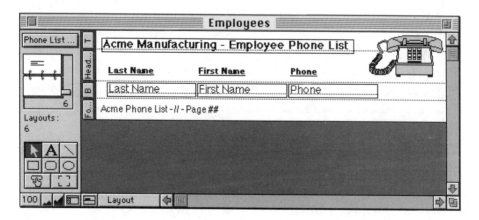

You can see the new title header part label above the header label, and a new part boundary line extends across the top of the layout just below the phone list title.

When you drag the part tool onto a layout, you see the boundary line extending from it in the exact position where it will appear when the part is defined. In this case, the boundary line cuts through the layout title and the telephone graphic. Having added this title header part to the layout, we would now want to resize it and put the fields, graphics, or layout text we wanted in it. (See *Resizing and deleting parts*, on p. 205.) In this case, we'd want to enlarge the title header part and move the layout title and phone graphic down into the page header, and then add a larger title and perhaps a larger graphic to the title header itself.

Using the Part Setup... command

The Part Setup... command is the alternative way to add parts to a layout, and it also lets you work with existing parts. To use this command:

1. Choose Part Setup... from the Mode menu. The Part Setup dialog box appears, listing all the currently defined parts in the layout, like this:

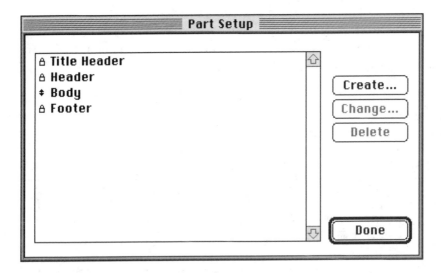

2. Click the Create... button. The Part Definition dialog box appears, as described on p. 202.

3. Choose the part you want to add and select its options, then click the OK button. You'll be returned to the Part Setup dialog box, and you'll see the new part's name on the list of parts. (If you choose a sub-summary part,

FileMaker Pro will display a dialog box asking whether to print the information above or below the records being summarized. Click the Print Above or Print Below button to indicate the position you want.)

4. Click the Done button. The part is added to the layout.

You can also display the Part Definition dialog box by double-clicking on any part label in a layout.

TIP

Resizing and deleting parts

Part sizes are set automatically when you create a layout or add parts to it with the Part Setup… command. When you add a part with the part tool, you determine its size by where you place it relative to the part boundary above it. In any case, at some point you'll probably want to either enlarge parts (to make room for the fields or other objects you want to put in them) or shrink them (so they don't take up any more space in the layout than necessary). To resize a part, just drag its boundary line up or down.

If you change your mind about adding a part after it's on the layout, you can delete it in the Part Setup dialog box (by selecting the part name there and clicking the Delete button), or by selecting the part's label on the layout and pressing the (Delete) key.

When you delete a part using one of the above methods, FileMaker Pro deletes any objects inside the deleted part as well. You'll see a warning asking you if you want to delete all objects inside the part. If you don't want to delete the objects inside the part, drag them into another part first.

IMPORTANT NOTE

If the part doesn't contain any objects, you can also delete it by dragging its lower boundary line up until it overlaps the boundary line above it.

Rearranging parts

The header, title header, footer, title footer, and grand summary parts on a layout must remain in certain positions at the top or bottom of the layout, but you can rearrange the positions of the body and any sub-summary parts. You can do this with the Part Setup dialog box:

1. Choose Part Setup… from the Mode menu. The Part Setup dialog box appears as on p. 204. The parts that can be rearranged have double-arrow icons next to their names; the parts that can't be moved have padlock icons next to their names.

2. Select the part you want to move and drag it up or down to rearrange it relative to the other parts.

3. Click the Done button to return to the layout.

Placing Objects in Parts

To add a field, text or graphics to a part, you use the standard Layout mode tools discussed in Chapter 6. Reviewing the basics, you can:

-   Add fields by dragging the field tool to the location you want, releasing the mouse button, and choosing the field you want from the list that appears.

-   Add fields inside text objects by using the Merge Field... command on the Paste Special... submenu on the Edit menu.

-   Add text by clicking on the text tool, clicking or dragging a box in the location where you want text to begin, and then typing or pasting in the text you want.

-   Add graphics by selecting the graphic tool you want and drawing the graphic where you want it, by pasting in a graphic from the Clipboard, or by importing a picture or a movie with the Import Picture... or Import Movie... commands on the Import/Export submenu on the File menu.

Putting an object in the right part

When you're designing reports, be careful that objects you place on a layout are actually in the part where you want them to be. As far as FileMaker Pro is concerned, an object is in a part if the *top* of that object is in the part. For example, look at this layout:

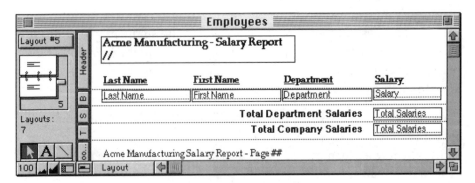

Everything looks okay at first glance, but on closer inspection you can see that the top of the Salary field is overlapping the header part boundary line, instead of being just below it like the other fields in the body. As a result, the Salary field is actually in the header part. When you view this layout in Browse mode, you'll see that the field shows up only in the header (and it shows the data from the first record on the page), like this:

≡ Employees ≡

Layout #5 ..	**Acme Manufacturing - Salary Report** June 21, 1996				↑
	Last Name	**First Name**	**Department**	**Salary**	
	Anderson	John	Accounting	$23,500	
Records: 34	Pak	Jennifer	Accounting		
	Jefferson	Freida	Accounting		
Semi-sorted	Acme Manufacturing Salary Report - Page ?				↓
100	Browse				

Sometimes it's hard to see when fields or other objects overlap part boundaries, but if a field's data doesn't appear in every record in Browse or Preview modes, this is the most likely reason. If you're not sure whether an object is overlapping a part boundary, use the zoom controls in the lower left corner of the document window to magnify the layout so it's easier to see the exact positions of objects.

TIP

Adding graphics

Because graphics are placed and managed in layers on a FileMaker Pro layout, you can put graphics on top of one another or on top of text or fields. In most cases, graphics should be contained completely inside a part. If not, remember that the *top* of the graphic is what determines which part the graphic is in. If the graphic's top is in a header, for example, then the graphic will only appear once at the top of each page in a report.

Because the top of a graphic determines its part placement, you must overlap graphics if you want them to appear across more than one part. For example, to draw a vertical line that extends from a header and down the page through the body of a layout (visibly dividing one column of data from another, perhaps), you must draw a line beginning in the header and extending into the body, and then draw a second line overlapping the first one, beginning in the body and extending to the bottom of the body.

Even if the body is very short (as in the examples in this section), you must draw a second, overlapping line that begins in the body itself if you want the line to extend down the entire page. If you only draw a line that begins in the header and extends down to the bottom of the body in Layout mode, the report will look like this:

Employees

Layout #5..	**Acme Manufacturing - Salary Report** **June 21, 1996**			
	Last Name	**First Name**	**Department**	**Salary**
	Richman	Linda	Accounting	$27,500
5	Hong	Rita	Administrative	$22,300
Records:	Rogers	Wanda	Administrative	$41,000
34	Suraci	Jane	Administrative	$23,200
Semi-sorted	Acme Manufacturing Salary Report - Page ?			

Here, the vertical line extends down about a quarter of an inch, because that's how tall the body is in Layout mode.

Using Headers and Footers

So far, we've discussed the mechanics of making, changing, and deleting parts and adding objects to them, but this information is pretty abstract unless you can relate it to database reports in the real world. In this section, we'll see how you might use headers and footers in printed reports.

In a standard layout, FileMaker Pro includes header and footer parts that are a little less than ½ inch high. You can drag their boundary lines to make these parts bigger or smaller, as you like. When you add text to headers or footers, though, remember that this data will appear at the top or bottom of every page in the report.

TIP   Choose the Graphic Rulers command from the Select menu in Layout mode to display rulers so you can see exactly how tall headers or footers are.

Adding header or footer text

Adding text to a header works the same way as adding text anywhere else in the layout:

1. Select the text tool in the tool palette.

2. Click in the header or footer part where you want the text to begin.

3. Type the text or paste it in from the Clipboard.

Once you've entered the text, you can select it as an object and move it or reformat it using the commands on the Format menu.

It's faster to add all of a layout's text first and then worry about the formatting afterwards. Once you've got the text where you want it, choose Text Ruler from the Show menu and use the ruler's controls to adjust the font, size, style, alignment, and line spacing of text.

TIP

Adding layout text using special symbols

FileMaker Pro has special symbols you can use to insert the current date, time, user name, page number, or record number on a layout. These symbols tell FileMaker Pro to insert this information in their place, but the symbols don't work in every part of a layout.

You can insert these symbols by typing them or choosing them from the Paste Special submenu off the Edit menu.

*   To add the current date (at the time the data is browsed, previewed or printed), type // (two slashes), or choose the Date Symbol command from the Paste Special submenu. This symbol works in any part of a layout.

*   To add the current time, type :: (two colons), or choose the Time Symbol command from the Paste Special submenu. This symbol works in any layout part.

*   To add the current user name (as supplied by the Sharing Setup control panel or the General Preferences you set for FileMaker Pro), type | | (two vertical bars) or choose the User Name Symbol command from the Paste Special submenu. This symbol works in any layout part.

- To add the page number, type ## (two pound symbols), or choose the Page Number command from the Paste Special submenu. This symbol also works in any part of a layout, but only when a report is previewed or printed.

- To add the record number, type @@ (two "at" symbols), or choose the Record Number command from the Paste Special submenu. This symbol works in any layout part when a report is printed or previewed, but it only shows the current record number when it's used in the body of a layout. And when the symbol is used in the body of a layout, you can also see the current record number when you view records in Browse.

IMPORTANT NOTE

Each special symbol you add to a layout appears as a text object on the layout. Make sure that each text object is large enough to display all the information inside it, such as dates in long formats or long user names. To change the format of a date or time symbol, add the symbol as a separate text object, then select the object and use the Date... or Time... command on the Format menu.

Aligning header text within page margins

In word processing programs, you can use alignment or ruler commands to position a header at the center, left, or right of the page, because you're aligning text within the page margins. In FileMaker Pro, the Align Text commands on the Format menu or the alignment controls in the text ruler control the alignment of text *within text boxes*. You may have text left-aligned within a text box, but if the text box itself isn't at the left edge of a layout, the text inside it won't be aligned with the left page margin.

To align header text (or any other text, for that matter) relative to the page margins on a layout, size text boxes so they stretch from the left edge of a layout all the way to the right edge. This way, aligning text within the text box also aligns it within the page margins.

TIP

To see the left and right page margins, choose Page Margins from the Show menu in Layout mode.

For example, suppose we want to center the report title in a header.

1. Choose the Show command from the Layout menu and select the Page Margins command from the submenu that appears. FileMaker Pro shows the page margins, like this:

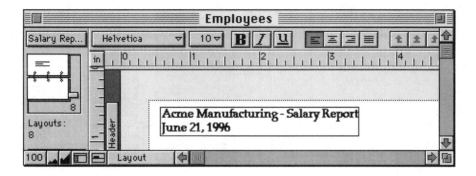

2. Select the text object containing the report title so selection handles appear around it.

3. Drag one of the left selection handles until the text box's outline lines up with the dotted line showing the report's left margin.

4. Drag one of the right selection handles until the text box's outline lines up with the dotted line showing the report's right edge. The text box now stretches from the left margin to the right margin.

5. Choose Text… from the Format menu. The Text Format dialog box appears.

6. Choose the Center command from the Alignment pop-up menu, then click the OK button or press ⌜Return⌟. The report title will now be centered between the edges of the report.

In the example above, the text ruler is showing, so you could also click the Center alignment button on the text ruler instead of performing steps 5 and 6 above. To display the text ruler, choose Text Ruler from the Show menu. Note that you can have the text and graphic rulers showing at the same time.

TIP

Using Summary Parts

Summary parts are used in layouts when you want to summarize data from multiple records. In a payroll report, for example, the body might contain rows of individual salaries, a sub-summary part might show the total of each department's salaries, and a grand summary part might show the total of salaries for the whole company.

In the following preview of a company salary report, the records are sorted on the Department field, and the Preview mode screen shows the salary totals by department. And since we're previewing the end of the report, the bottom line shows total salaries for the entire company:

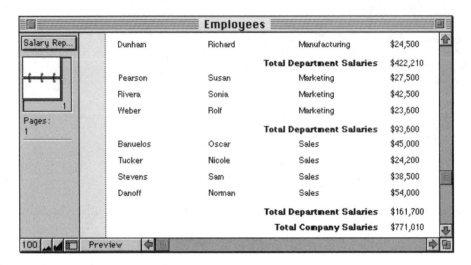

Here's how this report looks in Layout mode:

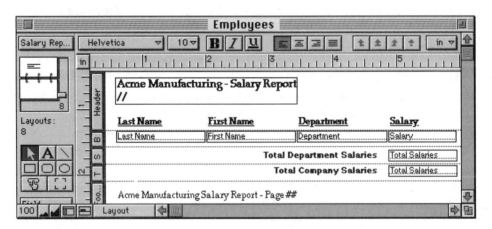

In Preview mode, the Total Department Salaries field's data appears once for each department in the company, but it only appears once in Layout mode. That's because this field is in a sub-summary part defined to produce a summary for each department when the file is sorted on the Department field.

To summarize data like this, you must create a sub-summary part, and you must have a summary field to put into it. To make sub-summary fields calculate and display their data properly, you have to sort the records on the proper field, as specified in the sub-summary part definition.

You'll also notice that there's a trailing grand summary part that contains the same Total Salaries field that appears in the sub-summary part above. When it's located in the trailing grand summary, the Total Salaries field totals all the salaries in the report, rather than by department.

Let's step through the process of creating the summary parts in this layout to see how all this works.

Defining a summary field

We'll assume that the Employees file this report is based on is already open and that it already contains First Name, Last Name, Department, and Salary fields. To produce the report, we'll need a Total Salaries field to calculate departmental and company salary totals.

1. Choose Define Fields... from the File menu. FileMaker Pro displays the field definition dialog box.

2. Type *Total Salaries* as the field name, and click the Summary button to choose a summary field type. Then click the Create button. FileMaker Pro displays the summary field options dialog box, like this:

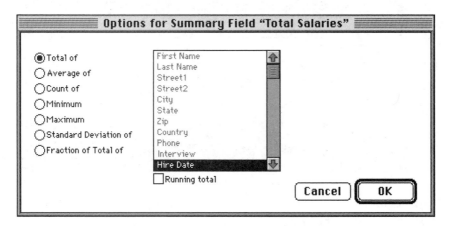

3. The Total of button is automatically selected at the left, because this is the most common summary calculation. At the right, scroll down the field list and select Salary as the field whose data will be totaled, then click the OK button. FileMaker Pro creates the field.

Normally, FileMaker Pro adds each new field you define to the body of the current layout and enlarges the body part to make room for it. If you don't want the field in the body, delete it and drag the part boundary back up to its former location. To prevent fields from being added to layouts automatically, choose the Preferences... command from the Edit menu, choose Layout from the pop-up menu in the Preferences dialog box, and uncheck the Add newly defined fields to current layout option.

Creating a columnar report layout

Now let's create the new report layout:

1. Switch to Layout mode if you're not already in it, and press ⌃⌘Ⓝ to create a new layout.

2. Choose Columnar report in the New Layout dialog box, type *Salaries by Dept.* in the Layout Name box, and then click the OK button. FileMaker Pro displays the Specify Field Order dialog box.

3. One after the other, double-click on the First Name, Last Name, Department, and Salary field names, to move them into the Field Order list; then click the OK button. FileMaker Pro displays the layout, as shown here:

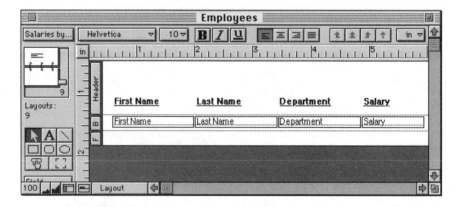

This layout contains the fields we need in the body of the report, and shows the field names as column headings in the header.

Adding summary parts

Now we'll add the summary parts. Since we're adding two parts, it's simpler to use the Part Setup... command than the part tool.

1. Choose Part Setup… from the Mode menu, then click the Create… button in the Part Setup dialog box. FileMaker Pro displays the Part Definition dialog box.

2. Click the Sub-Summary when sorted by button, then click on Department in the field list so FileMaker Pro knows how the database will be sorted for the summary.

3. Click the OK button to create the part. FileMaker Pro displays an alert message like this:

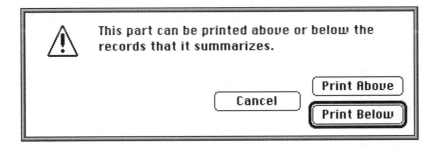

4. Click the Print Below button or press ⟨Return⟩ to place the part below the body in the report. FileMaker Pro creates the part and displays the list of parts now defined for the layout.

5. Click the Create… button again, and then click the Trailing Grand Summary button.

6. Click the OK button to create the part, and then click the Done button in the Part Setup dialog box. FileMaker Pro displays the new parts in the layout, like this:

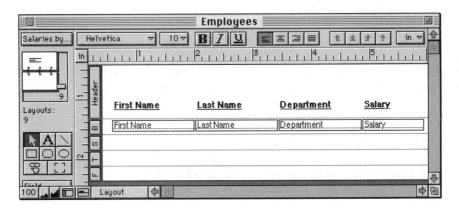

Adding fields to the summary parts

Now we'll add the Total Salaries field to the sub-summary and trailing grand summary parts so FileMaker Pro can show the calculated totals there.

1. Drag the field tool into the sub-summary part, right underneath the Salary field in the body part above. Release the mouse button. FileMaker Pro displays a list of fields in the file.

TIP

If the new field's outline doesn't line up directly below the Salary field when you drag it onto the layout, drag it as close as you can. Then, choose AutoGrid from the arrange menu to turn off the AutoGrid, and use the left or right arrow keys to nudge the Total Salary field and field name so that the field outline is directly below the Salary field above.

2. Select the Total Salaries field name, click the Create field label checkbox, and then click the OK button. FileMaker Pro adds the field to the sub-summary part, like this:

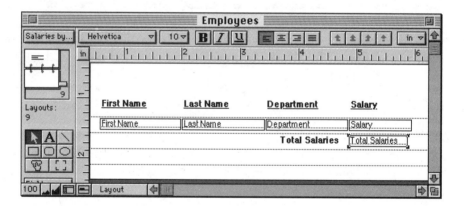

3. Drag one of the right-hand selection handles on the new Total Salaries field to make this field as wide as (or a bit wider than) the Salary field above it.

TIP

Hold down the ⟨Shift⟩ key as you drag the field's handle. This way, the field will only grow horizontally, not vertically, when you enlarge it.

4. Click the text tool and edit the Total Salaries field label so it reads "Total Department Salaries," like this:

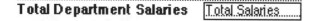

5. Repeat the four steps above, but this time put the Total Salaries field in the trailing grand summary part, and edit its label to read *Total Company Salaries*.

To format the Salary and Total Salary fields on this layout so they show numbers in dollars and cents, hold down the [Shift] key and then click on all three fields to select them all. Then, use the Number... command on the Format menu to set a decimal format with currency notation and a comma thousands separator. Also choose the Text... command and choose the Right alignment option so the values align right. (See *Changing Field and Object Formats*, on p. 138 in Chapter 6, for more on formatting field data.)

Finally, we won't need the footer in this report, so select the footer part label and press the [Delete] key to delete it. (Scroll the layout to the left so you can see the footer part label, if necessary.)

The layout is now complete, but before the report is actually printed, you'll have to sort the records on the Department field to put them into the groups required by the sub-summary field. (For more on sorting records, see Chapter 8.)

This example gives you a pretty good idea of how summaries are used to create reports in FileMaker Pro.

Creating Form Letters

One last type of report we'll look at is a form letter, which is a full-page layout with a body that prints once per page. In this case, most of the layout contains text, with just a few merge fields included for the information that changes in each letter.

Merge fields in FileMaker Pro 3 allow you to combine field data with text on layouts much more easily than simply adding fields themselves, because merge fields automatically expand to allow enough space for the data they contain, and they automatically slide together to close up any gaps in text between fields.

NEW FEATURE

Look at the example on the next page:

Acme Manufacturing Company
4500 Old County Road
San Jose, CA 95115
408-555-6700

June 21, 1996

Susan Pearson
135 Walnut St.
Pasadena, CA 91002

Dear Susan:

I'd like to personally take this opportunity to compliment you on your work in the Marketing department. You've been a real inspiration to the rest of us at Acme, and richly deserve the enclosed bonus check.

Thanks for helping make Acme tops in our industry. I have no doubt that with workers like you, we'll stay a step ahead of the competition.

Best wishes,

Buster Sessions
President

This finished form letter shows the data from one record of our Employees file.

Creating a new layout

This layout began as a single page form. When you create a single page form, FileMaker Pro automatically adds as many of the fields from your file as will fit on the form. Since most of our layout is text, the first step after creating the layout is to delete all the fields that were automatically placed on the form.

1. Type ⌘L to switch to Layout mode, and then type ⌘N to create a new layout.

2. Click on the Single Page Form button, type *Form Ltr* in the Layout Name box, and press the Return key to create the layout.

3. Press ⌘A or choose the Select All command from the Edit menu to select all the objects on the new layout, and then press the Delete key to delete them.

Creating the logo and return address

Now, we can add our own text and fields to create the form letter. First, we'll create the logo and return address.

1. Choose the Page Margins command from the Show menu to display the edges of the layout.

2. Choose the text tool and drag a text box from the upper left corner of the layout out to about the 1½-inch mark on the horizontal ruler and down to about the 1⅜-inch mark on the vertical ruler. Then type *A*.

3. Choose the text tool again, and create a second text box directly next to the first one, the same height as the first one and about 5 inches wide.

   Since the border of the first text box disappears when you select the text tool a second time, begin the second text box just to the right of the 1½-inch mark on the horizontal ruler at the top of the layout, and drag it down 1½ inches and then to the right until the pointer is beyond the 6½-inch mark on the horizontal ruler.

   TIP

4. Type the company name and address as shown in the example.

(If the name and address you just typed overlap the original letter A, select the text box containing the company name and address and drag it to the right. If the company name and address text is centered instead of left-aligned inside the text box, select the company name and address and choose the Left command from the Align Text submenu on the Format menu.)

5. Select the text tool again, and then select the letter *A* in the first text box you drew. Format this letter as 60-point Palatino Italic using the Font, Size and Style submenus on the Format menu or the controls on the text ruler. (The 60-point size won't be on the Size menu. Choose the Custom… command from the Size menu and enter *60* to create this size.)

6. Select the text tool again, then select the company name and address text and format it as 14-point Palatino Bold.

    (If the company name wraps around inside the box when you do this, just select the whole text object with the pointer tool and drag one of its right selection handles to the right to make the box wide enough to fit the company name on one line.)

7. Select the company address text and format it as 12-point Palatino Bold.

8. Choose the rectangle tool with no fill pattern and a 2-point black line, and draw the box around the letter A. (See *The fill, pen, and line controls*, on p. 106 in Chapter 6, for instructions.)

9. Drag or resize the two text boxes and the rectangle to align them properly, if necessary.

Typing the letter

Now, we'll enter the rest of the letter in the body. We'll create the entire letter as one text object, using merge fields to supply the employee name and address, the first name in the greeting line, and the department name in the second line of this letter.

1. Select the text tool, click about 1 inch directly below the right edge of the box surrounding the company logo, and drag a box about ½ inch high extending to beneath the 6-inch mark on the tab ruler, like this:

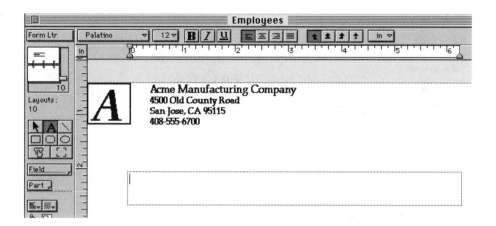

By setting the horizontal size of the text box here, we can ensure that the letter's body will have a 1-inch right margin. When you specify the size of a text box, any text typed in it will automatically wrap around to fit inside it. If you simply click with the text tool and begin typing instead, you must indicate each line ending by pressing (Return). With the auto-wrap feature enabled, we know that FileMaker Pro will end every line in the body of the letter as close to the edge of the text box as possible. FileMaker will automatically adjust the length of the second line in the body of the letter to accommodate Department field data of varying lengths.

IMPORTANT NOTE

As an alternative to dragging a text box to align with ruler markings, create a text box of any size, type a couple of characters in it, and then select the text box and resize or change its position precisely by using the Size window. See p. 123 in Chapter 6.

TIP

2. Choose the Palatino font and 12-point type size with the font and size controls in the text ruler, or with the Font and Size submenus on the Format menu.

3. Type // to have FileMaker Pro insert the current date at the time the letter is printed.

4. Press (Return) twice to move the insertion point down two lines, and then press (⌃⌘M) to display the Specify Field dialog box.

5. Double-click on the First Name field's name. A merge field marker is added to the layout, like this:

 Acme Manufacturing Company
4500 Old County Road
San Jose, CA 95115
408-555-6700

6. The insertion point is blinking just to the right of the merge field inside the text box. Press the [Spacebar] and then press [⌘M] again to display the Specify Field dialog box, and double-click on the Last Name field there. This field's merge marker is now added next to the First Name field's marker, like this:

```
//
<<First Name>> <<Last Name>>|
```

7. Press [Return] to move the cursor down one line, press [⌘M] again to display the Specify Field dialog box, and double-click on the Street field's name.

8. Press [Return] to move the cursor down another line, press [⌘M] again to display the Specify Field dialog box, and double-click on the City field's name.

9. Type [,] and then press the [Spacebar], and then press [⌘M] and add the State field's merge marker.

10. Press the [Spacebar], and then press [⌘M] and add the Zip field's merge marker. The entire address block now looks like this:

```
<<First Name>> <<Last Name>>
<<Street>>
<<City>>, <<State>> <<Zip>>|
```

11. Press ⏎Return three times to skip two more lines, and then type *Dear* followed by a space.

12. Press ⌘M again to display the Specify Field dialog box, double-click on the First Name field's name to add a merge marker, and type a colon immediately after the merge marker.

13. Press ⏎Return twice, and then type the first part of the letter text shown on p. 218, up to and including the word *the* just before *Marketing* in the second line.

14. Press the ⎵Spacebar to add a space after the word *the*, and then press ⌘M and add the Department field's merge marker.

15. Type the rest of the letter text, including the sign-off and signature lines. (Just press ⏎Return to begin new lines or add blank lines between the sign-off and signature lines. Do *not* press return to end lines in the body of the letter itself.)

Finishing touches

When you're done entering the letter text, look at it in Preview mode to make sure the text box containing the letter itself lines up with an appropriate amount of left margin and is centered in the space between the logo and address and the bottom of the page. If not, just select the text box with the pointer tool and drag it left or right, up or down, until it looks right.

IMPORTANT NOTE

The current date symbol you added at the beginning of the letter will probably be formatted as MM/DD/YY. To format this date so the month name is spelled out, select the entire text box with the pointer tool and choose the Date... command on the Format menu. Even though this text box contains a lot of text and merge fields in addition to the date symbol, FileMaker Pro recognizes that it contains a date symbol and allows you to choose the date format. See *Formatting date fields*, on p. 143 in Chapter 6.

When you print this form letter, you can select the employee records for which the letter is printed by using Find mode. You could search for records by the employee's last name, department, salary, or other field criteria. And, because you used merge fields, those fields will grow or shrink as necessary to accommodate longer or shorter data, with no extra gaps between them.

For a one-page letter like this, it wasn't necessary to put the company name and logo in a header part. However, if you wanted to create a multiple-page form letter, you could put a company name and logo in a title header at the top of the layout so it would only print on the first page. Then, you could add a regular header to print the letter name, page number, date, or other information at the top of subsequent pages.

These examples just scratch the surface of what you can do with FileMaker Pro reports. By experimenting on your own and studying the layouts in the template files supplied with FileMaker Pro, you can learn more about creating reports to suit any purpose.

Troubleshooting

Now let's look at some common problems you might have in creating or printing reports, and see what to do about them.

Rows of information are too close together or too far apart in a columnar report layout.

If rows of data seem too close together or too far apart when you view the layout in Browse or Preview mode, just drag the body part boundary to make the part shorter or taller. Make a part taller to leave more space between rows of data, or make it shorter to move rows of data closer together. Just make sure the objects inside the body remain completely inside it. Remember, an object is considered to be in a part if its *top edge* is in that part. If an object's top edge overlaps the part boundary above, it will appear in that part.

TIP

To precisely set the height or width of fields or parts, use the Size window. Just click on the part label to select it, and then type in the part's height as described in *The Size window*, p. 123 in Chapter 6.

Data in different parts doesn't line up.

Since you have to place fields or other objects onto a layout separately, it's sometimes hard to line them up vertically. There are several ways to align objects more precisely:

- Zoom the layout to twice or four times its normal size when you drag objects on the screen so you can see the edges of fields in different parts more clearly and line them up better. Use the arrow keys to nudge objects a pixel at a time.

- Select all the fields that you want to line up vertically and choose the Set Alignment... command from the Arrange menu. Then click the appropriate button to align all the objects along their left or right edges.

- Choose T-Squares from the Layout menu and drag the vertical line to the edge of a field in one part. Then line up the edges of fields in other parts along the same line.

For more on these techniques, see *Moving Objects in Layouts*, p. 119 in Chapter 6.

A field shown in Layout mode shows up only in the top record in Browse mode.
When arranging fields, be careful not to accidentally position a field so it overlaps the boundary between the body and header part of a layout, particularly when you're working with a columnar report layout. If any part of a field is in a header when you're working with a columnar report, the field will become part of the header, and only data from the first record on the page will appear in Browse mode.

Check the field's position in Layout mode, and reposition it if necessary. This problem will also occur on any layout when you have View as List checked on the Select menu. When this command isn't checked, FileMaker Pro just shows the current record's data in the header or footer.

A sub-summary doesn't appear in Browse mode.
Sub-summaries don't show up when you're browsing records. You must sort the records and then either display them in Preview mode or print them.

A sub-summary doesn't appear when you preview or print a report.
This means the records haven't been sorted on the field specified when you created the sub-summary part. As in our example earlier in this chapter, if you create a sub-summary part that totals data within departments, you have to sort on the Department field to make it appear.

The text in a multipage letter won't print after the first page, or it doesn't print at all.

You've probably got the printing options for the body part set improperly.

If text prints on the first page but won't print on subsequent pages, you probably have the option set to discard the remainder of the part before a new page. To fix this, choose the Part Setup... command from the Mode menu, select the Body part in the list, and click the Change button. Because you're printing a multipage letter, the option Allow part to break across page boundaries should be checked. (This way, letter text will break at the end of the first page and continue onto the second page.) However, if the option Discard remainder of part before new page is also checked, FileMaker Pro will delete any text that didn't print on the first page. Make sure this last option isn't checked in the Part Definition dialog box.

On the other hand, if text in a multipage letter doesn't print at all, you probably haven't checked the Allow part to break across page boundaries option. Since the body of a multipage letter will spread across more than one page, you must allow the part to break across page boundaries for the text to print.

10 Previewing and Printing Reports

- Preparing Records for Printing
- Choosing a Page Setup
- Using Preview Mode
- Basic Printing
- Troubleshooting

Printing FileMaker Pro reports on paper is a very simple procedure, but getting them to look exactly the way you want can be pretty complicated. Most of that work is done in Layout mode, but the page setup you select plays a significant role, too. In any case, you can't see how a layout will really look when printed unless you actually print it or view it in Preview mode.

In this chapter, we'll look at the basics of using FileMaker Pro's page setup and printing options and the uses of Preview mode. Then we'll focus on some common problems you may have in producing the reports you want.

Preparing Records for Printing

Printing your data properly involves more than just selecting Print... from the File menu. Most of the time, you'll want to use a particular layout, select a specific group of records, and perhaps sort them in a certain way before printing them. Here's a checklist of steps to take before printing:

1. Select the printer you want to use with the Chooser, and then set the page setup options you want with the Page Setup... command on the File menu.

2. Select the group of records you want to print using the Find or the Find All command.

3. Sort the records in the order you want them, using the Sort... command.

4. Select the layout you want your data to print on.

Now let's take a closer look at the options Page Setup... gives you.

Choosing a Page Setup

Before you preview or print a report, you need to specify the size of paper you'll be printing on. Depending on your layout's size and content, you may also want to adjust the page reduction, orientation, and print area options so that all of the layout's data, text, and graphics will fit on the printed page. You select these options with the Page Setup dialog box.

The specific dialog box you see when you choose Page Setup... from the File menu will depend on which printer and system software version you're using. The LaserWriter Page Setup dialog box for a Mac using System 7.5 software (without QuickDraw GX installed) looks like this:

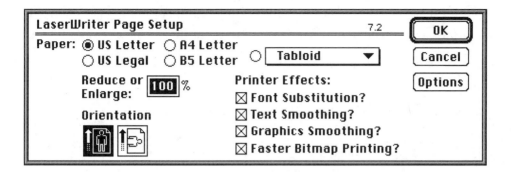

Here's how these options affect a layout's printable area in FileMaker Pro. In the Paper section, the buttons let you select a predefined paper size. The four letter and legal sizes are standard U.S. and European paper sizes, and the Tabloid option is a pop-up menu that lets you select other sizes, including envelopes. The default setting is US Letter, which is 8½ by 11 inches. If you choose a smaller size (such as A4 letter), you'll have less width on the layout for adding fields or other objects. Choosing a bigger paper size, such as Tabloid, will give you more room.

The Reduce or Enlarge box lets you shrink or expand the size the layout will have when it prints. The default setting is 100% — that is, actual size — 1 inch on a layout prints on 1 inch of paper. If you select a reduced size (such as 90%), data and objects will be scaled down proportionally, so you'll be able to fit more on a page. Setting a size greater than 100% will enlarge layout objects, and you won't be able to fit as many on a page.

Another way to fit more items on a page when you're using a LaserWriter is to enlarge the area of the page that will be printed on. To do this, click the Options button at the right side of the dialog box. Another dialog box will appear, with another group of options. Clicking the Larger Print Area checkbox there will enable the layout to print closer to all four edges of the page (although it will limit the number of downloadable fonts your layout can use).

TIP

The Orientation option in the Page Setup dialog box lets you choose which direction your layout will print on the page. The vertical orientation option is standard. Choosing the horizontal option causes records to print across the paper's length, rather than across its width, giving you more horizontal room on a page for columnar reports and other wide layouts.

IMPORTANT NOTE

It takes longer to print layouts in the horizontal orientation, because your Mac and printer have to do additional processing to flip the layout sideways.

If you have a StyleWriter selected in the Chooser, the Page Setup dialog box looks like this:

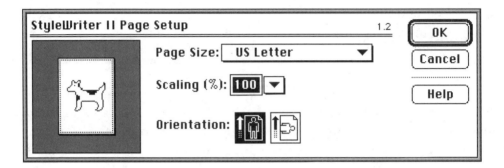

You can choose among preset paper sizes with the Paper Size pop-up menu. You can also set page reduction (Scaling) and orientation options in this dialog box.

To see how these options affect the size of a layout's printable area, try different paper size, reduction, and orientation options, and then look at the layout's boundaries in Layout mode. (The bottom of the printable area is indicated by a heavy dashed line whenever the layout is taller than a single page. To see the top, left, and right page boundaries, select Page Margins from the Show menu in Layout mode.)

Now let's see how Preview mode works.

Using Preview Mode

The way layouts appear in Browse or Layout mode doesn't always match the way they'll look when printed. If a layout uses sliding objects, non-printing objects, sub-summary parts, or the Display in columns option, or if you've used the Reduce or Enlarge page setup option, only Preview mode will display the layout as it will look on the printed page. If you're preparing a multipage report, Preview mode can show you what each page will look like.

With Preview mode, you can spot formatting problems without wasting the time, paper, and ink or toner used in printing. (Once you identify such problems, you can fix them in Layout mode.) Previewing layouts also lets you see data in sub-summary fields without printing.

We'll look at some common formatting problems at the end of this chapter, and you'll find others in the troubleshooting sections of Chapters 6 and 9. Right now, though, let's take a quick look at the Preview screen.

The Preview screen

To preview any layout, choose Preview from the Mode menu or press ⌘⌘U. FileMaker Pro displays the Preview screen, like this:

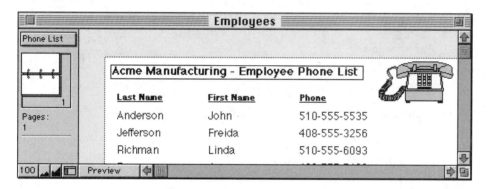

As in FileMaker Pro's Browse and Layout modes, the layout pop-up menu in the upper left corner of the screen lets you choose the layout you want to preview. Click the pages in the book icon to view different printed pages of the report.

If you want FileMaker Pro to preview a particular page in a report, select the current number below the book icon, type the page number you want, and press (Return).

TIP

If you've used the book icon to display the last (or only) page of the report, the total number of pages in the report appears in the status area; otherwise, you'll see a question mark there.

The Preview screen represents the entire printed page, including margins. If the whole page won't fit on your screen at once, use the scroll bars to view other parts of it.

To exit Preview mode, just choose another mode from the Mode menu or from the mode selector at the bottom of the window.

~~~~~~

Basic Printing

Once you're satisfied with the appearance of your report in Preview mode, you're ready to print it.

1. Choose Print... from the File menu or press ⌘P. FileMaker Pro displays a dialog box for the printer you've chosen. For example, here is the Print dialog box for a LaserWriter (on a Mac running System 7.5):

```
┌──────────────────────────────────────────────────────────┐
│ LaserWriter  "Personal LaserWriter IINT"      7.2   ( Print )│
│ Copies:[1]        Pages: ◉ All  ○ From:[  ] To:[  ]          │
│ ┌─Paper Source───────────────────────────────┐  ( Cancel )   │
│ │ ◉ All   ○ First  From:[ Cassette        ▼] │  ( Options )  │
│ │         Remaining from:[ Cassette       ▼] │              │
│ └────────────────────────────────────────────┘              │
│ Destination:  ◉ Printer        ○ PostScript® File           │
│ Number pages from:  [1]                                      │
│ Print:  ○ Records being browsed                             │
│         ◉ Current record                                    │
│         ○ Blank record, showing fields [ as formatted ]     │
│         ○ Script: [ All scripts           ]                 │
│         ○ Field definitions                                 │
└──────────────────────────────────────────────────────────┘
```

2. Choose the options you want, and then click the Print button or press the Return key to print your report.

The options in the Print dialog box are all standard for every Mac program except for those in the Number pages from box and in the Print area at the bottom.

The Number pages from box is where you specify the starting page number for your report. This option only matters if you've included page number symbols in the header or footer part of a report. (See *Using Headers and Footers,* on p. 208 in Chapter 9.)

The Records being browsed button prints all the records in the found set. The Current record button prints only the record that's currently showing or selected on the Browse screen.

The Blank record, showing fields button lets you print a record showing only the fields from a layout, not the data. The pop-up menu for this option lets you print fields as formatted (using whatever format options you set for each field in Layout mode), with boxes around each field (the default option), or with underlines beneath each field. (These last two options show you the size of each field on the layout.)

The Script button lets you print script definitions you've defined for the file, depending on which option you choose from the pop-up menu at the right. The All scripts option is the default, and it prints the definitions of all the file's defined scripts. The name of every script you've defined also appears on this pop-up menu, so you can select an individual script definition to print if you like. (For more on script definitions, see Chapter 12.)

Finally, the Field definitions button prints a list of all the field names, field types, and any formulas or entry options set for them, much like the list of fields in the Define Fields dialog box. (See *Defining Fields*, on p. 50 in Chapter 4.)

Troubleshooting

The Page Setup, Preview, and Print procedures in FileMaker Pro are fairly straightforward, but there are lots of things that can go wrong between creating a layout and realizing you didn't get what you wanted on paper. In this section, we'll look at some common printing problems and solutions.

You try to print but nothing happens.
This is usually caused by one of five things, so ask yourself:

- Is the printer connected to your Mac?

- Is the printer cable plugged into the printer port, and not the modem port?

- Is the printer on, and does it have paper in it?

- Is the printer's Select or Ready light on?

- Did you select the printer and the correct port with the Chooser?

If you can answer yes to all these questions, you should be able to print your file with no problems. If you can't and you're using a networked printer, it could be that your Mac or your printer has become disconnected from the network.

Try selecting the printer in the Chooser again. If the printer's name doesn't show up in the Chooser window, either the printer is off or there's a broken connection between it and your Mac on the network. Check all the network connections for your Mac and the printer, and restart the printer if necessary.

Some fields or items on the layout don't print or don't print the right data.
This usually means you don't have the fields in their proper locations or the file isn't sorted properly. If a field is supposed to be in the body of a layout and its upper edge is in a summary or header part above the body, the field is actually located in the part above, as far as FileMaker Pro is concerned. Therefore, the field will print only once (in the header or summary part) rather than once for each record in the body. Try zooming the layout on the Layout screen and checking for fields or other objects whose upper edges overlap part boundaries. If your file has a summary field and the data in it isn't printing properly, you haven't sorted the file on the field that will make the summary calculation possible. (See *Using Summary Parts*, on p. 211 in Chapter 9.)

Finally, the field or other object may be formatted as a non-printable object. To find out, switch to Layout mode, select the object that isn't printing, choose the Sliding/Printing... command from the Format menu, and see whether the Do not print the selected objects checkbox is checked. If it is, uncheck it to make the object appear on the printout.

The left or right margin is too small or too big.
FileMaker Pro doesn't have margin-width settings. You control the width of the left and right margins by moving objects on the layout. To see how much margin space you have, choose the Page Margins command on the Show menu in Layout mode. (See *Page margins*, on p. 124 in Chapter 6.) Then, you can make decisions about how much extra margin space you want and put objects in the appropriate places to create that space. To check the overall look of a page with its margins, use Preview mode and reduce the layout so you can see the whole page on the screen at once.

To create larger margins on a layout, use the Page Setup... command to either reduce the size of objects on the layout or enlarge the print area.

A header or footer is too big.
If the header or footer takes up too much vertical space on your page, make it smaller by dragging its part boundary in Layout mode. You may have to move objects up or down so there's room to drag the part boundary line—FileMaker Pro won't let you drag a boundary past an object contained in that part. (See *Adding and Changing Parts*, on p. 201 in Chapter 9.)

Columns are too narrow to show the data in fields.

In this case, you'll have to widen the fields whose data isn't visible. When you widen fields, make sure you don't overlap any fields on the left or right. If you can't widen fields without overlapping other fields and you don't have any more horizontal space on the layout, try one of these solutions:

- Select all the fields and field names and choose a smaller font size.

- Choose the horizontal orientation option in the Page Setup dialog box (so records print across the length of the page), then widen the fields in Layout mode.

- Specify a reduced size in the Reduce or Enlarge box of the Page Setup dialog box, so you can squeeze more data into the same space. Then widen the fields in Layout mode.

Check the Preview screen to see how these remedies affect your report.

Dates or times in a header or footer are wrong.

FileMaker Pro supplies the current date or time at the moment you print a report. It gets this information from your Mac's internal clock and calendar, so if it's wrong in the report, it's wrong on your Mac. Use the General Controls or Date & Time control panel to reset the Mac's clock or calendar.

Page numbers are wrong.

This can only happen for one of two reasons: either you've specified the wrong starting page number in the Print dialog box or you're using a layout part that restarts page numbers after it prints.

The Number pages from box in the Print dialog box is where you tell FileMaker Pro which page number to start with in a report. If you want to start with a number other than 1, type it into this box before you print.

If you're using a title header, leading grand summary, sub-summary, trailing grand summary, or title footer part, you have the option to restart page numbering after the part is printed. If page numbers are restarting and you don't want them to—or they're not restarting and you do want them to—choose the Part Setup... command, select the name of the part you want to change, click the Change... button, and click in the checkbox labeled Restart page numbers after each occurrence.

Subtotals or grand totals are wrong.

If you're getting the wrong subtotals in a sub-summary or grand summary part, it's probably because you don't have the right records in the current found set or they're not sorted properly. If you're getting inaccurate grand totals, you probably haven't got the right records in the found set.

1. Use the Find command to select records for the report.

2. If it's a subtotal that was incorrect, choose the Part Setup… command, select the sub-summary part's name in the dialog box, and click the Change… button to see which field is specified for sorting in the sub-summary part's definition.

3. Make sure the file is sorted on that field.

View the report in Preview mode to see if the correct summary information appears.

If it's still wrong, the next thing to check is that you're using the correct field in the sub-summary or grand summary part. Ordinary fields won't summarize data just because you place them in a summary part—you need to use a summary field. And, of course, the field must be defined to perform the calculation you want on the field whose data you want to summarize. Check the field's definition, as follows:

1. Choose Define Fields… from the File menu.

2. Select the name of the summary field in the field list that appears. "Summary" should show in the Type category of the field's definition.

    If it doesn't, click the Summary type button and click the Save button. A warning dialog box will appear. Click the OK button, and then specify calculation options in the dialog box that appears. (See *Defining summary fields*, on p. 61 in Chapter 4 for more information.)

    If "Summary" does show as the field's type, click the Options… button and check the formula in the Summary Options dialog box to make sure it's calculating the right type of summary on the field you want. (See Chapter 16 for more information on calculation options.) Make whatever changes are necessary and click the OK button.

3. Click the Done button in the Define Fields dialog box.

11

Working with Data in Multiple Files

- About Lookups and Relational Databases
- Defining Relationships
- Defining Lookups
- Creating a Relational Database
- Working with Related Fields
- Troubleshooting

The most important improvement in FileMaker Pro version 3 is its ability to manage data in relational databases. Previous versions of FileMaker Pro allowed lookups, but FileMaker Pro version 3's relational database capability offers far more data-handling power. In this chapter, we'll explore lookups and relational databases.

NEW FEATURE

About Lookups and Relational Databases

Lookups and *relational databases* make it possible to collect and store data in one file but display or manipulate that data in other files. With a lookup, data from one file is copied into a field in another file. In a relational database, on the other hand, data is always stored in just one file, but it can be displayed or manipulated in other files as needed. Because a field's data is only stored in one place in a relational database, changing the data anywhere the field occurs, no matter which file it is in, changes the stored data.

Lookups vs. relational databases

FileMaker Pro's previous versions provided a partial solution to the data-growth jumble by offering lookups. In a lookup, data from a specific field in another, *related file* is copied into a field in the current file you're working in (called the *master file*). Lookups are a one-way, one-time relationship: Information is copied from the related file to the master file at a particular time, and then the relationship has done its job. For example, a lookup might copy a product's price from the Price field in a Products file into the Price field in an Invoices file. If someone later changes that particular price in the Products file, the price in the Invoices file remains as it was when it was first copied. (If necessary, however, you can reactivate a lookup to copy updated information into a field. See *Updating lookup values*, on p. 250.)

In a relational database, on the other hand, you use two-way, continuous relationships between the data in different files. Rather than copying information from a related file to a master file, a relational link simply allows you to *display* a field's information from a related file in a master file. Since it isn't copied, the data always exists in only the related file.

For example, let's look at a sample relational database that came with prerelease versions of FileMaker Pro 3. This database is designed to handle ordering and business-contact information. It consists of eight files, each of which has a specific purpose, yet information among the files is exchanged as necessary. The main files in this database are Products, Line Items, Invoices, and Contacts. Here's a view of the Invoices file:

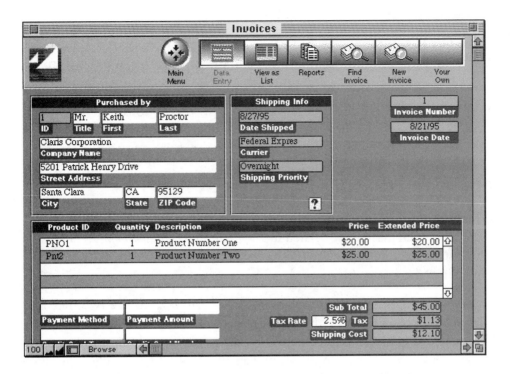

This file uses data from several different files. The Invoice Number and Invoice Date fields at the upper right belong to the Invoices file. The customer information fields in the Purchased by area at the upper left are from the Contacts file. And the data about items purchased is from the Line Items file.

By combining information from several files and showing it all as if it were part of the Invoices file, we gain several advantages over keeping all the information in just one file:

- **Efficiency.** Each file has fewer fields and is easier to maintain. When users need to enter data about a new customer, for example, they can use the Contacts file, where all the fields collect customer contact information.

- **Economy.** Information in each file is stored only once. For example, we might create several dozen invoices for one customer, but that customer's name and address information is stored only once, in the Contacts file. In a flat-file database, the same customer contact information would be stored over and over again in each new invoice record, making the file larger than necessary.

- **Accuracy.** Since data is stored in only one file, it only needs to be updated in one file. If a customer's address changes, for example, changing it in any file where it is used automatically changes it in the Contacts file, where it is stored.

If you have a data set that only requires you to define a handful of fields, you can probably do very well without using FileMaker Pro's relational and lookup features. But if you find your files gaining in complexity as you add new fields to meet new needs, then lookups and relational databases are a way out of the maze.

About relationships and match fields

Whether you're using a lookup or a relational database, you establish each connection between master and related files by defining a *relationship*. A relationship is an instruction FileMaker Pro uses to locate information in the related file and copy it into the master file.

To define a relationship, you must specify *match fields* in the two files that FileMaker Pro uses to locate the specific record that contains the data you want. Typically, this is a field that contains the same data in both files, and which is unique in each file. For example, a Contacts file and an Invoices file might both contain a field called Customer Number. If you set up a relationship using Customer Number as the match field, entering a customer number in this field in the Invoices file tells FileMaker Pro to locate a record containing the same customer number in the Customer Number field of the Contacts file. A record in the related file whose match field contains the same data as a record in the master file is called a *related record*.

IMPORTANT NOTE

Before specifying a relationship, you must have two existing FileMaker Pro files whose data you want to work with. All files used for relational databases or lookups must be FileMaker Pro version 3 files. If you're using files from older versions of FileMaker, convert them to version 3 format. (See *Converting files from earlier versions of FileMaker*, on p. 296 in Chapter 13.)

How lookups work

In a lookup, you choose a relationship to specify the match fields that locate the right record in a related file. Then you must also specify a *lookup source* field and a *lookup destination* field. This tells FileMaker Pro that, once the correct record is found in the related file using match fields, it must copy data from the lookup source field in the related file and paste it into the lookup destination field in the master file. Here's how it works:

1. You type data into the match field of the master file.

2. FileMaker Pro automatically opens the related file without showing it on the screen. (The file's name appears in parentheses on the Window menu.)

3. FileMaker Pro compares the data you just entered in the match field of the master file with data in the match field of the related file.

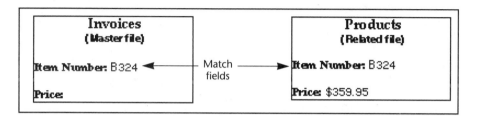

4. If it finds a record with matching data in the related file, FileMaker Pro copies the data from the lookup source field of that record in the related file into the lookup destination field of that record in the master file, like this:

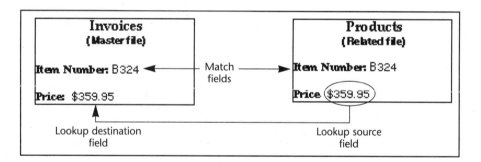

If there's no match between the comparison data in the two files, no information is copied. (You can set options to have FileMaker Pro enter other data automatically or to leave the lookup field blank. See *Lookup options*, on p. 249 below).

A lookup like this is useful, because it ensures that the invoice price never changes. You might later change the price in your Products file, but the price that was previously copied into the Invoices file wouldn't change.

How relational databases work

In a relational database, you establish relationships by specifying match fields, just as you do with a lookup. But once the relationship is established, you can use any of the fields from the related file in the master file by adding them to layouts, referring to them in calculations, specifying them in scripts, exporting their data, or using them in searches or sorts.

You use relational databases when you want to make sure that any changes you make to a field's data are always immediately reflected in any other files where that data is used. For example, suppose you have two files called Inventory and Suppliers. You maintain information about product names, costs, and descriptions, and suppliers in the Suppliers file, and information about the stock on hand in the Inventory file. But when you run low on stock of an item, the Inventory file creates an order form for your supplier. In this case, you would always want the supplier's name and address to be current in the Inventory file, so you would use a relational database to make sure that happens, like this:

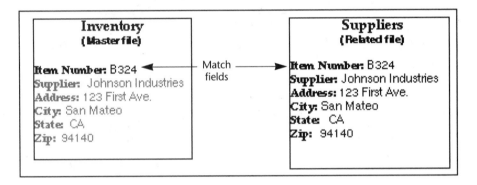

The relationship between these two files is based on the Item Number match field. The Supplier, Address, City, State, and Zip fields in the Inventory file are *related fields*—they are displayed in the Inventory file, but they're actually stored in the related Suppliers file. When you type in an item number in the Inventory file, FileMaker finds the record with the matching item number data in the Suppliers file, and then the contents of the other fields from the Suppliers file are displayed in the Inventory file. As a result, any change to the supplier information in the Suppliers file is automatically shown in the Inventory file.

Any file can be a related file or a master file, as long as they're all FileMaker Pro 3.0 files. In fact, a file can be both a related file (supplying information to a mater file) and a master file (displaying information from another related file) at the same time.

When you add a field from a related file to a layout, you can place it in the layout by itself, or you can place it in a *portal*, which is a special layout window that displays data from related fields.

- When you place a field by itself, you see only the data from one record in the related file. If the related file contains more than one related record, the field displays the first such record from the related file. (For example, if Customer ID is the match field in an Invoices file, there could be several invoice records for the same customer.)

- When you place a field in a portal, you can display data from several related records in the related file. For example, the Product ID, Quantity, Description, Price, and Extended Price fields in the Invoices file shown on p. 239 are all related fields from the Line Items file. Because these fields are located inside a portal, each row in the portal represents a different record from the Line Items file. You determine how many rows (or records) to display in a portal when you create the portal (see p. 254).

When you open a file that contains related fields, FileMaker Pro automatically tries to open the related file as well, so it can display information from the related fields in your master file. When related files are open, their names appear on the Window menu in parentheses. If a related file is protected by a password, you'll be asked to enter the password for that file when FileMaker Pro tries to open it (see p. 257).

Defining Relationships

Since both lookups and relational databases are based on relationships between files, you need to define relationships to use either feature. You can define relationships at any time in FileMaker Pro, as long as you have two or more files whose data you want to relate.

There's a Define Relationships… command on the File menu, but this command is also an option on the pop-up menu that appears at the top of any dialog box where you can specify fields for use in FileMaker Pro, including the Specify Field dialog box, the Sort Records dialog box, and the Specify Calculation dialog box.

Suppose we want to create a relationship between a Payroll file and an Employees file, so employee addresses stored in the Employees file are always up to date in the Payroll file. To do this, we'll use the Employee Number field in both files as the match field, since this data will be unique in both files.

1. Open the Payroll file and then choose Define Relationships... from the File menu. The Define Relationships dialog box appears, like this:

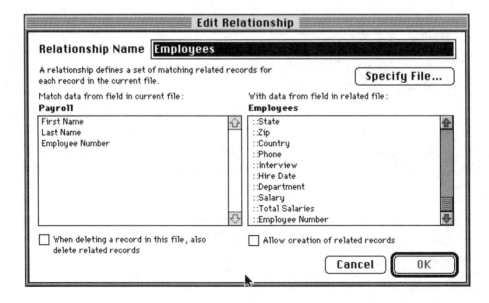

This dialog box shows all the relationships you have defined for the file you're currently working in.

IMPORTANT NOTE

You must always define a relationship from the master file where you want to use the related field or fields.

2. Click the New... button. You'll see a dialog box where you're asked to choose the related file. Select the name of the related file and click the Open button. The Edit Relationship dialog box appears, like this:

In the Relationship Name box, FileMaker Pro proposes the name of the related file as the name of the relationship. You can type a different name for the relationship if you like. Below the relationship name, you see a list of the fields in each of the files you're relating. In this case, we're relating fields in the Payroll file (the master file, on the left) with fields in the Employees file (the related file, on the right).

FileMaker Pro shows related field names with a double colon (::) before them, so you can distinguish them from fields in the master file. Because colons are part of the way related field names are shown, don't use colons when defining field names or relationship names.

IMPORTANT NOTE

3. Select the names of the Employee Number fields from the two lists. This is the match field that will link these two files. (The match field has the same name in both files in this example, but the field names don't matter as long as both fields contain the same data.)

4. Click the OK button to return to the Define Relationship dialog box, and click the Done button there to return to your database file.

The two checkbox options in the Edit Relationship dialog box let you enhance the linkage between the related fields by allowing operations in the master file to affect the data stored in the related file.

The When deleting a record in this file… checkbox tells FileMaker Pro to delete the record in the related file when it's deleted in the master file. For example, if an employee resigns from the company and you're working in the Payroll file, deleting the employee's record there will also cause it to be deleted in the Employees file.

The Allow creation of related records checkbox tells FileMaker Pro to create a new record in the related file when you create a new record in the master file. For example, if you're creating a record for a new employee in the Payroll file, a new record is also created in the Employees file.

If you choose the wrong related file when you begin defining a relationship, click the Specify File… button in the Edit Relationship dialog box to select a different related file.

Editing relationships

After you've defined a relationship, you can edit it at any time.

1. Choose the Define Relationships... command, and select the name of the relationship you want to edit in the Define Relationships dialog box.

2. Click the Edit... button to display the Edit Relationship dialog box.

3. Make the changes you want.

4. Click the OK button to return to the Define Relationships dialog box.

Duplicating and deleting relationships

The Define Relationships dialog box also allows you to duplicate or delete relationships easily.

To duplicate a relationship, select the relationship name and click the Duplicate button. To delete a relationship, select the relationship name and click the Delete button. You'll see a warning like this:

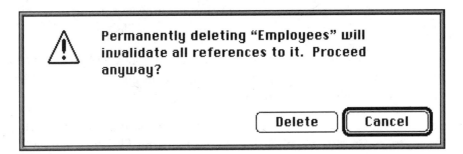

Click the Delete button to delete the relationship from the list.

When you delete a relationship that you've used to display fields, the fields disappear. If you delete a relationship that you've used in a script or calculation, the script or calculation will no longer work properly.

Once you've defined one or more relationships, you can use those relationships to define lookup fields or to create a relational database.

Defining Lookups

A lookup field is a field in a master file into which you want data copied from a related file. When you create a lookup field, you:

- choose the relationship that links your master file with a related file

- and then specify the *lookup source field* from which you want the data copied in the related file and the *lookup destination field* where you want the copied data pasted in the master file.

For example, let's assume we have two files, Employees and Payroll. The Employees file contains employee names, number, addresses, and other personnel information. The Payroll file contains employees' first names, last names, and numbers. We want to use the Employee Number field as the match field that triggers lookups that will copy the employee name information from the Employees file.

Let's assume we've already defined a relationship between the Employee Number fields in the two files, as explained above.

1. Open the Payroll file and choose Define Fields... from the File menu.

2. Double-click on the First Name field in the Define Fields dialog box. This is the first field we want to contain looked-up data. You'll see the field's entry options, like this:

Entry Options for Field "First Name"

Auto Enter ▼

⦿ Nothing

◯ Creation Date ▼

◯ Serial number

next value | 1 | increment by | 1 |

◯ Value from previous record

◯ Data | |

◯ Calculated value [Specify...]

◯ Looked-up value [Specify...]

☐ Prohibit modification of value

☐ Repeating field with a maximum of | 2 | repetitions

[Storage Options...]   [Cancel]   [OK]

3. Click on the Looked-up value button. You'll see the Lookup dialog box, like this.

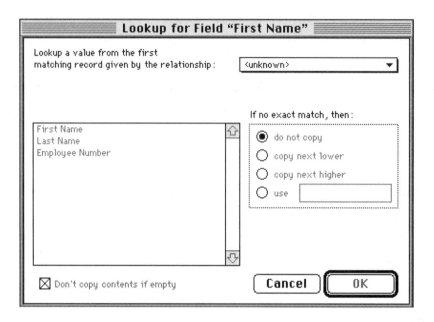

4. Choose Employees from the relationship pop-up menu in the upper right corner. With this relationship selected, we now see all the fields defined for the Employees file, like this:

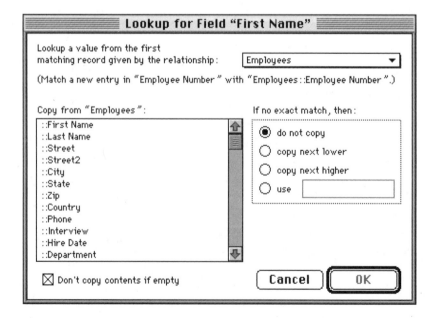

We now choose the lookup source field from which we want data copied. We're creating the lookup for the First Name field in the Salary file, so we want the data from the First Name field in the Employees file copied into it.

5. Select First Name from the field list, and then click the OK button to complete the lookup definition. You'll see the Entry Options dialog box again. Click the OK button there, and you'll be returned to the Define Fields dialog box. There, you'll see that the First Name field's definition now has its option set to Lookup, like this:

```
╔═══════════════ Define Fields for "Payroll" ═══════════════╗

                                                   3 field(s)
      Field Name          Type       Options      View by  creation order ▼
   ⬦ First Name          Text        Lookup                              ⬆
   ⬦ Last Name           Text
   ⬦ Employee Number     Text
```

6. Now repeat this procedure for the Last Name field.

Once these lookups are set up, the lookup will occur when you type a valid employee number into the Employee Number field of the Payroll file. FileMaker Pro will find the record in the Employees file whose employee number matches, and it will then copy and paste the First Name and Last Name fields' data into their respective fields in the Payroll file.

Lookup options

Let's take another look at the Lookup dialog box on p. 248. At the right, a set of radio buttons lets you decide what FileMaker is to do when there's no exact match between the match fields specified in the relationship.

The do not copy button is the default: it tells FileMaker Pro to leave the lookup field blank.

The copy next lower and copy next higher buttons tell FileMaker Pro to substitute the record whose match field contains the next lower or higher numeric value and then copy its lookup source field data into the lookup destination field. For example, say you type *12* into the Item Number field in an Invoices file, but the related Inventory file doesn't contain a record whose Item Number field contains this number. You could make FileMaker Pro copy information from a record whose Item Number field contained 11 or 13, depending on whether you clicked the copy next lower or copy next higher option here.

The use button lets you specify a particular value or text string for FileMaker Pro to enter if there's no exact match. For example, if an employee number isn't found in the related file, you could have FileMaker Pro enter the text, "Employee not found!" instead of leaving the First Name and Last Name fields blank in the Payroll file. Text strings or values you supply for the use option can be up to 255 characters long.

Below the field list on the left, the Don't copy contents if empty checkbox prevents FileMaker Pro from copying if the lookup source field is empty.

Creating multiple lookups

You can set up as many lookup fields in a file as you like, but you have to set the lookup option for each field in which you want information copied. (In the example above, you had to define both the First Name and Last Name fields with the lookup option.) You could use the same relationship to define many different lookup fields (which is likely to happen when you want to copy several fields of related data, such as the parts of an address), or you could use a different relationship for each lookup field.

Using picture lookups

The examples we've seen so far cover data lookups, but you can also create lookups that transfer picture, sound, or movie data. If you maintain an inventory file that contains drawings of different parts, for example, you can have a part drawing looked up when you enter its corresponding part number.

Updating lookup values

Once a lookup is performed, the information in the lookup destination field in your master file doesn't automatically change if the data in the related file changes. But there are two ways to make FileMaker Pro perform a lookup again at a later time:

1. Change the data in the match field of the master file. This will automatically trigger the lookup again for that particular record.

2. Select the match field in the master file and choose Relookup from the Mode menu. When you use the Relookup command, you're telling FileMaker Pro to recopy data for all the records in the current found set, based on the lookup you've defined for that match field.

You'll see a warning box like this:

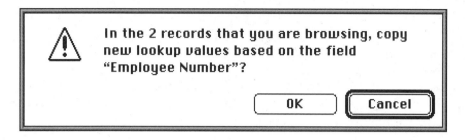

Click the OK button to perform the lookup.

Creating a Relational Database

When you create a relational database, you're simply taking data stored in one file and using it in another file. There's no need to specify source or destination fields as you do with a lookup, so the procedure is simpler. In this section, we'll see how to use related files in layouts and in portals.

Planning a relational database

The whole point of using a relational database is to manage data efficiently in a series of small related files. To do this, you plan a series of files so that each one contains at least one field whose data is unique, and so each pair of related files contains a match field on which the relationship is based. In an order-entry system, for example, you might have three files:

- An Inventory file that contains item names, item numbers, counts, costs, prices, supplier names, and supplier addresses

- An Invoices file that contains item numbers, descriptions, prices, customer numbers, customer name and address information, and shipping information

- A Customers file that contains customer names, numbers, and addresses

In this example, you'll notice that each of the files contains such a match field:

- The Inventory file stores the item number data (since it's likely that you'll create new item numbers as you receive new merchandise and enter counts and descriptions and names at the same time). However, the item number data is also used in the Invoices file, so that file contains an Item Number field as a match field.

- The Customers file contains the customer number, name, and address information, but this data is also used in the Invoices file, so the Invoices file also contains a Customer Number field as a match field.

In this scenario, there are two relationships:

- A relationship between the Invoices file and the Customers file is based on the Customer Number field. Entering a customer number into the Invoices file causes the customer name and address data from the Customers file to be displayed in a new invoice record.

- A relationship between the Invoices file and the Inventory file is based on the Item Number field. Entering an item number in an invoice causes the item's name, description, and price from the Inventory file to be displayed in a new invoice record.

In planning a relational database, consider how to distribute your data among several files so that it must only be stored once. For example, customer name and address data is stored in a Customers file, but it can be used in an Invoices file.

Also, think about each file that actually stores information as one that contains records in which at least one field's information is unique for each record. In a Customers file, for example, each record represents a different customer, so the Customer Number field in this file contains unique data in each record. The same is true for the Item Number field in an Inventory file. In an Invoices file, you would probably store item counts and invoice totals, but the data about the customer or the descriptions of items would come from other files.

Before you begin defining database files, sketch out file names and the fields they will contain on paper. You'll quickly be able to see whether or not each file contains a field with unique data, and you'll also see how to set up relationships between the files based on match fields.

Once you've arrived at a workable plan on paper, create the files and define the fields you'll need for each one, and enter the appropriate data into each file. At this stage, each file contains its own set of fields, and you can then define relationships between those files (see p. 243).

Adding a related field to a layout

Let's assume we've defined a few relationships in advance, linking files called Contacts, Phone Numbers, and Activity Log.

- The Contacts file stores customer numbers, names, and addresses.

- The Phone Numbers file stores customer numbers, phone numbers, and hours of availability at each phone number.

- The Activity Log stores customer numbers, names, and records of individual calls made to each customer.

(The Customer ID field is the match field that links these files in relationships.)

Now, suppose we want to add a Phone Number field to a layout in the Activity Log file.

1. Switch to Layout mode in the Activity Log file.

2. Drag the field tool onto the layout and release the mouse button. You'll see the Specify Field dialog box.

3. Choose the name of the relationship from the pop-up menu at the top (probably Phone Numbers, the name of the related file you want to use). The fields defined for that related file appear in the list below, like this:

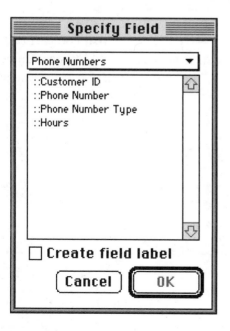

Double-click on the name of the Phone Number field. The field is added to the layout, like this:

Notice that the field name is shown with double colons in front of it to indicate that this is a related field.

You can use related fields in any layout part, and you can move, resize, or reformat related fields just as you would other fields. See Chapter 6 for more information.

Creating a portal

A portal is a container for related fields that allows you to display data from more than one record in a master file. Here's an example:

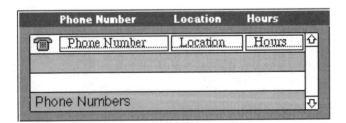

This portion of a layout from the Contacts file is a portal that contains related Phone Number, Location, and Hours fields from a file called Phone Numbers. It is set up to display four records at once. This portal is useful because one person's contact information might contain two or more phone numbers. In Layout mode, the portal looks like this:

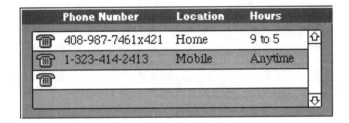

You can see that the portal has a name (Phone Numbers) at its lower left corner, and each of the fields is in the top row. (As in a columnar report layout, you only add each field once, and its data is repeated in subsequent rows, one row for each record.) Also, notice the phone icon next to the Phone Number field: You can add graphics or other objects inside portals.

You can't place a portal inside a portal. If you draw one portal that overlaps another one, it will simply cover up the one underneath.

IMPORTANT NOTE

To create a portal:

1. Select the portal tool [ ] in the tool palette and then draw the portal's outline on your layout. The Portal Setup dialog box appears, like this:

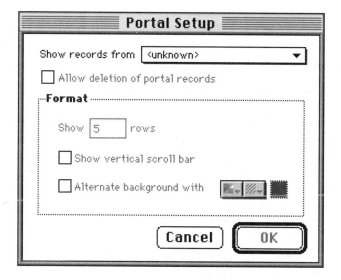

2. Choose a relationship from the pop-up menu at the top to specify which relationship you want to use to supply the contents of this portal. (Each portal's fields must all come from the same related file.)

3. Choose the options for formatting and portal behavior.

4. Click the OK button. The portal is created, like this:

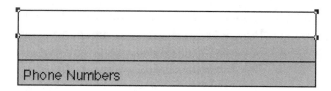

5. Now you can add fields inside it using the field tool. When you use the field tool, its relationship pop-up menu will already be set to the same relationship you specified in the Portal Setup dialog box. When dragging fields inside the portal, place them in the top row (shown in white in this example).

TIP

Make sure the AutoGrid is on when you drag fields into a portal. The first field you drag will align to the upper left corner of the portal, and the rest will align precisely next to the first field.

Portal setup options

Now, let's look at the options in the Portal Setup dialog box.

The Allow deletion of portal records option tells FileMaker Pro to delete the related record in the related file when you select and delete a row from a portal in your master file.

In the Format area, you can specify the number of rows you want the portal to contain. This determines the number of records the portal can show at one time.

**IMPORTANT
NOTE**

The physical size of the portal doesn't determine how many records it will show. When you set the number of rows with this option, the row heights are determined by the overall height of the portal you drew.

The Show vertical scroll bar option adds a right-hand vertical scroll bar to the portal, like the one on p. 254. You'll want to add a scroll bar when the portal might contain more rows of records than you can see at once.

The Alternate background with option lets you choose a fill color and pattern that will apply to alternate rows of the portal.

Changing a portal

A portal can contain related fields as well as text and graphic objects. You can add or delete related fields in a portal at any time by using the field tool. You can draw graphic objects or text inside a portal using the tool palette. However, a portal cannot contain fields from the master file.

To change a portal's setup, double-click in a blank area of the portal when you're in Layout mode. You'll see the Portal Setup dialog box again, and you can change the options there.

If you change the relationship for a portal, any related fields that are in the portal at the time become "disconnected" from the portal and appear on your layout as stand-alone related fields. In other words, the field data will appear only once on the screen (rather than in rows representing different records), and it will over-lap the portal.

IMPORTANT NOTE

You can select, move, resize, or change the fill color or pattern of a portal just as you would any other graphic object on a layout (see Chapter 6).

Deleting a portal

To delete a portal, select it by clicking in any blank area inside it and press the ⌈Delete⌋ key. Any related fields inside a portal must be deleted separately.

Working with Related Fields

Once you've placed a related field in a layout, you can use the same data entry and manipulation features discussed in Chapters 5, 7, and 8. However, since related fields really belong to another file, there are some differences in how FileMaker Pro behaves when you work with related fields.

Accessing related files

If a related file is protected by a password, you'll be asked to enter that password when you open a master file that contains related fields connected to the related file. For example, if a file called Employees requires a password, and a Payroll file contains a related Salary field from the Employees file, you'll be asked for the Employees file's password when you open the Payroll file, like this:

```
╔══════════════════════════════════════╗
║═══════════ File "Employees" ═════════ ║
║                                        ║
║  Password  ┌──────────────────────┐   ║
║            │                      │   ║
║            └──────────────────────┘   ║
║                                        ║
║            ┌──────────┐  ┌──────────┐ ║
║            │  Cancel  │  ║    OK    ║ ║
║            └──────────┘  └──────────┘ ║
╚══════════════════════════════════════╝
```

If you don't know the password needed to open a related file, you can click the Cancel button in the dialog box and the file won't be opened. When FileMaker can't open a related file, the message *File Missing* appears in any related fields from that file.

For more information about passwords and controlling access to files, see Chapter 14.

Changing field definitions

To change the definition of a related field, you must redefine the field in the related file itself. Remember, the related field actually belongs to the related file, so its definition must be changed there.

Changing field formats

To change the display format of a related field, just select the field in Layout mode and then use one of the options on the Format menu, as explained in Chapter 6.

Entering and changing data

A related field displays data as currently stored in the related file. When you select a related field and change the data in it, that data is also changed in the related file.

TIP

You can also use the Replace command to replace data in related fields. See *Replacing data in several records at once*, on p. 78 in Chapter 5.

Deleting data

When you delete data from within a related field, you also delete that data from that field in any related files. But to delete an entire record from a related file when you delete the record in a master file, you must check the option When deleting records in this file, also delete related records in the Edit Relationship dialog box (see p. 244).

TIP

Another way to prevent users from changing or deleting the data in a related field is to format it on the layout so it doesn't allow changes. In the master file, select the field in Layout mode, then choose the Field Format... command from the format menu and deselect the Allow entry into field option in the Field Format dialog box. (See *The Field Format... command* on p. 147 in Chapter 6.) When you use this method, however, remember that the field format applies only to the selected field in the current layout. So, to prevent changes in this field in every layout where it appears, you would have to reformat the field in every layout.

If you select a row in a portal and delete it, and you have the Allow deletion of portal records option checked in the Portal Setup dialog box, the record is also deleted from the related file. (See p. 256, in this chapter.) If you don't have this option checked, the record can't be deleted from the portal.

Creating new records

When you create a new record in your master file whose match field data doesn't exist in a related file, the record will normally be created in the master file only. However, a new record will also be created in the related file if you've checked the Allow creation of related records option in the Edit Relationship dialog box (see p. 244).

To create a new record inside a portal, select the rightmost field in the last row of the portal (you may have to scroll down the portal to see this row), and then press the Tab key. A new, blank row will appear, representing a new record in the related file. Naturally, you must also have checked the Allow creation of related records option in the Edit Relationship dialog box to enable the creation of records in the related file.

Duplicating records

When you duplicate a record in the master file and that record contains related fields, the record is not duplicated in the related file, unless you've checked the Allow creation of related records option in the Edit Relationship dialog box (see p. 244).

Copying fields and portals

You can select and copy related fields and portals just as you can other objects on a layout. When you copy a portal, however, you must also select the fields or other objects inside it if you want to copy them as well.

When you copy a related field to another layout, it is copied with the same relationship you specified in the original version. But when you copy a related field or portal to another file, the relationship becomes invalid.

Printing related records

When you print a layout that contains related fields, all data in those related fields prints as well.

When you print a record containing a portal with a scroll bar, FileMaker Pro prints only the records that appear in the portal in Preview mode. Any records in the portal that would ordinarily have to be scrolled into view will not be printed.

Using related fields in sorts

You can sort on related fields just as you would sort on the master file's fields. To include one or more related fields in a sort, choose a relationship from the pop-up menu in the Sort Order dialog box to display fields from the related file, and then select the field you want to add to the sort order list.

When you add a related field to the sort order list, its name appears along with the related file name, like this:

Here, the Action Status field from the Activity Log file is part of the sort order.

Related fields can appear anywhere in a sort order.

Using related fields in searches

To include a related field in a find request, display a layout that includes the related field, and then choose the Find command from the Mode menu. You then create a find request just as you would normally. See *Creating a Find Request*, on p. 162 in Chapter 7.

Using related fields in calculations

To include a related field in a calculation field formula, just choose a relationship from the pop-up menu at the upper left corner of the Specify Calculation dialog box. (See *Defining calculation fields*, on p. 57 in Chapter 4.)

To summarize the data from records inside a portal, define a calculation field that contains an aggregate function such as Sum, Average, Min, or Max, and then refer to the related field in the formula (see Chapter 16).

Using related fields as merge fields

To use a related field as a merge field in a layout, choose a relationship name from the pop-up menu in the Specify Field dialog box, and then choose the name of the merge field from the list of fields. See *Adding special text or symbols*, on p. 132 in Chapter 6.

Troubleshooting

FileMaker Pro can't find a related file.

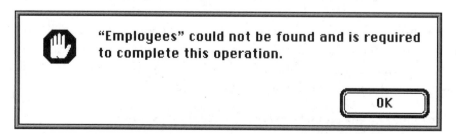

If you open a file containing related fields or you type into the match field that triggers a lookup and FileMaker Pro displays this message, the related file has been moved to another disk or deleted. Click the OK button to display a directory dialog box where you can locate the file on another disk, then select the file and click the Open button.

A related field shows the data *<File Missing>*.

This means that either the relationship on which the field is based has been deleted, or the file supplying the data is missing.

If the file isn't open or is missing, use the solution outlined in the previous section.

To determine if the relationship has been deleted, choose Define Relationships… from the File menu and make sure the relationship on which the field is based is listed in the Define Relationships dialog box. If it isn't, define a new relationship. Then delete the field containing the <File Missing> tag and add it to your layout again. (The old field must be deleted because it's based on a relationship that doesn't exist anymore.)

A lookup field contains the wrong data, or is blank.

This probably means that the lookup relationship didn't find the record containing the right data in the related file. For example, if an entry in the Employee Number field of a Payroll file locates a record in the Personnel file that contains no data in the Salary field, then the Salary field in the Payroll file will be empty.

This could also mean that you've set the copy next lower or copy next higher option in the Lookup Field dialog box, and there's no record that contains your match field's data. For example, suppose your database has no item 13 and you enter this number in the Item Number match field. If you've set the copy next lower option, the related fields in your master file will contain the data from the record for item 12.

You want to choose a relationship from a pop-up menu, but the relationship doesn't appear there.

If you're defining a lookup field, creating a portal, or adding a related field to a layout, and you can't find a relationship on the pop-up menu in the dialog box, it's because you haven't defined one. Choose Define Relationship… from the pop-up menu and then define a new relationship (see p. 243).

You want to select a portal but you keep selecting fields inside it.

To select the portal itself, click on the portal name in the lower left corner, not on any part of a field, text, or graphic object that's located inside the portal.

You delete a portal but the fields and objects inside it are still on the layout.

You have to delete fields and objects inside a portal separately.

A related field's definition doesn't appear in the Define Fields dialog box.

To see a related field's definition, you must view the Define Fields dialog box inside the related file. The field definition, like the field's data, belongs to the file where it is actually stored, not to any master files where it happens to be used.

You scroll a portal to display a different group of records, but when you print or preview, you see the records that show at the top of the portal when it isn't scrolled.

FileMaker Pro will only preview or print the records that show in a portal's unscrolled state. The only way to print or preview records that aren't normally in view is to enlarge the portal itself so those records are showing.

12 Using Scripts and Buttons

Scripts and buttons allow you to execute a series of FileMaker Pro commands by simply clicking an object on a layout or choosing a command from a menu. In this chapter, we'll see how to create and use scripts and buttons.

~~~~~~

About Scripts

Once you've put together a FileMaker Pro database file, you'll probably use it for certain recurring activities that require a series of commands to carry out. For example, when preparing a monthly mailing, you might want to find a group of customer records by a range of zip codes, sort them by zip code, and print them on a label layout. At other times, you might want to sort the same records by last name and print them on a columnar report layout for a telephone list. With scripts, you can have FileMaker Pro perform tasks like this automatically.

A *script* is an automated procedure that you set up to perform one or more FileMaker Pro functions. To create a script, you use the ScriptMaker utility: choose the ScriptMaker... command from the Scripts menu. (See *Creating a Script*, on p. 268, below.)

Once a script is defined, you can display its name on the Scripts menu and then play back, or *perform*, the script by choosing its name there. When you perform a script, the FileMaker Pro commands or operations stored in it will be repeated automatically.

Script capabilities

In a script, each operation or command is called a *step*. Script steps include most of the things you'd do with the program by choosing commands or selecting data yourself, along with tasks such as checking the sort status of a file. In FileMaker Pro version 3, the ScriptMaker utility is far more powerful than in previous versions. There are script steps that perform virtually any FileMaker Pro operation you would otherwise do manually. Script steps are divided into 11 categories:

- Control steps, such as performing, pausing, or resuming another script or performing certain steps inside a script only if certain logical conditions are met.

- Navigation steps, such as switching to a particular mode, choosing a layout, or selecting a record or field.

- Sort, find, and print steps, which perform those tasks.

- Editing steps, such as cutting, copying, or pasting data.

- Field steps, which insert special types of information (such as dates or the current user name) into a field.

- Records steps, which create, duplicate, replace, delete, and otherwise work with records.

- Import and export steps, which handle importing of data, pictures, or movies or the exporting of data.

- Windows steps, which control the appearance of the FileMaker Pro window.

- Files steps, which let you create, open, or save copies of a file.

- Spelling steps, which are used to run the spelling checker.

- Miscellaneous steps, which include operations like dialing a telephone, opening the Help system, sending Apple Events, performing AppleScript commands, and quitting FileMaker Pro.

A single script can perform one or all of the operations described above. One script can contain commands to perform other scripts, so you can cause a very long and complex series of events to occur by playing just one script. In addition, a script can be paused and resumed, so a script might display a data entry screen, wait for input from the user, and then continue after the user clicks a Resume button. Finally, scripts can be set to play automatically when you open or close a file.

A script can also contain a *loop step*, which repeats itself. For example, a script might add a new record for a file, wait for data input, and then repeat itself and add another new record.

Script limitations

Scripts can be extremely powerful, containing dozens of steps, but there are a few limitations to keep in mind as you create and use them.

- FileMaker Pro automatically assigns ⌃⌘ key shortcuts to the first ten scripts listed on the Scripts menu. To determine which scripts get these shortcuts, you can rearrange the order of scripts on the menu.

- A script can store only one version of the following settings:

—find requests

—sort order

—import order

—export order

—page setup

A script can *contain* more than one of these steps, but each repetition of the step will implement the same settings. For example, you might begin a script by sorting a file on the Customer Number field to browse records in that order, then unsort the file to add more records to it, and then sort it again on the Customer Number field to print invoices.

TIP

To specify more than one find request, sort order, import or export order, or page setup, define a subscript containing the new setting and then include it in the main script. See *Using Subscripts and External Scripts*, on p. 277.

Creating a Script

Now, let's go through the process of creating a script to see how this all works.

Preparing your file

When you begin any script, the current settings for the layout, mode, find requests, sort order, import or export options, and page setup are automatically included in the script definition. So the easiest way to add these options to a script is to set them up before you begin defining the script. Here's a checklist of preparatory steps to take before defining a new script:

1. Create the find request(s) you want using Find mode. You don't have to actually execute the find itself, although you can if you want to be sure it produces the right group of records.

2. Set up the sort order you want. Here again, you don't have to actually sort the records unless you want to be sure you get the desired result. Otherwise, just click the Done button in the Sort Records dialog box to store the sort order you've created.

3. Choose the page setup options you want.

4. Create the layout you'll want to use. (If you're planning to include a page setup in the script's definition, be sure to select the right layout first.)

5. Create any scripts or AppleScript commands you'll refer to in the script.

6. Store the import or export options you want if you plan to include an import or export step.

Defining a new script

Once you've prepared the file using the above steps, here's how to create a new script:

1. Choose ScriptMaker... from the Scripts menu. FileMaker Pro displays the Define Scripts dialog box, like this:

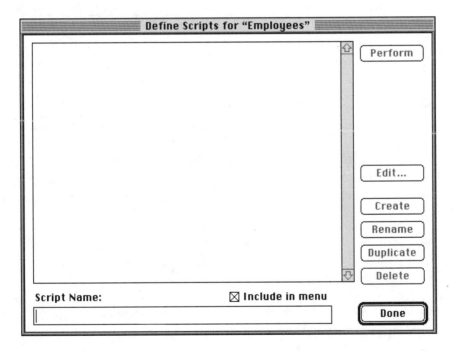

The names of any existing scripts are shown in the list, and the check mark at the right of a script name means it's listed on the Scripts menu. You can select any script name here and perform the script, edit it, rename it, duplicate it, delete it, or remove it from the Scripts menu. (See *The Define Scripts dialog box*, on p. 272 for more information.)

2. Type a name for the script in the Script Name box.

3. Click the Create button or press [Return]. FileMaker Pro displays the Script Definition dialog box, like this:

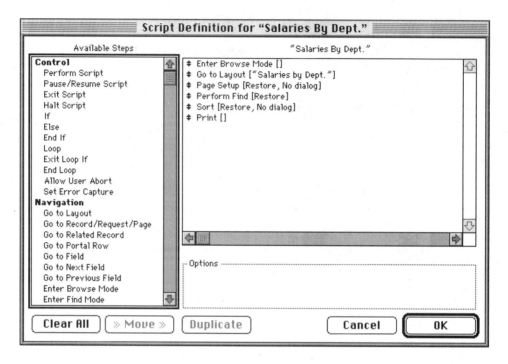

The Available Steps list at the left shows the steps you can include in a script. Steps that offer a subset of options are shown with brackets after their names. Notice that the steps are grouped in categories, as explained on p. 266.

At the right, the list shows the steps currently included in the script you're defining. (As you can see, the mode, layout, page setup, find, and sort set-.tings that are currently active in the file are already shown in the list.)

In the lower right corner, the Options area shows the options (if any) for the script step you've selected at the left.

IMPORTANT NOTE

With steps that ordinarily display a dialog box, such as Sort or Print, you have the option to display the dialog box or not while the script is being performed. If you choose to display the dialog box, the script pauses when the dialog box is displayed so the user can select options from it and then click a button (such as Print or Sort) to continue the script.

4. If you want to build a new set of steps from scratch, click the Clear All button to clear the existing steps from the list at the right. To clear one or more individual steps from the list, select the step name and then press the $\boxed{\text{Delete}}$ key or the Clear button.

5. To add a step to the list, either double-click on the step name or select the step name from the Available Steps list and click the Move button.

6. Select any options, if necessary, for the step you've added to the list. The options you choose will be shown in the brackets following the step name.

7. Once you've added all the steps you want, scan the list of steps to make sure they're in the right order. FileMaker Pro always executes the steps in the order shown in the list.

To change the order of a step in the list, point to the arrows icon at the left of the step name and drag it up or down in the list.

TIP

8. Click the OK button to create the script. FileMaker Pro adds the script name to the list in the Define Scripts dialog box.

9. Click the Done button to put the Define Scripts dialog box away.

Now let's look more closely at the various options available in the Define Scripts and Script Definition dialog boxes.

The Define Scripts dialog box

The Define Scripts dialog box displays all the scripts you've created for the file. It also lets you make new scripts, change existing ones, delete scripts, and perform scripts. Refer to the sample dialog box on p. 269, earlier in this chapter for a look at this dialog box, or choose the ScriptMaker... command from FileMaker Pro's Script menu to see it on your own screen.

Script names are added to the list in the order they're created, but you can move them up or down the list by dragging the arrows icon next to the script name you want to move. The order of the script names on this list determines their positions on the Scripts menu, if you've chosen to display their names there. To prevent a script from appearing on the Scripts menu, select the script name and click the Include in menu option below the list of scripts to remove the check mark from it.

The Script Name box is where you type in a new script name or edit an existing one. To edit a script name, select it in the list, type a new name in the Script Name box, and then click the Rename button at the right.

The Perform button in the upper right corner tells FileMaker Pro to play back the script whose name is selected in the list.

The Edit… button displays the Script Definition dialog box. This dialog box is automatically displayed when you're creating a new script, but you can also display it when you want to view or edit an existing script's definition. Select the script's name in the list and click the Edit… button to display its definition.

Double-clicking on a script's name in the Define Scripts dialog box also displays the script's definition.

TIP

The Create button creates a new script, displaying the Script Definition dialog box after you type in the script's name.

The Rename button lets you change the name of an existing script after you select the script and edit its name in the Script Name box.

The Duplicate button duplicates the selected script, adding *Copy* to the end of its name and adding it to the list. This is useful when you want to copy a complex script that already exists and then change a few steps in it.

The Delete button deletes the script whose name is selected in the list at the time. (You'll see a warning message when you try to delete a script, because this operation can't be undone.)

The Done button puts the Define Scripts dialog box away.

The Script Definition dialog box

After you click the Create button to make a new script or the Edit… button to display an existing script's definition, FileMaker Pro displays the Script Definition dialog box, as shown at the top of the next page. Let's take a closer look at this dialog box.

When you first create a script, your file's current mode, layout, page setup, find, and sort settings are automatically included as a series of steps in the list at the right. FileMaker Pro performs the steps in the order in which they appear on the list. Here's what the steps would do in the example following:

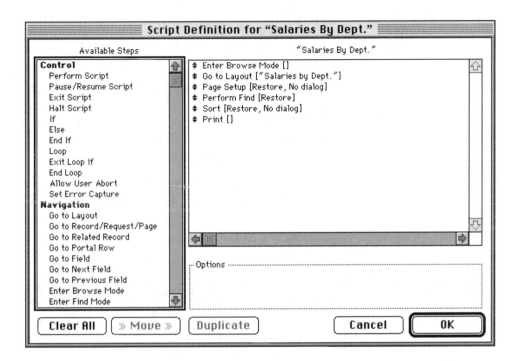

Enter Browse Mode switches the file to Browse mode. This step has an option (hence the brackets after its name), but the option wasn't selected in this particular case (which is why the brackets are empty). Different options are available for different steps. For a list of the options and what they do, see Step options, in the next section.

Go to layout tells FileMaker Pro to switch to the layout indicated in the brackets (*"Salaries by Dept."* in this case). When you first create a script, the layout your file is currently using will be chosen for this step, but you can make the script switch to any layout in the file by selecting the step name here and then specifying a different layout in the Options area below.

Page Setup tells FileMaker Pro to set page setup options. Inside the brackets, the two options set for this step are separated by a comma. Restore means to restore the current page setup options (as set when you began defining this script) and No dialog means to do so without displaying the Page Setup dialog box.

Perform Find tells FileMaker Pro to select records in the file to match the current found set.

Sort means to sort the file. The options inside the brackets are to Restore the sort order in effect when you began defining the script, and to do so with No dialog box on the screen.

Print tells FileMaker Pro to automatically choose the Print... command. Since the brackets after this step are empty, FileMaker Pro will display the Print dialog box during the script.

Step options

When you add a step that has brackets after its name, the Options area of the dialog box displays options you can choose for that step. For example, if we added the Open step to the script shown earlier (to open another file), the dialog box and Options area would look like this:

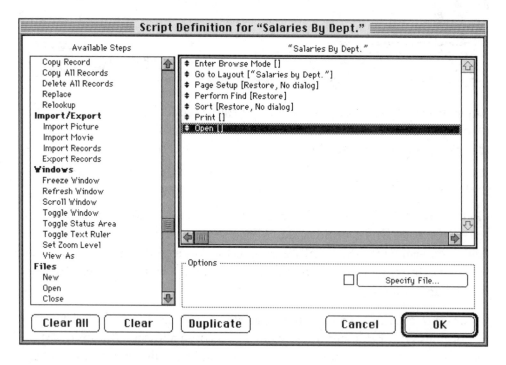

Let's look at some of the options you might have when you choose a step name that has a pair of brackets after it.

The Perform without dialog option means the step is one that normally displays a dialog box, but that you want it performed without the dialog box. The Print... command is an example: You normally see the Print dialog box when you choose this command, but if you know you don't want to change any of the print options, you could perform this command without having the script display the dialog box. On the other hand, you may want to display a Print, Page Setup, or Import Records dialog box so you'll be able to choose different options in it each time the script is performed.

Clicking the Perform without dialog option makes scripts execute more quickly because it takes extra time to display various dialog boxes on the screen.

TIP

Specify buttons display a pop-up list, menu or dialog box where you select or enter a file name, field name, text string, Apple Event command, or other options for the step you've chosen. In the previous example, the File step in the script has the Specify File... option, because you must choose the file you want opened.

The Select entire contents option selects all the data in a field or of a record.

The Pause option temporarily halts the script so you can perform some manual tasks before continuing. For example, the step to enter a particular mode has the pause option, because you might want to have a script select Find mode and then wait for you to enter a request before continuing. (In such a script, the next step would probably be Perform Find.)

When you insert the Pause option in a script step, FileMaker Pro adds Continue and Cancel buttons to the status area on the screen so you can resume the script after the pause. This shows a script that has been paused:

First Name	Last Name	Department	Salary
Susan	Pearson	Marketing	$27,500
John	Anderson	Accounting	$23,500
Joe	Bruno	Manufacturing	$31,000
Sonia	Rivera	Marketing	$42,500
Rolf	Weber	Marketing	$23,600
Laura	Brandeis	Manufacturing	$26,760
Freida	Jefferson	Accounting	$42,500
Oscar	Banuelos	Sales	$45,000
Don	Williams	Manufacturing	$26,500
Diane	Parssinen	Manufacturing	$28,000

Employees

Salaries b...

Records: 34

Found: 26

Unsorted

Script:

[Continue]

[Cancel]

100 | Browse

The script control buttons that are used to resume and cancel the script are in the lower left corner.

The Refresh screen option redraws the screen when the step containing this option is performed. FileMaker Pro normally redraws the screen when you switch layouts, but since it can take extra time to redraw the screen when you're displaying a complex layout or lots of graphics, you can make a script execute more quickly if you don't use this option.

The Restore option tells FileMaker Pro to restore the find request, sort order, import or export order, page setup, or other options that were in effect when you began creating the script.

There are other options that appear with various steps. Select any step name in the FileMaker Pro Help Index for more information on its options (see p. 34 in Chapter 3).

Playing Scripts

Once you've defined a script, there are four ways to play or perform it.

- Select the script name from the Scripts menu.

- Choose the ScriptMaker... command to display the Define Scripts dialog box, then select the script and click the Perform button.

- Click a button that's been defined to perform the script. (See *Using buttons*, later in this chapter.)

- Set a file's preferences so a script is played automatically each time you open or close the file. (See *Document preferences*, on p. 40 in Chapter 3.)

Pausing or stopping a script

You may want to pause a script at certain times during its execution to allow yourself or other users a chance to review data on the screen, add or edit data, create or edit find requests, or perform other activities. There are two ways to pause a script:

- Use the Pause option when you add a step, if that option is available.

- Add the Pause/Resume step to a script.

When a script is paused, many of the menu commands in FileMaker Pro are inactive.

IMPORTANT
NOTE

When a script is paused, you can resume it by clicking the Continue button in the status area or pressing the ⌨Enter key.

To cancel a script while it's paused, click the Cancel button in the status panel, switch to another mode, close the file's window, or quit FileMaker Pro.

To stop a script while it's running, press ⌨⌘.. (You could also close the file or quit FileMaker Pro, but doing these may damage your file.)

Using Subscripts and External Scripts

So far, we've covered the basics of creating and playing scripts. Now, let's look at two of the most powerful scripting capabilities in more detail.

Subscripts are scripts that are played from within a script using the Perform Script step. Using subscripts, you can define separate tasks such as preparing individual reports, and then perform them all at once from within a single script. In a sales-order file, for example, you could create separate scripts to produce reports for sales by part number, sales by geographic region, and sales by employee, and then use the Perform Script step three times in one main script that automatically prepares and prints all three reports at once. Or you could prepare a report of your highest volume customers, print it, and then print a form letter inviting customers to a special sale. Subscripts also allow you to specify a second find request, sort order, or import/export order within a script, since each script can contain only one of these.

External scripts are subscripts that are stored and performed in other FileMaker Pro files. External scripts give you the ability to perform complex operations in other files from within the current file. In a relational database, for example, you might define a script in the Invoices file that includes an external script that sorts the Customers file by company name.

The possibilities are truly mind-boggling when you use subscripts and external scripts. It all starts when you add the Perform Script step to an existing script.

Adding a subscript

To add a subscript to an existing script, you must first create the subscripts you want to use. (If you want to specify external scripts, you must first open the external files and create the scripts you'll want to use in them—see *Adding an external script*, below.) Once you've created all the scripts you need, adding subscripts to a script is simple. Here are the steps:

1. Create the individual scripts you'll need, one at a time.

2. Define or modify the script that will contain or activate the subscripts, adding the steps you want to perform before each subscript is performed.

3. Add the Perform Script step to the script. You'll see a set of options like these:

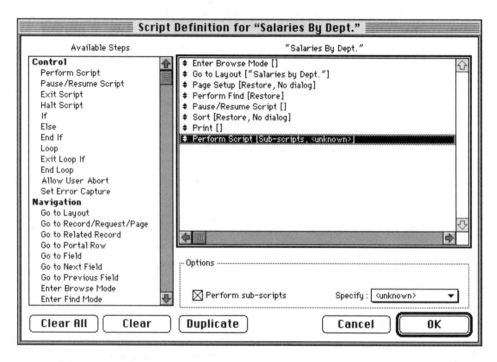

The Perform sub-scripts option is checked by default, because you'll usually want FileMaker Pro to perform any subscripts within the script you're performing with this step.

4. Select the name of the subscript you want to run from the Specify pop-up menu.

5. Add any other steps you want the script to perform, and then click the OK button to return to the Define Scripts dialog box.

6. Click the Done button to put the Define Scripts dialog box away.

Adding an external script

To add an external script to your script definition, the procedure is much the same, except you must specify the name of the external file whose script you want to run before choosing the script name. Here are the steps:

1. Follow steps 1 through 3 to add a subscript, as described above.

2. Select External Script... from the bottom of the Specify pop-up menu. FileMaker Pro displays the Specify External Script dialog box like this:

3. Click the Change File... button. You'll see a dialog box where you can navigate to and open another FileMaker Pro file.

4. Select the file you want to open and click the Open button. You'll be returned to the Specify External Script dialog box, but now the filename will be listed and you'll see a pop-up menu of script names below it, like this:

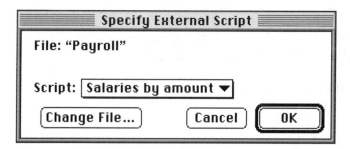

5. Select the script name from the pop-up menu and click the OK button. You'll be returned to the Script Definition dialog box, and the subscript definition is finished. You can now add more steps or complete the script definition.

TIP

When a subscript is an external script, FileMaker Pro will automatically open the external file containing that script—you don't need to include a step in the main script to open the external file first. And, since playing the subscript is only one step in the script you're defining, any steps you add after it will take place in the current file—you don't have to put a step in the external script that returns you to the current file.

Changing scripts

It's not always easy to create the exact script you want. Fortunately, you can change scripts whenever you want to correct any mistakes you've made, or to accommodate new needs. You can change a script name or add, remove, or edit the steps it contains by editing the script in the Define Scripts dialog box.

To change a script's name:

1. Choose the ScriptMaker… command, and select the script's name from the list in the Define Scripts dialog box.

2. Edit the script's name in the Script Name box.

3. Click the Rename button, and then click the Done button to put the dialog box away.

To change a script's definition:

1. Set up any new Find request(s), page setup options, or field orders for sorting, importing, or exporting that you want the script to use.

2. Choose the ScriptMaker… command.

3. Select the script's name in the Define Scripts dialog box, and click the Edit… button. FileMaker Pro displays the Script Definition dialog box, showing the script's current steps.

4. Include new steps, delete steps, or select existing steps and choose different options for them.

5. Click the OK button. If the script contains no page setup, find, sort, import, or export steps, you'll be returned to the Define Scripts dialog box. From there, just click the Done button and you've finished editing the script. If your script *does* contain any of these functions, FileMaker Pro will display the following dialog box:

```
╔═══════════════ FileMaker Pro ═══════════════╗
║                                              ║
║  The following information is needed to perform this
║  script. You can:
║
║  • Keep the information already saved for this script
║  • Replace it with the information currently in use
║
║        Page Setup:  ⦿ Keep   ○ Replace
║      Import Order:  ○ Keep   ○ Replace
║     Find Requests:  ⦿ Keep   ○ Replace
║        Sort Order:  ⦿ Keep   ○ Replace
║      Export Order:  ○ Keep   ○ Replace
║
║                          ┌────────┐ ╔════════╗
║                          │ Cancel │ ║   OK   ║
║                          └────────┘ ╚════════╝
╚══════════════════════════════════════════════╝
```

Nothing in the Script Definition dialog box tells FileMaker Pro whether to keep the Find requests, page setup options, and sort, import, and export orders in the script's original definition or replace them with those currently in effect. So FileMaker Pro uses this dialog box to ask you whether it should keep the originals or replace them with the ones you set up in step 1. (Some of the options are dimmed in the above example because they don't apply to the current script.)

6. Click the appropriate buttons to tell FileMaker Pro whether to keep existing settings for each item or replace them with new ones.

7. Click the OK button. The changes are made, and FileMaker Pro displays the Define Scripts dialog box again.

8. Click the Done button to put the dialog box away.

Deleting scripts

To delete a script, select the script name in the Define Scripts dialog box and click the Delete button. You'll see a warning box, and you can then click the Delete button inside the box to confirm the deletion.

IMPORTANT NOTE

When you delete a script, the script name is *not* deleted automatically from any other script or button definitions where it appears. If you click a button or try to perform a script that plays a script you've deleted, you'll see a message saying the script wasn't found.

Managing script names on the Scripts menu

If a script name appears on the Scripts menu and you want to remove it from the menu (but you don't want to delete it), select the script name in the Define Scripts dialog box and uncheck the Include in menu option. Conversely, you can add a script's name to the menu by selecting it and checking the Include in menu box.

To rearrange a script name on the Scripts menu, choose the ScriptMaker… command, select the script you want to move, and drag the arrows icon next to the script name up or down in the list. And remember, the first ten script names on the menu automatically get their own ⌘ key shortcuts.

You can create a dividing line between two groups of scripts on the Scripts menu by creating a script, naming it "——————————" or "================," dragging the new script between the two groups you want to separate, and adding the script name to the menu.

Using AppleScript Commands in Scripts

AppleScript is a scripting language you use to control programs on the Macintosh. To use AppleScript commands, you must have either the AppleScript extension or the Apple Event Manager and QuickTime extensions installed in your System Folder. To create scripts with AppleScript, you need to understand the AppleScript language (see your Apple dealer for more information), but let's look at how you would use AppleScript commands in a FileMaker Pro script.

To use AppleScript commands in FileMaker Pro scripts:

1. Define the script that will contain the AppleScript command, or select a script in the Define Scripts dialog box and click the Edit... button.

2. Choose Perform AppleScript step from the list of steps (it's under Miscellaneous, near the bottom of the list), and click the Move button to add it to the list of script steps.

3. Click the Specify... button in the Options area. You'll see a dialog box like this:

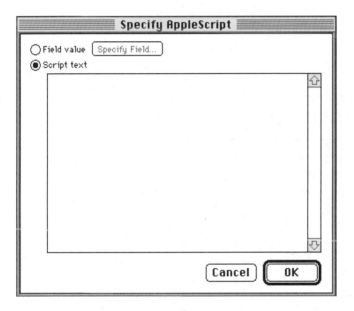

In this dialog box, you can either type in the AppleScript commands you want to send in this script step or have FileMaker Pro send AppleScript commands that are stored in a field.

4. To send a script that's stored in a field, click the Field value button, and then click the Specify Field... button next to it to select the field that contains the script text.

    Or, to enter the text of a script, click the Script text button and then type in the AppleScript commands you want to send in the box below.

5. Click the OK button, and then finish defining the FileMaker Pro script as explained above.

Using Apple Events in Scripts

Apple Events are commands that control various operations in programs. Apple Events in FileMaker Pro are primarily for use by application developers as a way to automate interactions between FileMaker Pro and other programs. For example, an Apple Event might send data from FileMaker Pro to a spreadsheet program so a chart can be made from it.

But exchanging data between FileMaker Pro and other programs involves more than simply opening another program or opening or printing one of its documents. In addition to understanding the basics of sending an Apple Event, you'll probably also need to include script commands in the Apple Event you send.

In effect, the Apple Event sends instructions to the target program in that program's own scripting language (AppleScript, for example). The Apple Event can open a specific program and document, but the script tells the program what to do after that. For example, an Apple Event that opens an Excel document might also play an Excel script that takes data currently on the Clipboard, pastes it into certain cells, and then makes a chart out of it.

If you're a developer and want more information about which Apple Events are supported in FileMaker Pro, look in the FileMaker and Apple Events folder inside the FileMaker Pro 3.0 folder on your disk, or contact the Apple Program Developer's Association through Apple Computer.

To learn how to write scripts for the target program to which you're sending an Apple Event, consult the AppleScript manual or the scripting manual that came with the target program. You can exchange Apple Events with other programs that support Apple Events, including HyperCard and Excel.

Apple Events are individual commands. The events are grouped into *suites*, and different programs may support different suites of events. Like every program that supports Apple Events, FileMaker Pro supports the Required suite of Apple Events. These events perform the fundamental operations of opening and closing documents, loading and quitting programs, and printing. FileMaker Pro also supports the Core, Menu, and Database suites of Apple Events. These other suites support more sophisticated operations, such as selecting data in a particular field in a particular record.

To send an Apple Event from FileMaker Pro, you must create a script that contains the Send Apple Event step, and then define the Apple Event you want to send (see *Sending an Apple Event*, below). To send an Apple Event from another program to FileMaker Pro, you must have a local copy of FileMaker Pro on the same Macintosh as the program from which you're sending the event.

Apple Events are primarily for use by developers, and a comprehensive discussion of Apple Events is well beyond the scope of this book. To give you a basic orientation about Apple Events in this section, however, we'll discuss the basic procedures for sending and receiving Apple Events, go through the steps of adding an Apple Event command to a script, and look at the options you have when you do so.

Sending an Apple Event

To send an Apple Event, you first define a script that includes the Send Apple Event step, and then you perform the script. When you include the Send Apple Event step in a script definition, you'll have options about which event to send. Here's the procedure.

1. Choose the ScriptMaker... command from the Scripts menu, type a name for the new script, and click the Create button. FileMaker Pro displays the Script Definition dialog box.

2. Select the script steps you'll want to perform before sending the Apple Event and move them into the list of defined steps.

3. Add the Send Apple Event step to the list of defined steps. (Send Apple Event is in the group of Miscellaneous steps near the bottom of the list of steps, so you'll have to scroll the list to see it and select it.)

4. Click the Specify button in the Options area. FileMaker Pro displays the Specify Apple Event dialog box, like this:

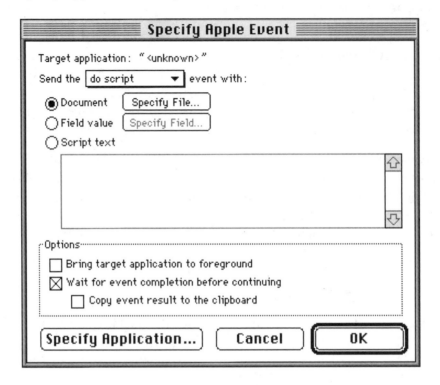

FileMaker first needs to know the name and location of the program to which you want to send the Apple Event (the *target application*). Notice that the name shown for the target application at the top of this dialog box is "*<unknown>*."

5. Click the Specify Application... button to display a dialog box where you can locate and open the target application. The program's name will then appear at the top of the Specify Apple Event dialog box.

6. Choose the event you want to send from the pop-up menu below the target application name. Depending on the event you choose, you can then specify a document name or a field name or enter script text. For example, if you choose the open document event from the pop-up menu, you would then click the Document button below it, and then click the Specify File button to select the document you want to open. If you send the do script event, then you would click the Script text button below and enter the script text you want to send.

7. Set the other options at the bottom of the dialog box (see below for more information).

8. Click the OK button and finish defining the rest of the steps for the script, as described earlier.

Once you've finished defining the script, you can send the Apple Event by performing the script that contains it.

Apple Event options

Now, let's look at the options in the Specify Apple Event dialog box.

On the pop-up menu, the choices are open application, open document, do script, and Other.... Depending on which type of event you send, you have further options with the radio buttons below the pop-up menu and the checkboxes at the bottom of the dialog box.

Opening applications

When you choose the open application event, FileMaker Pro will open the target application you selected when you first began specifying the Apple Event (see step 4 in the preceding section). None of the radio buttons below the menu are active, because the Apple Event's only purpose is to open the target application, and you've already specified the target application you want opened (see step 5 above).

Opening documents

When you choose the open document event, you can click any of the three radio buttons to select:

- the name of the document you want opened (the document to which the event will be sent)

- the field whose value you want sent with the event

- the script text you want sent with the event

When you specify the field, you see a list of fields in the current file from which you can select.

Playing scripts in the target application

When you choose the do script event, you're asking the target application to perform a script. In this case, the script is in the target application's own scripting language. To perform a script in the target application, you must specify which document to open (the target application document where the script will be performed), and then specify the script text or the script name. If you specify a script name, there must already be a script by that name stored with the target program's document.

You can select a target application document to open by clicking the Document radio button and clicking the Specify File... button. To specify a script or script name, click the Script text button and enter the script text or script name in the box below.

When specifying a script or script text, use the script's name if you want to perform a script that's already stored in the target application's document, or enter script text in the target application's scripting language.

For example, suppose you had already created a script called Make Chart in an Excel document called Budget, and you wanted to send an Apple Event from FileMaker Pro that sent some data and ran the Make Chart script. In this case, you would use the do script event, specify the Budget document to open it, click the Script text button, and enter *Make Chart* as the name of the Excel script in the box below it. The Apple Event would then open Excel, open the Budget document, and play the Make Chart script stored with that document.

Sending other kinds of Apple Events

When you choose the Other... event, FileMaker Pro displays a dialog box where you can enter the Apple Event class and ID number, like this:

Obviously, you need to know a lot about Apple Event class and ID names to use this dialog box. Ask your Apple dealer about an Apple Events reference book.

Finally, the three checkboxes at the bottom of the Specify Apple Event dialog box work as follows:

The Bring target application to foreground checkbox displays the target application on your screen when the Apple Event is being performed. For example, if you send an event to copy data from a record in HyperCard, HyperCard will become active on your screen, and you'll see the stack where the data is being copied from. Uncheck this box if you don't need to see the target application: The event will be performed in the background, and your FileMaker Pro file will remain active on the screen throughout it.

Uncheck the Bring target application to foreground box to make scripts perform as quickly as possible. It takes extra time for your Mac to redraw the screen when it brings a target application to the foreground.

TIP

The Wait for event completion before continuing box is checked by default, because FileMaker Pro assumes you want to wait for an Apple Event to play itself out before you do other work with your file. If you're running a lengthy Apple Event, however, and you don't need to wait for the data that results from that event before you can continue working, you can uncheck this option.

The Copy event result to the clipboard option does just that. For example, if the event creates a chart in Excel from some data you've sent out of FileMaker Pro, you may want the Excel chart itself (which is the result of the event) copied to the Clipboard. With this box checked, you would probably have a later step in your script that takes the data from the Clipboard and pastes it into a field or layout in FileMaker Pro.

Using Buttons

Buttons are objects on layouts that you click in Browse mode to execute a particular FileMaker Pro script or command. With buttons, you can make your FileMaker Pro file much simpler and more intuitive to use.

For example, instead of teaching a new user about the New Record command, you can add a button to your layout that says "Create New Record." In fact, you could create an entire layout filled with buttons to present your users with a graphic menu of options they could simply click to create different reports, choose different layouts, or perform other FileMaker Pro commands.

Creating a button

To make a button with the button tool:

1. Select the button tool 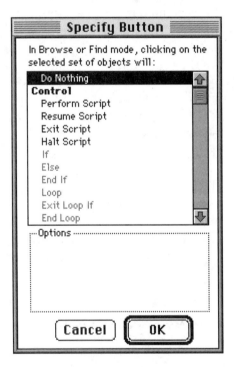 and draw an outline on your layout where you want the button to appear. When you release the mouse button, the Specify Button dialog box will appear, like this:

2. Select the name of the step you want the button to perform, and then click the OK button. The button appears on your layout with the text cursor blinking in the center of it, like this:

There are several script steps that can't be directly performed by a button. These steps are dimmed in the Specify Button dialog box. If you want a button to perform one of these functions, however, you can define a script that does it and then create a button to perform the script.

TIP

3. Type a name for the button, and then click outside the button's outline on the layout. The finished button appears, like this:

Phone List

The buttons you create with the button tool are pretty boring, visually, but you can also make a button out of any graphic object on your layout. For example, you can create interesting graphics or icons, or paste them into your layout from a clip art library, and turn them into buttons. To make a button from an existing layout object:

1. Switch to Layout mode and select the object you want to turn into a button.

2. Choose Button... from the Format menu. FileMaker Pro displays the Specify Button dialog box.

3. Select the step you want the button to perform.

4. Click the OK button to complete the definition.

For examples of nice-looking buttons created from graphic objects, look at the sample files in the FileMaker Examples or FileMaker Templates folder on your hard disk.

Copying a button

You may want to use the same button in several different locations. Once you've defined a layout object as a button, you can copy and paste that object to other layouts or other files, and the button definition copies with it. For example, if you copy a button defined to choose the Print... command, that button will also choose the Print... command in the new layout or file where you paste it. Here's how to copy a button:

1. Select the button in Layout mode.

2. Choose Copy from the Edit menu.

3. Switch to the layout where you want to copy the button, either in the same file or another file, and display it in Layout mode.

4. Click on the layout where you want the button to appear.

5. Choose Paste from the Edit menu.

IMPORTANT NOTE

Be careful when you copy a button that's defined to perform a script or switch to a different layout. When you copy such a button to a different file and use it there, it will choose a layout based on the original layout name's position on the layout pop-up menu. With buttons defined to perform scripts, a copied button will try to perform a script whose name matches the original script it was defined to run. If the file you've copied the button to doesn't have the same set of scripts or layouts as the file it was defined in, you'll get unexpected results when you use the button there.

Changing or deleting a button

You can select a button at any time in Layout mode and change its fill color or pattern or its pen color, pattern, or width. You can also resize the button or move it wherever you like.

You can also change a button's definition at any time. This is particularly handy when you copy a graphically elegant button from one file to another and it doesn't do what you want in the new file. To change a button's definition, just select it in Layout mode, choose the Button... command from the Format menu, and redefine it as if you'd just created it.

To delete a button, select it on the Layout screen and press (Delete) or choose Cut from the Edit menu. Deleting the object that represents a button deletes the button's definition as well.

IMPORTANT NOTE

Once you've created a button with the button tool, you can't change its name. To change a button name, you must delete the button and then create a new button with a different name.

TIP

Typically, you'll use buttons to give users control over FileMaker Pro when they're working in Browse mode, but you won't want the buttons to appear when you print a layout. To prevent buttons from printing, select them in Layout mode and click the Do not print the selected objects option in the Sliding/Printing... command's dialog box. See p. 155, in Chapter 6.

~~~~~~

Troubleshooting

Here are some common problems you might run into when using scripts or buttons and some advice on how to solve them.

A script doesn't select or sort records properly, or it produces the wrong Page Setup options.

The most likely cause of this problem is that the wrong Find request, sort order, or Page Setup options were in effect when you created the script. Remember, too, that if some of the file's records or data have been added, changed, or deleted since you created the script, it won't necessarily find the same records or sort them the same way as when you first created it. The simplest way to solve this problem is to replace the existing settings with the ones you want. See *Changing scripts* or *Deleting scripts,* pp. 280 and 282.

The wrong layout is showing after you play a script.

There are two possibilities here: Either the wrong layout was selected when you ran the script, or the script definition says to switch to that layout. A script may switch to different layouts many times before it finishes. You can check out what switches it makes by examining the steps in the Script Definition dialog box.

A script is paused and you can't select the command you want.

Many FileMaker Pro commands become unavailable when a script is paused. To access a command right away, you can cancel the script by clicking the Cancel button in the status area or switching to another mode.

One or more dialog boxes appears when you run a script.

This is because the script contains one or more steps that normally produce dialog boxes, and the Perform without dialog option for that step (or steps) isn't checked. If you want the script to run without showing dialog boxes, select each script step in the Script Definition dialog box and check the Perform without dialog checkbox if it appears in the Options area there.

A button doesn't work.

Usually, FileMaker Pro will give you a fairly specific message if a button doesn't work. This may occur when you've defined a button to select a particular script or layout and have later deleted the script or layout. It's particularly common when you copy a button from one file to another. It will also happen if the button is defined to execute the script step Do Nothing. If you get an error message or the button just doesn't do anything, select the button in Layout mode and redefine it using the Button... command on the Format menu.

An external file couldn't be found.

If you're performing a script that contains an external subscript, opens a lookup file, or sends an Apple Event, you may see a message that says the file can't be found. This means the file referred to in the script step has been moved, renamed, or deleted. To remedy this problem, click the OK button in the alert message, and FileMaker Pro will display a dialog box where you can manually locate and open the external file. If you can't find the file, click the Cancel button in the dialog box, and the entire script (not just the step that opens the external file) will be stopped.

You play a script containing an Apple Event and nothing happens.

First of all, make sure nothing really *has* happened. If the options you set for the Apple Event don't bring the target application to the foreground, and the result of the event isn't copied into your FileMaker Pro file, it may only *seem* as if nothing is happening. Check your Mac's desktop (or Application menu) to see whether the target program has been opened, and then check the target document opened by that program to see if, in fact, your event has been carried out.

If you're certain that nothing happens when you play the script, make sure you've specified a target application for the event and, if necessary, a target document.

If you've specified a target application and document, check that the application or document you're opening hasn't been moved or renamed. FileMaker Pro won't alert you when you play an Apple Event that refers to a document that can't be located—it will just play the event anyway, and nothing will happen.

13 Working with Files

- Opening and Converting Files
- Recovering Damaged Files
- Saving Files and File Structures
- Sharing Data with Other Programs
- Troubleshooting

Creating a file, designing layouts for it, and entering hundreds or thousands of records is a lot of work. If you're upgrading to FileMaker Pro 3 from a previous version, you'll be glad to know that you can convert your older files without losing any of the work that went into them. You'll also appreciate FileMaker Pro's built-in procedures that check your files for damage and repair them when they need it.

FileMaker Pro also offers several ways for you to reuse file structures with new data, or to reuse data in new files. You can save a copy of a file without its records or data and use its scripts, layouts, and field definitions for a new purpose. If you have data in another program's file, you can probably import it into FileMaker Pro. Likewise, you can export FileMaker Pro data for use in other programs.

In this chapter, we'll look at options for recycling your files and data.

~~~~~~

Opening and Converting Files

Opening FileMaker Pro files

You open a FileMaker Pro version 3 file the way you would any Macintosh file, by double-clicking the file's icon in the Finder. FileMaker Pro will load and then the file will open. To open a file when FileMaker Pro is already running, choose Open… from the File menu. You'll see a directory dialog box like this:

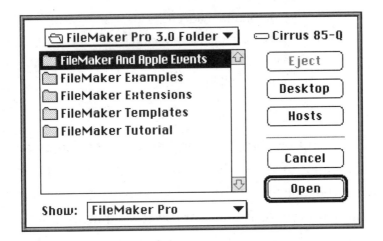

Normally, the list here will only show folders and FileMaker files, not files from other programs. Select the name of the FileMaker Pro file you want to open and press ⌊Return⌋. The file will open.

To view other types of files in this dialog box, choose a file format from the Show pop-up menu at the bottom. The list of choices includes formats that FileMaker Pro can import, such as tab-separated text and ClarisWorks or DBF files, as well as an All Available option that shows every file in the current folder, whether FileMaker Pro can open it or not.

To import data from another program, see *Importing data*, p. 305.

Converting files from earlier versions of FileMaker

The procedure for converting older FileMaker files is the same as opening FileMaker Pro files when the program is running, as described above. When you open a file from an older version of FileMaker, however, you'll see a message that the file will be converted for use with version 3, like this:

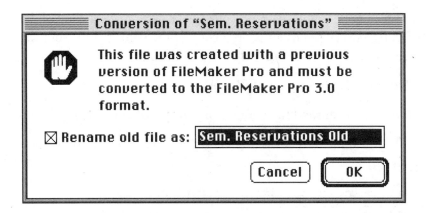

When FileMaker Pro converts a file from an earlier version, it offers to rename the original file so that you'll still have a copy of it in the older FileMaker Pro format. Once a file is converted to the FileMaker Pro 3 format, you'll no longer be able to open the file with the older version of FileMaker, so this process ensures that you'll have copies of the file in both versions.

Recovering Damaged Files

FileMaker Pro reads and writes to your disk frequently during the normal use of a file, so files are susceptible to damage caused by disk read or write errors. A small power surge that occurs when your disk is reading or writing can cause one or more records to be slightly damaged, making them difficult for FileMaker Pro to read.

FileMaker Pro checks a file for damage each time the file is opened, and displays a warning message then, or while you're using the file, if it has trouble reading a record from your disk.

If you try to open a file that's only slightly damaged, FileMaker Pro will perform minor repairs as it opens the file. If FileMaker Pro discovers damage on a file that's already open, it may ask you to close the file and reopen it. If the file has more extensive damage, you'll be asked to recover the file.

Sometimes, the minor repairs FileMaker Pro automatically makes will clear up a problem. But if you find that you're running into the same "minor damage" warning each time you open a file, you should recover the file as follows:

1. Make sure you've got enough space on your hard disk to make a copy of the damaged file. (Recovery builds a restored copy of the damaged file, but the copy is often 30 to 40 percent larger than the original.)

2. Close the file you want to recover, if it's open.

3. Choose Recover... from the File menu. A directory dialog box appears.

4. Select the file you want to recover and click the Open button. You'll see a dialog box like this:

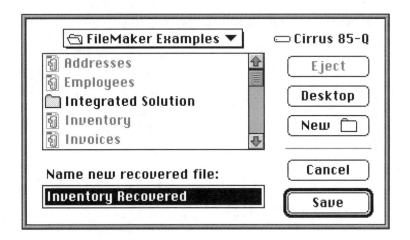

5. As the name of the new file, FileMaker Pro suggests the same name as the old file with "Recovered" after it. Type in a name for the recovered file, if you like, and select a location for it.

6. Click the Save button.

When it recovers a file, FileMaker Pro completely rebuilds it, taking the data, indexes, layouts, scripts, and other information from the old file and putting them in a completely new file. As the file recovery proceeds, messages will keep you informed about the various stages of the process. Once the process is complete, another message will tell you how successful it was and whether any data was lost. Click the OK button to put the message away. Then you can open the recovered file.

**IMPORTANT
NOTE**

File recovery is a complex process, and you should be prepared to leave your Mac alone while it takes place. A file containing 50,000 records and a dozen layouts may take an hour or more to recover.

Saving Files and File Structures

Although there's no Save command in FileMaker Pro, the Save a Copy As... command lets you make different kinds of copies of a file for different purposes. When you choose Save a Copy As... from the File menu, you'll see a directory dialog box like this:

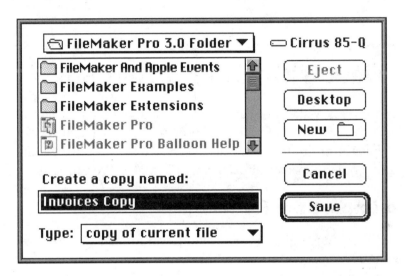

FileMaker Pro automatically enters the file's name with "Copy" after it, but you can type in any name you want.

The pop-up menu at the bottom of the dialog box contains three options for saving copies. The default option is copy of current file, which saves an exact copy of the file, including all the file's records.

The second option on the menu is compressed copy (smaller), which saves all the file's information in a compressed format so it uses less disk space. (It takes a while for FileMaker Pro to create a compressed copy, so be prepared to wait.) Compressed files can be opened just like regular FileMaker Pro files. Use this option to make a backup copy of your file.

The last option is clone (no records), which saves all a file's layouts, scripts, and field definitions, but not its data. After you've saved a clone of a file, you can open the clone, enter or import new data, and make any changes necessary to make the file suit its new purpose.

FileMaker Pro comes with a collection of template files that you can clone and modify. For example, you might save a clone of the file called Names and Addresses that's included in the FileMaker Pro Templates folder, change a few field definitions, and reuse it as a personal address file. With a few minor changes, layouts that have already been created in the Names and Addresses file will also work in your personal address file, saving you the work of creating new layouts from scratch. You'll save lots of work by cloning the FileMaker Pro templates and using them for various purposes.

Sharing Data with Other Programs

When you want to use FileMaker Pro data in another program, you'll have to put your FileMaker Pro data into a format that program can read. Conversely, if you want to use FileMaker Pro to work with data created by another program, you'll have to put the other file's data into a format FileMaker Pro can read.

Export and import file formats

FileMaker Pro can import and export data in ten different formats that are compatible with those used by most other programs:

Tab-Separated Text is a format supported by most other programs. Data in each field is separated by a tab character, and data in each record is separated by a carriage return.

Comma-Separated Text is like tab-separated text, except data in each field is separated by a comma. This format may also be called *comma-separated values*, or *CSV*.

Merge is a comma-separated text format that exports data containing smart quotes ("") differently than the comma-separated text format.

SYLK is a data interchange format supported by Excel. It arranges data in rows and columns, where each column is a field and each row is a record. Unlike the tab-separated or comma-separated text formats, however, SYLK distinguishes between text data and numeric data.

WKS is the data format used by Lotus 1-2-3. It also arranges data in rows and columns.

DIF is a row-and-column format used by older spreadsheet programs such as VisiCalc and AppleWorks.

DBF is the format used by dBASE III and dBASE IV files.

BASIC is like a comma-separated format; it's used by BASIC programs. BASIC format supports only 255 characters per field, so when you export data from a FileMaker Pro file to this format, you can only export the first 255 characters in each field.

Edition File format is used for exporting FileMaker Pro data only, and it formats data as an edition to which other documents can subscribe. *Publish* and *subscribe* are features of Macintosh System 7 and later. FileMaker Pro version 3 doesn't have publishing or subscribing commands on its menus, and you can't subscribe to data from within FileMaker Pro. With this format, however, you can export to an edition file. (For more on publishing and subscribing, consult your Macintosh System 7 user's guide.)

In addition, FileMaker Pro can import data directly from or export data in its own format. When you export in FileMaker Pro format, you export the file's data, but not the layouts or scripts as you do when you save a copy of a file.

Check the manual for the program you're moving data to or from for information on which data formats it can read or write. For example, if you're exporting data to a spreadsheet program that can import SYLK files, you'll want to export data from FileMaker Pro in that format. If you want to import data into FileMaker Pro, make sure to save it in one of the formats FileMaker Pro can read.

Exporting data

To export data from a FileMaker Pro file, you select the records you want to export, choose the data format you want, choose the fields whose data you want to include, and set up the order in which those fields' data is to be exported. File-Maker Pro then creates a file containing the selected data in the chosen format.

When you export data, you create an *output data file* which can then be imported by another program. Here's the exporting procedure:

1. Open the file from which you want to export data (the *source file*).

2. Use Find mode to select the group of records you want to export, or press ⌘J to select all the records in the file.

3. Sort the records in the order you want them to be exported, if necessary.

4. Choose Import/Export from the File menu, and choose Export Records... from the Import/Export submenu. FileMaker Pro displays a dialog box like this:

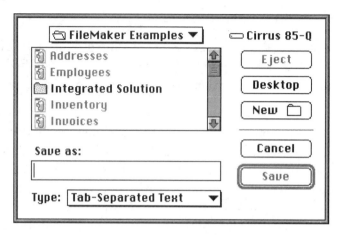

5. Type a name for the output data file (which will contain the exported data) and choose a location for it.

6. Choose the output data file type from the pop-up menu. (This is where you select the data format required by the program that will be importing this data.)

7. Click the Save button. FileMaker Pro displays the Export Field Order dialog box, like this:

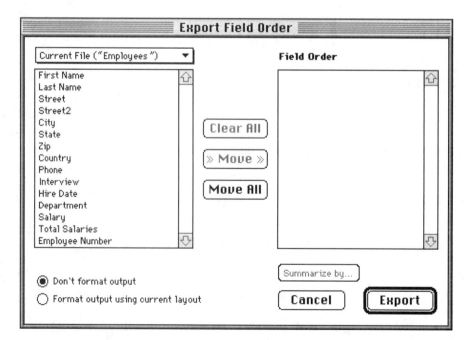

Each field in the source file is shown in the list at the left. To include a field's data in the export order, double-click on the field's name or select the field name and then click the Move button. (Click Move All to add all the fields to the Field Order list; click the Clear All button to clear the Field Order list.)

To export data from a related field, choose a relationship from the pop-up menu at the top of the Export Field Order dialog box, and then select one or more names from the list of fields that appears.

TIP

The Field Order list shows fields in the order in which you added them. You can rearrange the order in which field data is exported by moving the field names on the list. Just point to a field name so the double arrow pointer appears, and then drag the name up or down on the list.

8. Click a button to indicate whether you want the output (exported data) to be formatted. If you leave the Don't format output button selected, data will be exported as ordinary text. Choosing the Format output using current layout option tells FileMaker Pro to format the exported data with the number, date, and time formats used in the current layout. For example, if you were exporting data from a Unit Cost field, the data would be exported as "$1.50" instead of "1.5." (The Format output using current layout option isn't available if you're exporting in the SYLK, DBF, or DIF formats.)

9. If you're exporting data from a summary field and you want the records summarized by the contents of a certain field, click the Summarize by... button and select the field on which to summarize. (See *Exporting summary data*, below, for more information.)

10. Click the OK button to export the data. FileMaker Pro saves the data to the new output data file on your disk.

You can only export data from container fields if your output data file is in FileMaker Pro format.

IMPORTANT NOTE

Exporting summary data

If your source file contains one or more summary fields, you can export summarized data as well. If the summary field is in the body of a layout and it produces a summary for each record (such as a running total of the number of records), you export the summary field as you would any other field, and the summary data is included in each report.

If you're exporting sub-summary data (such as a total of employees or salaries sorted by department), you must tell FileMaker Pro how you want the data summarized before it can produce the proper totals and export them. Here's the procedure:

1. Follow steps 1 through 7 under *Exporting data,* above.

2. In the Field Order dialog box, select the summary field whose data you want exported, then click the Summarize by... button. FileMaker Pro displays a dialog box like this:

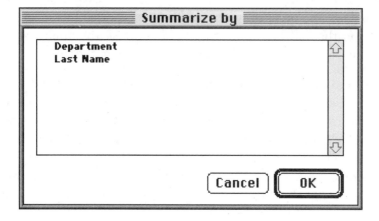

3. The dialog box lists the names of fields on which the file is currently sorted. You can only select one field at a time on which to summarize data, but you can select the same field again in the Field Order dialog box and then select another field on which to summarize if you want to export two different summaries of data. (In the example above, for instance, you could export total salaries sorted by the Department field, and then also export total salaries sorted by the Last Name field.)

4. Select the field on which you want the data summarized, click the OK button, and complete the export procedure as explained earlier.

Exporting repeating field data

Another special case is when you're exporting from a file that contains repeating fields. For example, on an order-entry form that contains repeating fields for the item number, description, quantity, unit price, and extended price, you would have several repeated values in any order for more than one item.

The way FileMaker Pro exports repeating field data depends on which file format you're exporting to. SYLK, WKS, and DBF formats won't support multiple values in a field, so when you export to these, you will only export the first value in a repeating field (you'll see a notice about this when you perform the export). All other formats will support repeating field data, so exporting from them is the same as for any other field.

To export repeating field data to a SYLK, WKS, or DBF file, you must first separate the repeating field data into individual records. Here's how:

1. Make a clone of the source file (a copy with no records in it—see *Saving Files and File Structures*, on p. 299, above).

2. Import the data from the source file into the clone, specifying that imported data from repeating fields in the source file should be split into separate records when they're imported. (For more on this procedure, see *Importing data*, below.)

3. Export the data from the clone to the SYLK, WKS, or DBF format.

Importing data

Using the Import Records... command on the Import/Export submenu, you can import data from other programs (in one of the file formats discussed in *Export and import file formats*, on pp. 300–301, above), or you can import data directly from another FileMaker Pro file. The procedure is basically the same in every case.

When you import data, every record from the source file gets imported, but you can choose which types of data to import and what fields to put it in. Here's the procedure:

1. Open the FileMaker Pro file to which you want to import data (the *destination file*).

2. Make a backup copy of the file, using the Save a Copy As... command, as described in *Saving Files and File Structures*, earlier in this chapter. The backup copy of the file is your insurance in case you accidentally replace data during the import process.

3. Choose Import Records... from the Import/Export submenu. FileMaker Pro displays a directory dialog box like this:

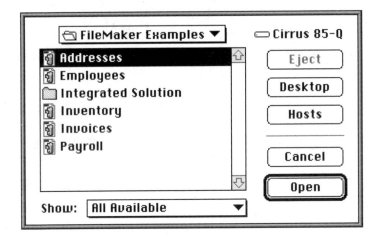

4. Select the name of the file from which you want to import data (the source file) by selecting it in the list.

TIP If the folder or disk from which you're importing contains dozens of files, you can make the list more specific by choosing the format of the source file from the pop-up menu: FileMaker Pro will then display only folders and files of the type you choose.

5. Click the Open button. FileMaker Pro displays the Import Field Mapping dialog box, like the one at the top of the next page:

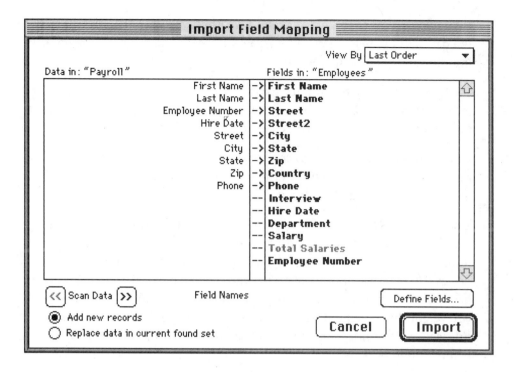

The Data in list shows the field names from the import file you've opened. To see data from this file, click the Scan Data arrows.

The Fields in list shows the fields in the destination file ("Employees") where the data will be placed. (The Total Salaries field name is dimmed because you can't import data into summary fields with the Import command.

The arrows in the column between the two lists indicate which data will be imported into which field. (The Interview, Hire Date, Department, Salary, Total Salaries, and Employee Number fields have dashed lines next to them, because nothing will be imported into them.)

6. Choose the fields whose data you want to import, and indicate which fields in the destination file each field's data goes in.

To change the field into which data will be imported, point to the field name in the right-hand list and drag it up or down until it's lined up opposite the data you want to import into it.

If you don't want to import a certain field's data, click on the arrow between the data and the field name. The arrow will change to a dotted line, indicating the data won't be imported.

If the field into which you want to import data doesn't exist, you can define it by clicking the Define Fields... button and following the steps discussed in Chapter 4.

7. Choose whether to add new records to the file or replace the data in the current found set by clicking one of the buttons at the bottom left corner of the dialog box. The default setting is Add new records.

If you choose Replace data in current found set, FileMaker Pro will replace the data in the records you're currently browsing with the data you're importing. This option is handy when you want to update records with newer data, but be sure to make a backup of your FileMaker Pro file beforehand, because the data being replaced will be lost for good. Also, make sure you've got the same number of records in the file you're importing as in the FileMaker Pro file's found set, and that they're sorted in the same order, before you import.

8. Click the Import button. You'll see the Import Options dialog box, like the one below.

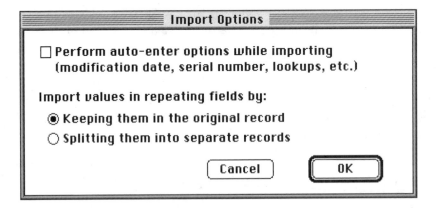

The checkbox option tells FileMaker Pro to perform your current file's auto-entry options on the imported data as it is added to your file. For example, if you import data into an Employee Number field and a new entry in the Employee Number field normally triggers a lookup in your file, you can check the box to have FileMaker Pro perform the lookup as each new entry in the Employee Number field is imported. Normally, FileMaker Pro won't perform auto-entry operations like this during an import, because it slows the import process considerably.

The Import values in repeating fields by options are only active when you're importing repeating field data, usually from another FileMaker Pro file. You can click one of the radio buttons here to have FileMaker Pro create a new record for each occurrence of repeating field data or to keep it all in one record, as it was in the source file.

Use the Splitting them into separate records option if you're exporting FileMaker Pro data from repeating fields into SYLK, WKS, or DBF format. Because these formats don't support multiple values in one field, the only way to export repeating data to them is to create a clone of the file you want to export, then import repeating field data as individual records from the original file, and then export the data from the cloned file.

TIP

9. Choose the options you want, and then press Return or click the OK button. The new records will become the found set in your destination file.

After this process finishes, the source file from which you imported the data will still be on your disk. Don't forget to delete it if you don't need it anymore.

Importing data from a remote database server

If you're using System 7 or later, you can use the built-in Data Access Manager facility and a query document to import data from a remote database server from within FileMaker Pro. To do this, you must have a third-party query document generator installed in your Mac. (If you'll be importing data from a remote database server, your local systems administrator or computer support person can help you install a query document generator.)

Once the query document generator is installed in your Mac, here's how to import data from a remote database:

1. Choose the Import Records... command from the Import/Export submenu. You'll see a directory dialog box like the one under *Importing data*, earlier in this chapter.

2. Select Data Access Manager from the File Type pop-up menu.

3. Select the source file from the list, and click the Open button. You'll see the query generator's log-in box, where you can enter your user name and password. (Remote databases control access by requiring a user name and password before you can open them.)

4. Type your user name and password and then click the OK button to start the Data Access Manager session. Because you're opening a file on a remote database server, this takes a while, and you'll see a message saying the Data Access manager session is starting up.

5. Click the OK button to continue. You'll see the Import Field Mapping dialog box, and you can select fields from which to import data, and then continue with the import as described earlier under *Importing data*.

IMPORTANT NOTE

If you scan remote database records in the Field Order dialog box, be prepared for some delays before data in different records is displayed. Because you're viewing data stored on a remote database server, it will take longer than scanning data from a file located on a disk connected directly to your Mac.

Troubleshooting

Now let's look at a few common problems you may have when working with files.

A message says a file is locked or in use.
This usually happens when you try to open a file that is available over a network and the file is already open on someone else's computer. You'll see a message like this:

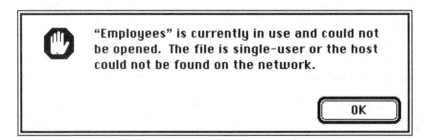

> "Employees" is currently in use and could not be opened. The file is single-user or the host could not be found on the network.
>
> OK

If you want to be able to use the file while other people are also using it, ask the person who first opened the file to choose the Single-User command on the File menu. Then the command name will change to Multi-User and the file will be accessible by several people at once. Otherwise you'll have to wait until the current user closes the file. (See Chapter 14 for more information on sharing files.)

A message says the file is damaged.
If this happens, close the file immediately and use the Recover… command on the File menu to recover it. It's possible you could repair the damage by simply opening the file again and having FileMaker Pro perform minor repairs, but it's best to be safe and recover the file.

Imported records replace data instead of adding to it.
If imported records replace records in your file instead of adding new ones, it's because the Replace data in current found set button was selected when you imported the data. If you made a backup copy of the file before you did the import, as suggested, close the current file and throw it away—its records are now changed for good—and then open the backup copy of the file. Run the import procedure again, but this time make sure the Add new records button is selected in the Import Field Mapping dialog box.

The wrong records appear after you import data.
If you import data into a destination file and then find that the current found set contains records you didn't want, it's because the source file from which you're importing contained the wrong records.

If you used the Replace data in current found set option to replace data in your destination file, your original records have been deleted and your only hope is that you made a backup of the destination file before doing the import. In this case, close the destination file, delete it, open the backup copy and start over, following steps 2 and 3 below.

If you used the option to add new records to the file, you'll have to delete the newly imported records and start over. Here's the procedure:

1. Choose Delete All from the Mode menu in Browse mode, and click the Delete button in the alert box that appears. (The newly imported records make up the current found set in Browse mode, so choosing Delete All will delete the records you just imported.)

2. Reopen the source file, carefully select only the records you want to import, and then export those records to a new file.

3. Open the destination file and use the Import Records… command to import the records from the new source file.

Data ends up in the wrong fields or is missing when you import from another file.
This means you haven't used the Import Field Mapping dialog box to properly match the field data from the source file with the fields in the destination file. Remember, in the Import Field Mapping dialog box, you match data types in the source file with field names in the destination file, and you can scan records in the source file to make sure the data you want is in each field you import. Finally, you can keep data from being imported at all by clicking the check mark between data in the source file and a field name in the output data file.

If you've used the Add new records option when importing the data, just delete the found set and try the import again. If you used the Replace data in current found set option, it's time to open your backup copy of the destination file (which contains your original, unmodified records) and try the import again. Before you do, though, you should use Save a Copy As... to make another backup copy of the file in case you goof a second time.

Finally, review the steps in *Importing data* above before trying the import process again.

There aren't enough fields in the destination file to contain all the data you're importing from the source file.
If the Import Field Mapping dialog box shows that there are more categories of data to be imported than there are fields in the destination file, you can either ignore the extra data or create new fields to contain it. To ignore the extra data, you don't have to do anything—FileMaker Pro automatically ignores it because there's no place to put it.

To create new fields to contain the extra data, click the Define Fields... button in the Import Field Mapping dialog box to create new fields to contain the extra data. (See Chapter 4 for more on defining fields.) Once the new fields are defined, make sure they match the fields from which data will be imported and that arrow icons point from the import fields to the new fields. Then finish the import procedure as you would normally.

14 Using FileMaker Pro on a Network

- How FileMaker Pro Shares Files
- Sharing Files
- Controlling Access to Files
- File Sharing Tips
- Troubleshooting

Because FileMaker Pro is a multi-user program, several people on a network can work on the same file at once. In this chapter, we'll look at ways you can share and control access to FileMaker Pro files on a network.

How FileMaker Pro Shares Files

This section tells you what you need to know about making a file accessible to others on a network and how FileMaker Pro handles the activities of many users working on a single file. Opening and working with shared files is covered in the next section, *Sharing Files*.

What you need to share files

To share FileMaker Pro files with others on a network you must have the following setup:

- Each Mac or PC must have its own copy of FileMaker Pro installed.

- All Macs or PCs sharing the files must be connected to a network. FileMaker Pro version 3 supports AppleTalk, TCP/IP, and MacIPX network protocols.

- You must have a network protocol selected. (See *General preferences*, on p. 39 in Chapter 3.)

Single-user and multi-user files

Once you've opened a file, you can make it accessible to other users by selecting the Single-User command on the File menu. When you select the Single-User command, its name changes to Multi-User, and the file can then be shared by others on the network.

You can make a multi-user file back into a single-user file in the same way: by choosing Multi-User from the File menu so its name changes to Single-User.

IMPORTANT NOTE

Once you've set a file for multi-user or single-user operation, it stays that way until you change it again. But remember, all files are single-user to begin with.

About hosts and guests

Several users can work with a multi-user file at the same time, but FileMaker Pro distinguishes between the *host* (the person who opens a file first) and the *guests* (those who open it afterwards).

If the file is available to users on a network, anyone who can access the file can open it and become its host. Otherwise, only the person on whose Mac the file is stored (the file's owner) can open it first. Once the owner of the file has opened it and has made it a multi-user file, other network users will then be able to open it.

If your shared file is stored on a network server, anyone may be the first to open a file, becoming its host. In that case, make sure everyone on your network who can access the file knows about the host's responsibilities, as covered in this chapter.

TIP

In either case, most work the guests do on the file is routed through the host's Mac. For this reason, the host can't close a file until all the guests have closed it on their machines.

Because the host is the last person to close the file, the saved file contains the sort order, found set, and page setup in effect on the host's Mac when he or she closed the file. The next time the file is opened, it will also show the layout that was displayed on the host's screen when the file was last closed (unless the host used the Preferences... command to make another layout appear each time the file is opened—see *Document preferences*, on p. 40 in Chapter 3, for more information).

The host is the only user who can:

• change a file from single-user to multi-user, or vice versa

• define user groups and set access privileges

• define fields or change field definitions

• reorder layouts

• save copies of the file with the Save a Copy As... command

However, the host can't perform these activities while others are using the file, so he or she must ask others to close the file on their Macs before undertaking any of these operations.

Once the host has opened a multi-user file, other users on the network can open it and:

• add, change, or delete records

• switch layouts or make new layouts

- sort or select records

- check spelling

- perform scripts

- change values in global fields

- print reports

- import or export data

When guests make changes to a file, the changes are automatically saved to the disk where the file is stored.

Although several people can be using a FileMaker Pro file at the same time, some operations can only be done by one person at a time, including:

- opening the ScriptMaker dialog box

- defining or changing passwords

- defining or changing relationships

- defining or changing the contents of a value list

- editing a particular record or layout

For example, two people can browse the same record or view the same script or field definition, but only one of them can make changes in it at a time. Once a user selects a field in a record, that record is locked against changes from other users, and it remains locked until the first user either selects another record or deselects the field in the current record by clicking away from it.

When you switch layouts or find or sort records in a multi-user file, those changes appear only on your Macintosh. Each user can be using a different layout, found set, and sort order without affecting the ones set up on other users' Macs.

Sharing Files

The way you open, close, and manage files varies a little, depending on whether you're a guest or a host.

Opening a file as a host

Opening a file as a host works the same way as opening it any other time, except that you must make the file multi-user, and you should also open any related files it's designed to access:

1. Double-click the file's icon in the Finder, or select and open it using FileMaker Pro's Open... command. (See *Opening and Converting Files*, on p. 296 in Chapter 13.)

2. Choose the Preferences... command from the Edit menu and choose a network protocol option. (See *General preferences*, on p. 39 in Chapter 3.) You can't set a file to multi-user if there's no network protocol set.

3. Check the File menu to see if the Single-User command is showing. If it is, choose this command so its name changes to Multi-User. The file is now available for others on the network to open.

4. Open any related files or files containing external scripts that the file you're opening is designed to use, and make sure they're set for multi-user operation also.

When you are a file's host, most work that guests do on the file is routed through your computer, which can only handle one task at a time. So you should be careful to avoid doing things that will tie up your Mac for long periods. For example, if you open a FileMaker Pro file as a host and then switch to a spreadsheet program and begin recalculating a spreadsheet for several minutes, guest users will have to wait until your computer is done recalculating the spreadsheet before they can open or work with the FileMaker Pro file. Ideally, you shouldn't use other applications while guests are working on a file you're hosting.

**IMPORTANT
NOTE**

If others are using a file that's stored on your hard disk, changes made by other users will be saved to your disk. Your Mac will then have to divide its time between your own work and other users' activity.

TIP

If you plan to have lots of people using a FileMaker Pro file at once, you'll get much better performance if you use the FileMaker Pro Server application. Consult your Apple dealer for more information.

Opening a file as a guest

Once the host has opened a file and has set it for multi-user operation, anyone else can open it as a guest. Here's how:

1. Start FileMaker Pro on your computer.

2. Choose Open... from the File menu. FileMaker Pro displays a dialog box like this:

3. Click the Hosts button at the right side of the dialog box. The cursor will change into a double arrow, indicating that FileMaker Pro is scanning the network for shared files. Once the network has been scanned, you'll see the Hosts dialog box, which looks like this:

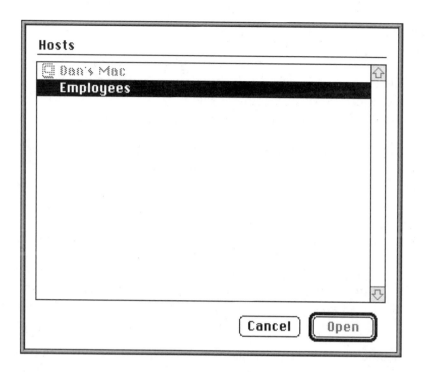

The list shows all the shared files currently open on the network, along with the names of their hosts. (In the example above, the only shared file is "Employees," and the only host is "Dan's Mac.") If your network has more than one zone, a list of zones appears below the list of hosts and files, and you must select a particular zone to see the available hosts and files in it.

4. Double-click on the name of the shared file you want to open. A message tells you FileMaker Pro is opening the shared file as a guest of the file's host, and then the file's window appears on your screen. (If the file has restricted access, you'll be asked to enter a password first. See *Controlling Access to Files* and *Troubleshooting*, later in this chapter.)

The above steps will work under any circumstances. However, if the host file is on a shared network server, you can also open it as a guest by simply navigating to a shared volume in the Open... command's dialog box and double-clicking on the file to open it (instead of clicking the Hosts button as in step 3 above).

TIP

Working with a file as a guest

When you're a sharing a file as a guest, any work you do on it will take longer than if the file were on your own disk, because commands have to travel over the network to be processed. Whenever there's a delay caused by FileMaker Pro sending your command to the host Mac, the pointer changes to a double arrow icon.

Your commands can also be delayed because the host Mac or server is busy processing other users' commands. When this is the holdup, FileMaker Pro displays a coffee cup symbol to indicate that you're on a forced coffee break (although it may only last a few seconds). So when you issue a command over the network, your pointer may change to a double arrow, then to a coffee cup icon, and back to a double arrow before you see the results. Be patient!

The layout, found set, and sort order that were in effect when the host last closed the file are the ones you'll see when you open a file as a guest. So don't be alarmed if the layout you see when you open a file isn't the one you had showing when you, as a guest, last closed it—just switch to the layout you want.

TIP

If you frequently switch to a particular layout, found set, or sort order when opening a file as a guest, create a script with those settings and set FileMaker Pro to perform it when you open the file. See *Document preferences*, on p. 40 in Chapter 3.

Closing a shared file

If you're a file's guest, you close a shared file just as you would close a single-user file: Close the file window or quit FileMaker Pro.

IMPORTANT NOTE

Never close a shared file by simply shutting down your Mac while the file is still open. You may damage the file.

If you're a file's host, you have to wait until all the guests using it have closed the file on their Macs before you can close it on yours. If you try to close a file while others are still using it, you'll see this message:

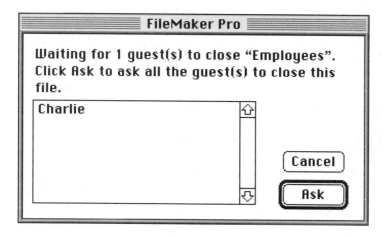

To send guests a message that you'd like to close the file, click the Ask button. The guests who have the file open will see a message requesting that they close the file. It's up to them to close the file, but as soon as they do, it will close on your computer, too.

Sharing files hosted from a PC

FileMaker Pro is cross-platform compatible, which means Mac users can open files created with FileMaker Pro on a PC, and PC users can open files created with FileMaker Pro on a Mac. Since both Macs and PCs can be on the same network, you can open a PC-hosted file from a Mac. When you do this, there are a couple of things to keep in mind:

- Because of the filename restrictions under Windows 3.1 and earlier, FileMaker Pro files hosted on a PC running these versions of Windows will have names no longer than eight characters, and all of the filenames will have the extension .FM. (For example, a file you might name "Employees" on a Mac would be named "EMPLOYEE.FM" on a PC.)

- Some fonts in PC-hosted files may not be the same as the ones you have installed on your Mac, so layouts may look different than they do in the original, Windows-based file.

- Where there are functional differences between the Windows version and the Mac version of FileMaker Pro, the guest user can only perform the functions allowed by his or her own computer.

Controlling Access to Files

Whether or not you share FileMaker Pro files on a network, you may want to control access to them. For example, you probably wouldn't want everyone on a network to see the salary information in a personnel file, although some users would need to be able to see or change it. And you may have some files that you only want to be able to open yourself.

To control access to a FileMaker Pro file, you create passwords and groups and then assign different access privileges to those passwords and groups.

By creating *passwords*, you can control whether others can open a file and what they can do with it. When you create more than one password for a file, you can assign different *access privileges* to different *groups* of users (based on which password a user has), and thereby control what users can see or do once they've opened a file.

Any file can have several passwords and groups, each of which allows a different level of access to a file. For example, you could:

- give yourself a password that allows you to do anything to a file

- give users in an administrative group another password that only lets them see and enter information

- give users in a marketing group a password that allows them to view certain information in certain layouts, but not to change anything.

Creating passwords

The whole point of creating passwords is to limit access to the file. When you create a file, there are no passwords and anyone can access the file. Once you create one or more passwords, a password is required to access the file (unless you define a password with the (no password) option—see the Tip on p. 324).

To begin with, you define a password for yourself that allows you access to the entire file. Here's the procedure:

1. Open the file, if it isn't open already, and set it to Single-User operation so nobody else can open it. You must be the only one using the file when you create or modify passwords.

2. Choose Access Privileges from the File menu, and choose Define Passwords... from the submenu that appears. FileMaker Pro displays the Define Passwords dialog box, like this:

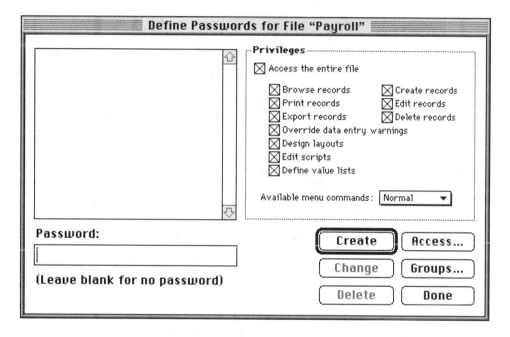

3. Type a password in the Password box.

Be careful not to accidentally enter spaces before or after the password itself when you create a password, since FileMaker Pro will treat spaces as part of the password and users will have to enter them to enter the password name correctly. Also, capitalization must be faithfully observed when users enter a password.

IMPORTANT NOTE

4. Click the Create button. FileMaker Pro will display the password in the list on the left.

Now you can create passwords for other users and restrict their access to certain parts of the file.

1. Follow steps 1 through 3 above.

2. Type in another password name and select privileges assigned to that password by checking the options in the Privileges area at the right.

3. Click the Create button to define the second password.

4. Create other passwords with other sets of privileges, if you like.

5. Click the Done button. FileMaker Pro asks you to enter a password that allows access to the entire file, like this:

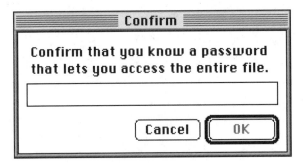

6. Enter the password that allows you full access to the file, and click the OK button.

The next time you open the file, you'll see a notice asking you to type in a password before the file will open.

TIP To allow users access to the file without having to enter a password, leave the Password box blank and click the Create button. You'll see a new password called (no password) in the list of passwords, and you can select it and assign a set of privileges to it.

About user access privileges

Here's a rundown of the access privileges available when you define a password.

Access the entire file is the highest level of access. A password created with this box checked will allow the user to do anything to a file, including creating, changing, and deleting passwords. If you uncheck any of the boxes below this one, this option is unchecked automatically, because the password no longer provides full access.

Browse records is the most basic privilege, so you can't uncheck it. If a person can't browse through records, he or she might as well not be able to open the file.

Print records lets the user print records from the file.

Export records lets the user export data from the file.

Override data entry warnings lets the user ignore FileMaker Pro's entry warnings, which enforce whatever restrictions you set up for fields when you defined them (such as requiring data entered in a certain field to be within a set range of values; see *Validation options*, on p. 67 in Chapter 4). Uncheck this option if you want to force users to enter data in the ways you've defined with field entry options.

Design layouts allows users to add new layouts or change existing ones. Uncheck this option if you have certain layouts you don't want changed.

Edit scripts allows users to create new scripts or modify existing ones. Uncheck this option if you've set up certain scripts or script buttons and you don't want them changed.

Define value lists allows users to create new value lists that are used to enter information into fields. (See *Validation options*, on p. 67 in Chapter 4.)

Create records lets users add new records to the file or edit existing records. Uncheck this option when you want to limit users to working with existing records.

Edit records allows the user to change the data in fields. Uncheck this option when you only want people to be able to view existing information in records.

Delete records lets the user delete any or all of the records in the file.

The Available menu commands menu at the bottom of the Privileges area lets you choose which menu commands are available under each password:

- The Normal option enables all menu commands associated with the access options you've set above.

- The Editing Only option enables only menu commands associated with data entry and editing for the options you've set above. For example, users can't create scripts with this option set.

- The None option disables all menu commands. With this option set, users can only open or recover files, switch among files, perform scripts, or browse records.

Changing and deleting passwords

Whether or not your password gives you access to an entire file, you can always change your own password. If your password does give you access to an entire file, you can change or delete any of the passwords defined for that file.

If you have access to an entire file, here's how to change or delete a password:

1. Open the file using the password that allows complete access.

2. Choose Define Passwords... from the Access Privileges submenu. FileMaker Pro displays the Define Passwords dialog box, as shown earlier.

3. Select the name of the password you want to change.

4. Edit the password and click the Change button to change it, or click the Delete button to delete it.

5. Click the Done button. FileMaker Pro asks you to enter a password that gives you access to the entire file.

6. Enter the password and click the OK button.

If you only have partial access to the file, the Access Privileges command isn't on the File menu. Instead, it's Change Password.... To change your password in this case:

1. Choose Change Password... from the File menu. FileMaker Pro displays a dialog box like this:

```
┌═══════ Change Password ═══════┐
│                               │
│  Old password:                │
│  ┌─────────────────────────┐  │
│  │                         │  │
│  └─────────────────────────┘  │
│                               │
│  New password:                │
│  ┌─────────────────────────┐  │
│  │                         │  │
│  └─────────────────────────┘  │
│                               │
│  Confirm new password:        │
│  ┌─────────────────────────┐  │
│  │                         │  │
│  └─────────────────────────┘  │
│                               │
│        ┌────────┐ ┌────────┐  │
│        │ Cancel │ │   OK   │  │
│        └────────┘ └────────┘  │
└───────────────────────────────┘
```

2. Type your old password and your new password in the spaces provided, and click the OK button. The password is changed.

If others have the same password as you, changing your password changes that password for them too. So, if you change your password from "sesame" to "alibaba," for example, anyone else who used "sesame" must now use "alibaba" instead. Therefore, if you change a password, make sure you tell other users with the same password that you've done so.

Setting group access privileges

When you create a password, you choose what general activities it will allow the user to perform on a file. To control which specific layouts or fields a password allows access to, you need to set up groups.

When you set up access privileges for others, you'll probably find that users' needs fall into certain categories. For example, people involved in marketing need to use certain kinds of information, and people involved in shipping or inventory need to use other kinds of information. You set up groups in FileMaker Pro in order to classify the kinds of information you want to allow or restrict access to.

Once you've identified and named a group, you specify which fields and layouts its members will be allowed to work in, which ones they'll only be allowed to see, and which ones they won't be able to access at all. For example, you might give a marketing group access to a layout of product information but not allow it to change the Price field. Or in a personnel file, you might deny access to the Salary field for everyone but the Personnel Management group—for other groups, the Salary field would be hidden.

Having set up groups, you decide which users' passwords will allow access to which groups' set of privileges. A password can allow access to more than one group's privileges, if you set it up that way. For example, a bookkeeper may need to use the fields and layouts set up for the marketing group *and* those set up for the inventory group; so you'd include his or her password in both group definitions.

Your password, which allows you access to the entire file, automatically makes you a member of every group you create.

Creating a group

To define a group, you must have full access to the file, and you must be the only one using it. Here's how to set up a group:

1. Open the file in which you want to create the group, using the password that gives you full access to the file.

2. Make sure no one else is using the file and that it's set to single-user operation.

3. Choose Define Groups... from the Access Privileges submenu. FileMaker Pro displays the Define Groups dialog box, like this:

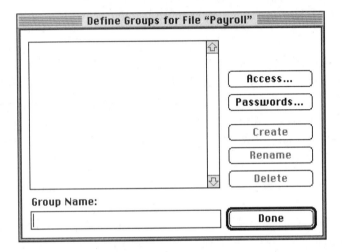

TIP
You can also display the Define Groups dialog box from within the Define Passwords dialog box by clicking the Groups... button; you'll then be asked to enter the master password before this dialog box is displayed.

4. Type a group name and click the Create button. FileMaker Pro adds the group name to the list.

Setting a group's access privileges

Once you've created a group, you set its access privileges. Starting from the Define Groups dialog box:

1. Select the group name in the Define Groups dialog box.

2. Click the Access... button. FileMaker Pro displays the Access Privileges dialog box, like this:

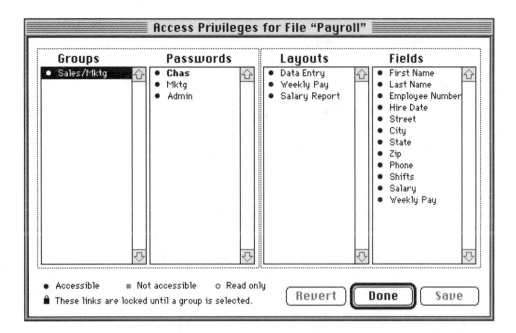

You can also display the Access Privileges dialog box by clicking the Access… button inside the Define Passwords dialog box, or by choosing Overview… from the Access Privileges submenu.

TIP

> The Access Privileges dialog box lists the current groups, passwords, layouts, and fields defined for the file. Notice that the new group, *Sales/Mktg*, is selected in the Groups list. When you select an item in either the Groups or Passwords list, the bullets next to each item in the Layouts and Fields list boxes indicate what degree of access the selected group or password has to those fields and layouts.

A quick way to find out which fields are included on a given layout is to select the layout name from the list in this dialog box. Fields included on that layout will have solid bullets next to them.

TIP

> The key at the bottom of the dialog box explains whether an item is accessible, not accessible, or read only (solid, dimmed, or open). In the dialog box shown above, you could use either the *Chas*, *Mktg*, or *Admin* passwords to gain access to the *Sales/Mktg* group. (The *Chas* password is in boldface because it's the master password, which allows access to the entire file.)

The passwords here are for illustration only. When defining passwords, you should use ones that are much more difficult to guess, such as combinations of letters and numbers.

IMPORTANT NOTE

3. Select a group name from the Groups list, and then click on the bullet next to any password(s) whose access you want to change. A dark bullet means the password grants access to this group, while a dimmed bullet denies access to the group—clicking on a bullet reverses its current setting.

4. Click on the bullets in the two right-hand columns to set the selected group's access privileges for specific layouts or fields in the file. Clicking a bullet moves it to the next of the three levels of accessibility. Starting with a dark, solid bullet, which allows full access to the selected item:

   • Clicking once on a bullet makes it open, or Read only, so users in this group can see the layout or field data but not change it.

   • Clicking twice on a bullet makes it dimmed, or Not accessible, so the selected group can't see the contents of this field or layout.

5. Click the Save button to save the changes. (If you make changes and want to return to the dialog box's original state at the time you opened it, click the Revert button.)

6. Click the Done button to return to the Browse screen.

After you've set up groups, passwords, and access privileges the way you want, remember to inform users of their passwords and to set the Multi-User command so it appears on the File menu.

Changing and deleting groups

You use the Access Privileges dialog box whenever you want to change a group's access, and you use the Define Groups dialog box to delete a group.

To change a group's privileges:

1. Choose Overview... from the Access Privileges submenu (or click the Access... button inside the Define Passwords dialog box) to display the Access Privileges dialog box.

2. Select the name of the group you want to change.

3. Click the password, layout, and field bullets you want to change.

4. Click the Save button, and then click the Done button.

To delete a group:

1. Choose Define Groups… from the Access Privileges submenu (or click the Groups… button inside the Define Passwords dialog box) to display the Define Groups dialog box.

2. Select the name of the group you want to delete.

3. Click the Delete button.

4. Click the Done button.

To change or delete groups, you must open the file with a password that allows full access.

IMPORTANT NOTE

File Sharing Tips

Everyone who shares FileMaker Pro files on a network has the ability to affect other users' productivity. Here are some tips to make life as easy as possible for yourself and other users.

Don't open a file unless you need to use it, and don't leave it open any longer than necessary.
Even if you're not working with a file, simply having it open prevents the host from closing it. So don't open a file and then leave for lunch or for the day without closing it. If you don't need a file, or if the host asks you to close a file, close it.

Don't perform time-consuming operations on a file when you know others need to use it.
Asking FileMaker Pro to perform lengthy operations such as finding or sorting lots of records means that other users won't be able to get their commands processed for long periods of time. Try to be sensitive to other users' needs when you work with a file. Postpone lengthy operations until times when others are less likely to be using the file.

If you're hosting a file from your own computer, be extra sensitive to the impact you're having on guest users' file performance. Anything you do like sorting large collections of records, working with other programs, recovering other FileMaker Pro files, or any other jobs that require lots of processing time on your computer will delay guests' work on the shared file.

Use descriptive layout names.
A layout that makes perfect sense to you may not mean a thing to other users. Since every layout you create is added to the layout pop-up menu, give new layouts descriptive names so others will know what they're for.

Don't clutter up a file.
If you make a layout or a script for a one-time purpose, delete it when you're through with it.

Use scripts to save guest settings.
The layout, find request, and sort order showing when you open a file as a guest are always the ones last used by the host. If you regularly use a particular layout, sort order, find request, or page setup, make a script to store it. Then you can restore those settings quickly whenever you need them by performing the script.

Don't make access any more complicated than it has to be.
You can go wild creating different passwords and groups and assigning different sets of privileges to each group, but the more complex your security setup, the more time you'll probably spend maintaining it. Invariably, there will be situations where people don't have the access they need, and when that happens, you're the one who will have to make the adjustments. The rule of thumb is to use as few access restrictions as you can get away with.

Troubleshooting

A message says the file is locked or in use.
This means someone else has the file open and it's set to single-user operation. Ask the person using the file to select the Single-User command on the File menu.

A message asks you to enter a password.

This box means the file's access is restricted. Ask the file's owner to give you a password that allows you the access you need to the file.

A message says the password is incorrect.
You've made a typing error or used an incorrect password. Remember, spaces and punctuation count. Try again or click the Cancel button and ask the file's host to give you a working password.

A message says a related file can't be found.
If you're a guest user, you can only open a related file if you have the appropriate access privileges and it's on a shared network volume. If the related file is on the host's computer, ask the host to open it. If you don't have the right access privileges to open a file on a network volume, ask the file's host for a password. (You may also get this message if the lookup file has been moved or renamed; ask the file's host about this possibility.)

You want to perform a task, but a message says someone else is using the file.
This means you're the file's host, and all other users must close the file before you can perform the operation you're attempting. Click the Ask button in the warning box to send a message requesting that other users close the file. When they've all closed the file on their Macs, you'll be able to continue with your work.

A field or layout is covered up.
If your password doesn't give you access to a particular layout, you'll see a screen like this one:

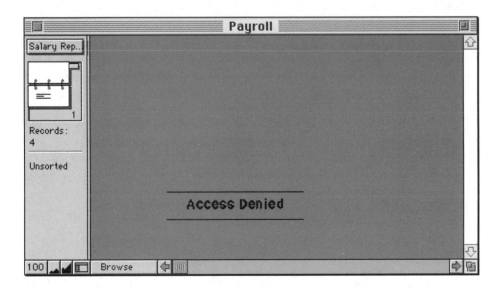

If you don't have access to certain fields, those fields will be masked, like this:

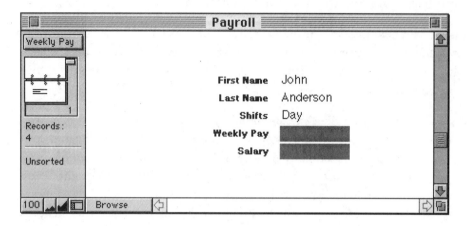

Ask the file's host for a different password if you need access to a field or layout that's currently offlimits.

A file is open on the host's machine, but it doesn't appear in your Hosts dialog box when you try to open it.

If the host computer's name doesn't appear in the Hosts dialog box and your network has more than one zone, be sure you've selected the right zone. If you know you've selected the right zone and the host computer's name still doesn't appear, you've probably got a bad connection in your network cabling. Check the cabling where it attaches to your computer, the host's computer, and any connections in between, to make sure they're all snug.

15 Using Functions

Chapter 4 covered the basics of defining calculation fields, but there are a lot of subtleties to using them. In this chapter, we'll go into more detail about how formulas work, what each FileMaker Pro function and operator does and how you might use it, and how calculations can make your files easier to use.

~~~~~~

The What and Why of Calculation Fields

As mentioned in Chapter 4, FileMaker Pro is capable of calculating information in two distinct ways.

- Summary fields calculate information in a group of records, taking the value from a specific field in each of several records and manipulating it. (For more information on summary fields, see Chapter 16.)

- Calculation fields, on the other hand, calculate information within individual records. All the data calculated in them comes from fields in the same record. (For the exception to this rule, see *The Summary function*, at the end of this chapter.)

The basic procedure for creating a calculation field is covered in *Defining calculation fields*, in Chapter 4. Here, we'll look at how calculation fields do their work.

Basically, calculation fields are used to make FileMaker Pro perform automatic calculations within individual records. Whenever you place a calculation field in the body of a layout, it performs its calculation automatically and displays the result. Calculation fields don't work when you place them in header, footer, or summary parts of layouts, because their formulas apply to specific fields in individual records and there are no individual records in headers, footers, or summary parts.

Calculation fields generate their own contents, so you can't type data into them. However, you can select the result in a calculation field and copy it to the Clipboard.

Changing calculation fields

After you've defined a calculation field, you can change its definition (or formula) at any time. As discussed in Chapter 4, you change a field's definition by selecting its name in the Define Fields dialog box, clicking the Options... button, and then resetting its options or changing its formula. This has specific implications with calculation fields. If you change the name of a calculation field, the name will automatically be changed in any other formulas where it is used. For example, if you change the field name TotalCost to Value, then a formula that used to read, "TotalCost * 1.075" will now read "Value *1.075."

When we refer to calculation formulas anywhere in this chapter, the formulas themselves are placed inside curly quotation marks (" "), as shown above. To type a formula, type what's *inside* the curly quotation marks, not the quotation marks themselves. On the other hand, straight quotation marks ("") are calculation operators that are used to identify text inside formulas, so when you see these inside a formula, be sure to type them.

IMPORTANT NOTE

Building calculation formulas

The result displayed by a calculation field depends on the formula you tell it to calculate. A formula can contain 32,767 characters, and includes the *values* (or data you want calculated) and the *functions* or *operators* that specify which calculations you want performed. Let's look more closely at how you use these building blocks when you define a formula.

Suppose we've just named a calculation field called Total and clicked the Create button. The Specify Calculation dialog box will look something like this:

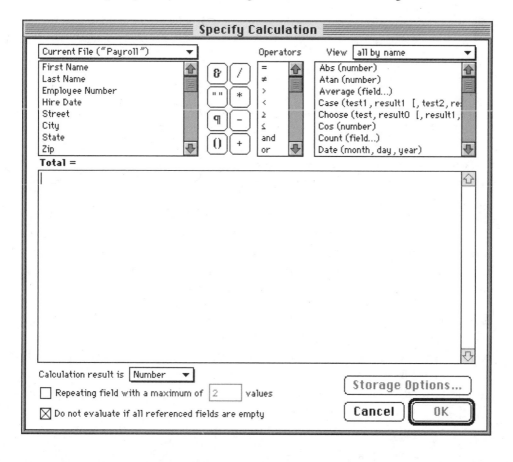

To build a formula, you double-click on field names, click on operators or numbers, or double-click on function names in the lists and button groups at the top of this box. As you select these items, they appear in the formula box, like this:

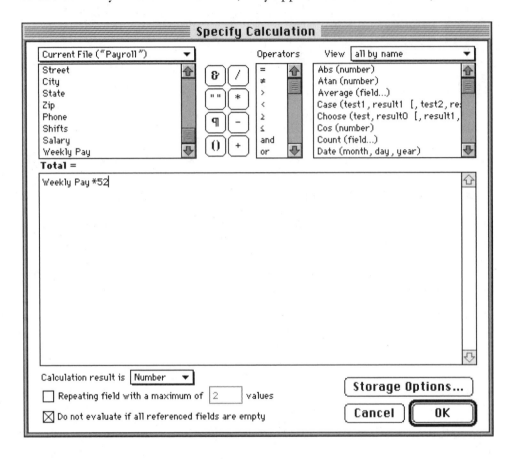

In this case, we're multiplying the contents of the Weekly Pay field by 52. Once the formula is complete, check the Calculation result is pop-up menu to make sure the result of the calculation has the correct data type. The default choice here is Number, because most calculations produce numbers, but you can also choose Text, Date, Time, or Container result types.

It's important to check the result type and make sure it's what you want before clicking the OK button to exit the dialog box. If you set the wrong result type you may get a warning message, but you won't always. For example, you could set a numeric formula's result type to Text and you wouldn't be warned. If you do this, however, you won't be able to use that formula's result in summary fields or other calculation formulas, because it's text. (For more on result-type problems, see *Troubleshooting*, at the end of this chapter.)

Defining a repeating field

The Repeating field with a maximum of *<number>* values checkbox at the bottom of the dialog box tells FileMaker Pro to make your calculation field repeat more than once inside the same record. To make a repeating field, you check the box and specify the number of values you want the field to contain. In a file where each record is an order-entry form, for example, you might want to have the Item No., Quantity, Item Description, Price, and Amount fields be repeating fields, so customers can order more than one item on a record.

You might not be sure how many repetitions you want for a field, so it's best to make a liberal guess. You don't have to display all a field's defined repetitions when you use the field in a layout, so having some extra repetitions defined won't hurt. If you guess wrong, you can always redefine the field or the number of displayed repetitions later. (See *Changing Field and Object Formats*, on p. 138 in Chapter 6, for more on displaying repeating fields in layouts.)

TIP

The Do not evaluate if all referenced fields are empty option is usually checked. This tells FileMaker Pro not to calculate a formula when all the fields referenced in the formula are empty. This saves a little processing time.

The Storage Options... button lets you set indexing options for a calculation formula. See *Calculation field options*, on p. 59 in Chapter 4, for more information.

NEW FEATURE

These are the basics of defining a formula and setting options in the dialog box, but there's a lot to building the formulas themselves. Now, let's look at the elements of a formula more closely.

Values

Values can be field references (the names of fields), constants, or expressions. In many formulas, all the values could be field references, like this: "Total Cost=Item Count*Unit Cost."

In this case, the calculation field's name is Total Cost. The Item Count and Unit Cost field references are the values, and the asterisk is the operator indicating multiplication. Because the formula uses field references, FileMaker Pro will multiply the data that appears in these fields.

You can now include related fields in a calculation formula. For example, you might calculate the Hours Worked field from a Time Card file by the Pay Rate field from a related Payroll file. To include a related field in a calculation

NEW FEATURE

formula, you must first establish a relationship to the related file. Then, choose the relationship from the pop-up menu at the upper left corner of the Specify Calculation dialog box, and choose the field name from the list below.

FileMaker Pro displays every field in the file in the Fields list, whether or not it would make sense to use it in any given formula. In the Specify Calculation dialog box shown earlier, for example, you could select the First Name field and use it in a numeric calculation formula. FileMaker Pro would allow this, but it wouldn't be able to calculate a proper result because the First Name field contains text.

IMPORTANT NOTE

FileMaker Pro evaluates text as zero when it's used in a numeric formula, so if you specify the name of a field that contains text, FileMaker Pro will treat the text as the number 0.

Along with field references, formulas can contain *constants*, which are specific numbers, dates, times, or strings of text you enter from the keyboard. For example, the value 52 in the formula shown on p. 338 is a constant.

You can enter numeric constants by clicking the number buttons in the calculation options dialog box or by simply typing numbers from the keyboard. If you want to enter text, you must type it from the keyboard.

IMPORTANT NOTE

The &, " ", and ( ) buttons represent operators, not text—see *Operators*, below.

Finally, a complex formula might include *expressions*, which are sub-calculations (or formulas inside a formula) containing their own values, functions, or operators. When FileMaker Pro evaluates a formula containing an expression, it calculates the expression first and then uses the result of the expression as a value in the formula that contains it. For example, if you wanted to calculate an order total by multiplying the subtotal by a tax rate, then adding the tax to the subtotal for a grand total, the formula might look like this:

"Total=Subtotal+(Subtotal*Tax Rate)"

Here, the portion in parentheses is an expression, which is calculated first and then added to the Subtotal amount.

Operators

Operators are the instructions that specify the types of calculations to be performed on the values in a formula. The Specify Calculation dialog box contains a series of mathematical, text, and logical operators you use to build formulas.

The eight buttons to the right of the field list let you specify operations to be performed. When you click one of these buttons, the operator symbol from the button is added to the formula in the formula box below. You can also type these operator symbols directly from the keyboard to add them to a formula. Here's what the operators do:

& joins, or *concatenates* one string of text with another. If you had separate First Name and Last Name fields, for example, you could join the information in them together into one Full Name field with the formula *"First Name &" "&
Last Name."* (There's a space between quotes in this formula so that a space will be inserted between the first name and the last name in the formula's result.)

" " encloses text that you want the computer to read as text, not as a field name or as instructions in the formula. In the example above, it's used to insert a space between the first and last names. (Without the quote marks, FileMaker Pro would assume the space was an extra one in the formula and would ignore it.)

¶ inserts a carriage return between two other pieces of data in a calculation field. For example, the formula "First Name ¶ Phone" would create entries in the calculated field that look like this:

> John
> 555-4321

¶ does not export as a carriage return when you export records. It only creates a carriage return inside calculation field formulas.

**IMPORTANT
NOTE**

( ) inserts a single opening or closing parenthesis to indicate the order in which operations should be performed. FileMaker Pro knows whether to insert an opening or closing parenthesis at any given time. For example, you could enter "Quantity*(Cost+Markup)" to calculate a final price. Without the parentheses, FileMaker Pro would multiply Quantity by Cost first, and the result would be wrong.

When you're in doubt about the order in which FileMaker Pro will perform operations in a formula, type in parentheses from the keyboard to force it to perform them the way you want.

TIP

/, *, -, and + are standard arithmetic operators for division, multiplication, subtraction, and addition, respectively.

The Operators list contains other operators for performing different calculations. Most of these are logical (or *Boolean*) operators used in formulas that tell

FileMaker Pro to display one of two possible results, depending on whether the logical condition proves true or false. Conditional formulas like this are made using logical functions. (For more information on conditional formulas, see *Logical Functions*, on p. 362 later in this chapter.)

At the top of the Operators list are the familiar equation symbols:

=	equals
≠ or <>	does not equal
>	greater than
<	less than
≥	greater than or equal to
≤	less than or equal to

Scrolling down the list reveals more operators:

and means the formula is true only if elements on both sides are true. For example, a field to calculate sales tax on California orders might read:

"If(State=CA and Tax Status≠"Exempt",SubTotal*.07,0)"

or means the formula is true if one element or the other is true.

xor means the formula is true if either element, but not both of them, is true.

not changes the value inside parentheses from false to true, or vice versa. "Not (true)" equals false, for example.

^ raises a value to an exponential power. "2^3" is the same as 2^3, or 8, for example.

We'll see many examples of these operators in use throughout the rest of this chapter.

Functions

The Functions list in the Calculation Options dialog box offers some 90 different functions for manipulating data in calculation fields. Most of the calculation field functions are for calculating single values, since most fields only contain single values.

However, since you can also define repeating fields so one field can contain several different values, FileMaker Pro includes a set of functions for calculating multiple values in a repeating field. These are covered in the section *Aggregate Functions*, which begins on p. 345.

In addition, three new functions in FileMaker Pro 3 let you extract information from repeating fields. See *Repeating Field Functions*, on p. 375.

NEW FEATURE

Finally, a special GetSummary function calculates values from summary fields; it's described on p. 360.

When you use most FileMaker Pro functions, you select the function name from the list and then select the field references or enter the values you want the function to calculate. The values you want a function to work on are always contained inside parentheses. The parenthetical part of a function formula is called the *argument*. Only a few functions can be used in formulas by themselves without an argument (for an example, see the Today function under *Date functions*).

The function list normally shows all the functions available in alphabetical order by name, but you can change the list. By choosing a function category from the View menu at the upper right corner of the Specify Calculation dialog box, you can limit the list to a specific category of functions (date, time, or financial functions, for example), or view the whole function list by category, rather than by name.

NEW FEATURE

Whenever you select a function that requires an argument, FileMaker Pro automatically adds the parentheses after it and indicates the type of data needed for the argument, like this:

Total =

Sum (field...)

The text inside the parentheses is just there to remind you what sort of value is required in the argument. Since this text is already selected, all you have to do to complete the formula is select the value or values you want the function to calculate (in this case a field name from the list). The value you select or type will automatically replace the reminder text inside the parentheses.

You can also enter function names by typing them, but when you do you'll have to add your own parentheses. When you enter the function name from the keyboard, you can use uppercase or lowercase letters—FileMaker Pro isn't particular about the capitalization of function names—and you don't need to insert spaces between function names and arguments.

Each function's argument has its own required format for specifying what you want calculated. Some arguments have just one parameter, such as Field..., while others require two or three parameters separated by commas in a particular order, as in "Date(Month,Day,Year)." This last argument has three parameters: Month, Day, and Year. You must enter the parameters in the order shown above or the function won't calculate a proper date. If you leave out a value, FileMaker Pro will display an error message and won't let you finish defining the field.

If you get an error message when defining a formula, check the function description in this chapter or in the FileMaker Pro manual to make sure you've entered the correct number of parameters in the proper format required by that function. If, while building formulas, you're stumped about the nature of the problem when you see an error message, check the *Troubleshooting* section at the end of this chapter.

Exploring FileMaker Pro's Functions

In the next sections, we'll look at all the FileMaker Pro functions. The functions are arranged in categories by the type of calculation they perform. Each function name is shown in the format required, so you can see at a glance what types of parameters are expected when you use the function.

Included are examples that show how each function might be used, along with some background information that will help you understand how these functions are calculated and how to use them most effectively. In some cases, we'll also look at alternate functions or formulas that accomplish the same result by a different method.

Aggregate Functions

Aggregate functions allow you to calculate multiple values, either in a series of regular fields or in a repeating field. Mostly, you'll use these functions in repeating fields. As discussed in Chapter 4, a repeating field is one that can contain more than one value in a single record. Although there's only one field name, the repeating field has spaces for several values. In the order form layout below, for example, the Product Name, Qty, Price, and Total fields are all repeating fields that have been formatted to display four repetitions vertically down the screen.

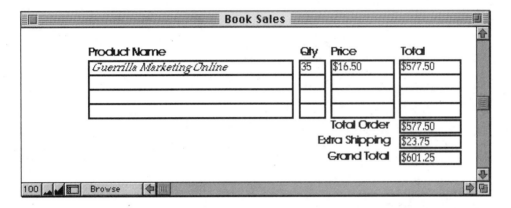

When you use FileMaker Pro's other functions on repeating fields, the functions calculate each of the values, one at a time. For example, the Total field above could be calculated with the formula, "Total=Price*Qty." If the above invoice were full, this calculation would be made four times, once for each value in the Price and Qty fields. A calculation field containing an aggregate function can also be displayed as a repeating field.

Because repeating fields can contain more than one value, however, FileMaker Pro has a special set of functions you can use to make calculations that apply to all the values in such a field at the same time. Let's look at those now.

Average(field name)

The Average function calculates the average of values in the field or fields whose names are referenced in the argument. In a grade reporting file, for example, there might be a different record for each test given, with all the grades for each test in a repeating field in one record. If you wanted to know the average score on a test, you'd use the Average function on the repeating field, like this:

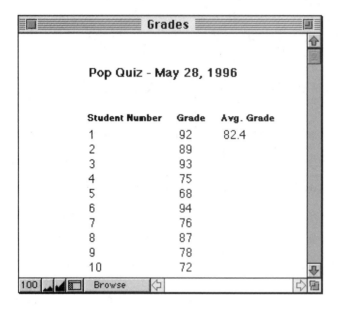

The Student Number and Grade fields here are repeating fields with ten repetitions showing, and the Avg. Grade field contains the formula "Average(Grade)."

TIP

The repeating field on which the average is calculated doesn't have to be on the same layout (or even in the same file) as the calculation field containing the function. The Avg. Grade field here could be on a layout that didn't contain the Grade field, or the Grade field could be in a related file.

Count(field name)

The Count function simply counts the number of entries in a repeating field or in a series of fields. Fields whose entries are being counted don't have to appear on the same layout where you use the Count function in a calculation field. The Count function ignores blank fields and invalid entries such as text entered into a number type field.

For example, you could use the Count function to determine how many students took the test in a grade report form, like this:

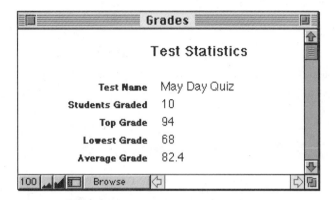

In this layout, the Students Graded field contains the formula "Count(Grade)." It counts the number of scores in the Grade field, which is a repeating field used in another layout (see the Average function in the previous section for this layout). The Count function formula here reports that there are ten valid entries in the Grade field, which means ten students were graded.

Max(field name)

The Maximum (Max) function determines the highest value among those in a repeating field or in a series of separate fields. In a grade-reporting file, you could use this to determine the highest score from a repeating field containing grades, like this one:

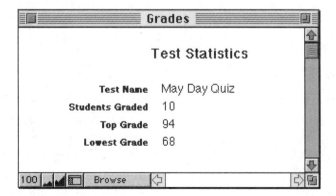

Here, the Top Grade field contains the formula, "Max(Grade)" and the Grade field is a repeating field in another layout that contains scores for the May Day Quiz. (See the Average function at the beginning of this section.)

Min(field name)

The Minimum (Min) function returns the lowest value among those in a repeating field. In the Maximum example above, the Lowest Grade field contains the formula "Min(Grade)."

StDev(field name), StDevP(field name)

The standard deviation is the average amount by which a group of values diverges from the arithmetic mean, or straight average, of those values. The StDev and StDevP functions calculate the standard deviation among values in a repeating field. You can use these functions to determine whether values in a repeating field or in a series of fields are within the typical range.

In a grade reporting file, for example, you could use the StDev function to find the standard deviation of test scores, like this:

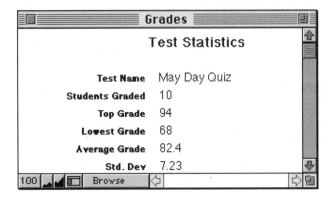

Here, the Std. Dev field contains the formula "StDev(Grade)," and the Grade field is a repeating field containing all the student scores for a test. Since this layout also contains the average score from the Grade field, we can add or subtract the standard deviation value from the Average Grade field's value to arrive at a range into which most of the grades fall. In this case, for example, the range containing most of the class grades is from 75.2 through 89.6 (82.4 plus or minus 7.23). Scores higher or lower than this are the unusual ones.

Consult a statistics textbook for more information about how to use the StDev and StDevP functions.

Sum(field name)

The Sum function adds up all the values in a repeating field. This comes in handy when you want to total up an order on an invoice, as in the order form layout shown on p. 345. There, the Total Order field contains the formula "Sum(Total)," so it sums all the values in the repeating Total field above it.

~~~~~~

Date Functions

Date functions let you do math with dates. To calculate dates, FileMaker Pro stores them as regular numbers. Each date is the number of days since January 1, 0001. For example, May 15, 1996 is day number 728,794. When you specify a date type field, FileMaker Pro automatically converts these numbers into standard MM/DD/YY format, but the real numbers are still used in calculations.

Since FileMaker Pro keeps track of dates as numbers, it's best to subtract earlier dates from later dates to make sure the result is always a positive number. (If you don't want to do this, you can always convert a negative number to a positive one with the Abs function. See *Numeric functions*, later in this chapter.)

In an invoicing system, for example, you might want to subtract the date an invoice was mailed from the current date to see how long it has been since the customer was billed, like this:

Today's Date:	9/4/96
Invoice Date:	7/2/96
Invoice Age:	64

Here, Invoice Date is a standard date field where the date has been entered by hand. The Today's Date and Invoice Age fields are calculation fields that use date math or functions.

- The Today's Date field is a calculation field that contains the formula "Today" and whose result type is set to Date. (The Today function displays the current date from the Mac's clock/calendar whenever the record is displayed—see *Today* on p. 354.)

- The Invoice Age field is a calculation field containing the formula "Today's Date-Invoice Date" and whose result type is set to Number. FileMaker Pro calculates the formula and returns the number of days.

Because FileMaker Pro stores dates as numbers, you can combine numbers and date field references in math calculations. For example, look at the following layout:

Today's Date :	9/4/96
Order Date :	7/2/96
Invoice Date :	07/16/96
Invoice Age :	50

Suppose you wanted the Invoice Date field to always show a date two weeks after the order date. To do this, you could make the Invoice Date field a calculation field with the formula: "Invoice Date=Order Date+14." If you set this field to a Date result, it will always show a date 14 days later than the one in the Invoice Date field.

Now, let's look at FileMaker Pro's time and date functions.

Date(month,day,year)

The Date function calculates a date that corresponds to the month, day, and year numbers entered inside the parentheses. For example, the formula "Date(10,5,1996)" would equal October 5, 1996.

IMPORTANT NOTE

The year in the Date function's argument must be entered as a four-digit number: if you enter only *96* after the second comma, for example, FileMaker Pro will think you mean the year 0096.

When you use the Date function, FileMaker Pro will automatically adjust a date and display it correctly, even if you specify a number of months greater than 12 or a number of days larger than the number in the given month. For example, the formula "Date(2,30,1996)" would equal March 1, 1996—FileMaker Pro knows there were 29 days in February 1996, and adjusts the date accordingly.

Although the examples above show the month, day, and year entered as ordinary numbers, it's probably more likely that you'll use this function when you're adding a specific number of days, months, or years to a date from another field. If so, the month, day, and year values can be derived from field references or from more complex expressions. For example, suppose you want an Invoice Date field to automatically show a date that's the first of the month following an item's ship date. In this case, the calculation formula for the Invoice Date field would use the Date function, and the argument would use values from the Ship Date field. The formula would read, "Invoice Date=Date(Month(Ship Date+1), 1,Year(Ship Date))."

The month value in the argument is actually the expression "(Month(Ship Date+1)." This tells FileMaker Pro to look at the Ship Date field, determine the month number, and add 1 to it (so the month following the month of the ship date is used). The 1 after the first comma returns day number 1, because we want the Invoice Date field to show the first of the month. The year portion of the formula tells FileMaker Pro to use the same year as the one in the Ship Date field.

When the ship date is in the month of December, this formula would have to be changed to: "Invoice Date=Date(Month(Ship Date+1),1,Year(Ship Date+1))."

IMPORTANT NOTE

DateToText(date)

This function converts a date to its text equivalent, so you can use the date-formatted text in formulas that use text functions or have Text result types. For example, you could use a text function in a calculated field to produce text in a form letter, and that text might contain a date from another field, like this one:

A Reminder...
This bill will become PAST DUE as of 05/13/96.
Your prompt payment is appreciated.

Here, the text below "A Reminder..." is produced by a calculation field containing this formula: ""This bill will become PAST DUE as of " &DateToText (Invoice Date+30)&". Your prompt payment is appreciated.""

The formula first evaluates the expression, (Invoice Date+30) so the past due date is calculated as 30 days after the invoice date. Then, the DateToText function turns this date into text. Without the DateToText function in the formula above, FileMaker Pro would use the date's numeric value and the text would read,

A Reminder...
This bill will become PAST DUE as of 728792.
Your prompt payment is appreciated.

The & operator concatenates (or joins) the result of the DateToText function with the rest of the text in the sentence. See *Text Functions*, on p. 382, for more on text formulas.

Day(date), Month(date), Year(date)

These three functions extract the number of the day, month, or year from the date supplied in the argument. For example, if an invoice's Ship Date field contains 5/15/96, the formula "Day(Ship Date)" will equal 15, the formula "Month(Ship Date)" will equal 5, and the formula "Year(Ship Date)" will equal 1996.

Remember, though, that when FileMaker Pro calculates the day number from information in a date field, it's really using the serial date number (for example, 728794 for 5/15/96) to determine the day. If you try to enter the formula "Day(5/15/1996)" you'll get an error message, because FileMaker Pro doesn't recognize 5/15/1996 as a date.

To make the right calculation by entering a specific date (rather than referring to a date field), you'd have to enter either the serial date number — "Day(728794)" — or use the TextToDate function described later in this chapter to turn the text date into a numeric value, like this: "Day(TextToDate("5/15/1996"))" (see *TextToDate*, on p. 392).

Use one of these functions when you want FileMaker Pro to recognize a certain day in each month or month in each year and then do something with that information. In a daily calendar file, for example, you might want FileMaker Pro to remind you to pay your mortgage on the 21st of each month, like this:

Today's Date 12/21/96
Reminder **Pay The Mortgage!**

The Reminder field here is a calculation field whose formula tells it to display this message only on the 21st day of each month. In this case, the formula is "If(Day(Today)=21, "Pay The Mortgage!"," ")." This formula uses the Today function to read the current date from the Mac's internal clock/calendar, and uses the If function to decide whether to display the warning text, depending on what day of the month it is.

(See *Today* and *Logical Functions* for more information.)

DayName(date), MonthName(date)

The DayName and MonthName functions return the name of the weekday or month upon which the given date falls. For example, if a record's Ship Date field contained 5/15/96, the formula "DayName(Ship Date)" would equal Wednesday.

Use one of these functions when you want FileMaker Pro to produce the name of a day or month so you can display it in a field or use it as part of a longer text formula. In the form-letter layout below, the word *Friday* in the fourth line is from a calculated field using the DayName function.

Just a friendly reminder that your account is past due by the following amount:

$1,939.50

It has been past due for over 60 days.

If we haven't received your payment by this coming Friday, we will be forced to refer your account to a collection agency. We appreciate your business and would like to continue serving you.

The formula is "DayName(Invoice Date+65)" and the field is set for a Text result. Thus, FileMaker Pro calculates the day of the week that falls 65 days after the invoice date and displays the day name as text. This entire formula is used in a larger text formula that produces all the text below the amount due.

An alternative to creating a long text formula that includes the date formula above is to simply create a calculation field with the formula "Invoice Date+65" specify a Date result, and then set the date format of the field to one that contains the day of the year. (See *Changing Field and Object Formats*, on p. 138 in Chapter 6.) In this case the date information would be in a separate field, but you could insert it as a merge field to make it align with the rest of the text so it would format consistently in a letter. (See *Creating Form Letters*, on p. 217 in Chapter 9, for more on this.)

TIP

DayOfWeek(date), DayOfYear(date), WeekOfYear(date), WeekOfYearFiscal(date,starting day)

These functions return the day of the year (from 1 through 365) or week of the year (from 1 through 52) represented by the date supplied.

For example, if the field's formula is "DayOfYear(Invoice Date)" and the Invoice Date field contains August 15, 1996, the number 228 will appear in this field.

In an appointment book database, for example, the layout might look like this:

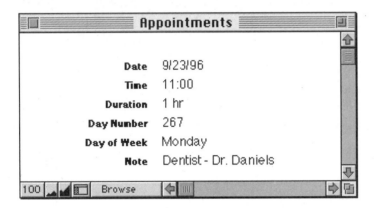

The Day Number field here is a calculation field that contains the formula, "DayOfYear(Date)." (Incidentally, the Day of Week field is a calculation field containing the formula, "DayName(Date)".)

NEW FEATURE

The DayOfWeek, DayOfYear, and WeekOfYear functions assume that the year starts on January 1, but the WeekOfYearFiscal function lets you specify when a year starts. For example, a payroll report might specify the week number of a pay period, but if you use a fiscal year that starts in October, the week number would be wrong unless you used the WeekOfYearFiscal function. In this case, you'd use the WeekOfYearFiscal function, to tell FileMaker Pro when to start the year, as in, "WeekOfYearFiscal(Pay Date,10/01/96)." This tells FileMaker Pro that your fiscal year begins on October 1, 1996.

Today

Today is the only date function that doesn't require an argument. Rather than calculating data you supply, it returns the current date as supplied by your Mac's internal clock/calendar. This is useful when you want to calculate or compare the current date with other dates or values.

You can use a field's entry options to automatically enter a record's creation or modification date, but you have to create or modify the record to update the date information in that field. The Today function *always* reads the current day whenever the field is calculated, so you can be sure today's date is always used in calculations.

In an invoicing database, for example, you might want to create a form-letter layout that reminds customers about their bills. You could create a calculation field called Aging that uses the Today function to determine the correct number of days between the current day and the day the customer was invoiced. If the date of invoicing is in a field called Invoice Date, the formula in the Aging field that determines the number of days since then would be "Today-Invoice Date." Although this is a date calculation, you want the result displayed as a number, so you can see the number of days, like this:

Just a friendly reminder that your account is past due by the following amount:

$1,939.50

It has been 251 days since you were originally invoiced.

If we haven't received your payment by this coming Wednesday we will be forced to refer your account to a collection agency. We appreciate your business and would like to continue serving you.

Thank you.

Here, the number of days in the second sentence is supplied by the Aging field. The rest of the sentence is layout text.

Since the Today function calculates the current day each time you open a file, it can take a long time to calculate it and insert it in every record in large databases.

IMPORTANT NOTE

For a smoother look that eliminates the extra spaces around the number of days, insert the Aging field as a merge field and include the rest of the text of the sentence around it when you add the merge field. See *Creating Form Letters*, on p. 217 in Chapter 9.

TIP

~~~~~~

Financial Functions

Financial functions have to do with calculating interest rates and how they affect the value or cost of money over time. Most people turn to spreadsheet programs for analyzing loan costs or investment earnings, but FileMaker Pro's four financial functions let you make basic financial calculations in a database.

The advantage to using FileMaker Pro for financial calculations is that you can easily make a new record for each of several different investment or loan-cost scenarios you want to calculate. For example, here's a simple loan-cost layout:

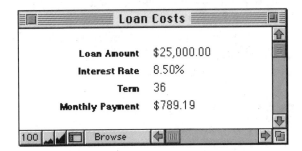

This record shows the monthly payment on a loan of $25,000 at 8.5 percent for three years. If these fields were cells in a spreadsheet, you'd have to delete the amounts in one or more cells and replace them to see the costs for a different loan. For example, to change the rate to 7 percent, you'd have to delete the existing value in the Interest Rate cell.

But because this is a database and the Monthly Payment field calculates the payment amount for any values in the three fields above it, you can simply create new records and enter different values in the top three fields to calculate this loan with different interest rates, amounts, or terms. Once the database contains several records representing different loan amounts, rates, and terms, you could use the Find mode to locate a record showing a particular loan, or you could print out a columnar report showing the costs of several different loans on one page so you could easily compare them.

**IMPORTANT
NOTE**

With all financial calculations, the values for the interest rate, term, and payment must all represent the same time period. If you want to calculate a monthly payment, you must specify a monthly interest rate and a term in months. In the example above, the formula in the Monthly Payment field automatically converts the annual interest rate shown to a monthly rate, like this: "Monthly

Payment=PMT(Loan Amount,Interest Rate/12,Term)." Also, remember that an interest rate is usually a decimal number. To enter 8.5 percent, you'd type, *.085*.

Now, let's look at FileMaker Pro's financial functions individually.

FV(payment,interest rate,periods)

The Future Value (FV) function calculates the future value of an investment, assuming a regular stream of identical payments at a steady interest rate. This is the basic means of determining how much regular investments such as monthly savings or yearly IRA contributions will be worth in the future.

Suppose, for example, that you planned to save $500 a month towards your retirement for the next 20 years. The layout might look like this:

Here, the Future Worth field is a calculated field containing the formula "FV(Amount Saved,Interest Rate/12,Periods)."

Notice that the interest rate portion of the formula divides the amount in the Interest Rate field by 12. This allows you to enter the yearly interest rate — you enter it as *.10*, but the field's formatting changes it to 10.00% — and have FileMaker Pro automatically convert it to a monthly rate when calculating the future value. Interest rates are usually specified as annual rates, but savings accounts compound interest monthly rather than yearly, so you'll want to use monthly interest rates in the formula. The value in the Periods field also specifies the number of months, to match the monthly interest rate.

NPV(interest rate,payments)

The Net Present Value (NPV) function calculates the current value of a series of unequal future payments at a given inflation rate. Use this function when you want to know whether or not the payback from an investment will keep pace with inflation and when the payments you'll receive are unequal amounts.

This function can only be used with a repeating field. If the payments you'll receive are of equal amounts, use the PV function. See *PV,* below.

For example, suppose you're asked to invest $10,000 in a new company. The company promises to pay you back over five years, with $1500 the first year, $2500 the next two years, and $3500 the final two years, for a total of $13,500. Looked at simply, this is a $3500 profit on a $10,000 investment over five years, or 35 percent for the period.

However, since the money is being paid back over time, you need to take inflation into account, because the dollars you're paid five years from now will be worth less than the dollars you're paid this year. This is where the NPV function comes in. The interest rate you enter is the inflation rate you anticipate, and the payments are the cash flows from your investment. Here's an example:

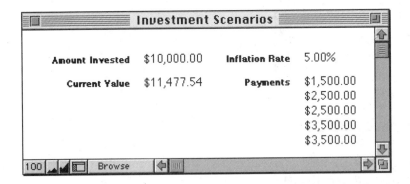

In this layout, the Current Value field is a calculation field containing the formula, "NPV(Inflation Rate,Payments)." The Payments field is a repeating field with five repetitions, as you can see, and the different payback amounts for the five years have been entered. An annual inflation rate of 5 percent is assumed, and the Amount Invested field is just there so we can compare the initial amount we loaned the business with the current value. As you can see, we still come out ahead on this investment if we assume a 5 percent inflation rate.

PMT(amount,interest rate,term)

The Payment (PMT) function is the one you use in calculating loan payments. The interest rate is usually expressed in months, because loan interest is calculated monthly, and the term must also be expressed in months so it agrees with the interest rate. The amount, interest rate, and term components must all come from number fields or from numeric constants.

For example, let's look again at the basic loan table from the beginning of this section:

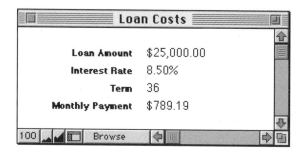

Here, the Monthly Payment field is a calculation field containing the formula "PMT(Loan Amount,Interest Rate/12,Term)."

As mentioned earlier, the Interest Rate field's amount here has been divided by 12. Interest rates are typically expressed as annual rates, so dividing by 12 in the formula lets us enter the rate as an annual amount. Otherwise, we'd have to enter the monthly interest rate.

PV(payment,interest rate,periods)

The Present Value (PV) function lets you determine the current value of a series of equal future payments, assuming a certain inflation rate. Use this function when you're trying to decide whether to loan someone money, they've promised to repay you over time with equal amounts, and you want to know if the total of their payments over time will keep pace with a specific rate of inflation.

Suppose, for example, that someone has asked to borrow $5,000 for five years, and they propose paying it back at the rate of $1200 per year. Because they propose to pay you back with equal amounts, you could use the PV function in a layout like this:

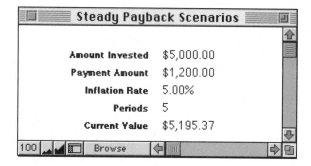

Here, the Current Value field is a calculation field containing the formula, "PV(Payment Amount,Inflation Rate,Periods)." You assume the annual inflation rate to be 5 percent during the loan period. Even though the total value of the payback is $6,000, the current value of that $6000 is only $5,195.37 when you take inflation into account.

The GetSummary Function

The GetSummary function extracts the value from a summary field so you can use it in another calculation or display it anywhere in a layout. To fully understand the difference between using this function and using a summary field, you need to understand summary fields, which are covered briefly under *Defining summary fields*, in Chapter 4, or at length in Chapter 16. You may want to look at these sections before reading on here.

You use summary field calculations in FileMaker Pro to produce totals, averages, and other calculations of values from groups of records. By sorting your file on different fields, you can arrange its records into different groups. (For example, an order-entry file sorted by the State field would arrange the records in different groups than if it were sorted by the Customer field.) Since summary calculations apply to groups of records, the values they produce depend on how a file's records are sorted.

The GetSummary function extracts the calculated value from a summary field. To use the GetSummary function, you specify the name of the summary field whose data you want to use, followed by the name of the *break field*, or the field on which records must be sorted to produce the summary totals you want. The GetSummary function format looks like this:

GetSummary(summary field name,break field name)

Summary fields alone can only display values on layouts, while the GetSummary function lets you use those values inside formulas. Further, calculation fields that use the GetSummary function will always display their values in Browse mode, while a summary field won't display its values in Browse mode if the summary field is located in a summary part of the layout. (Summary fields in summary parts of layouts only show their values in Preview mode or in printouts.)

Here's an example. Suppose you have a database of items sold at auction. The items are divided into several categories, and you want to know whether each item sold for more or less than the average price of items in its category. The layout might look like this:

Item No.	Class		Price	Relative Price
B138	Books		$10.00	Low
B139	Books		$10.00	Low
B140	Books		$9.00	Low
B141	Books		$21.00	High
B142	Books		$21.00	High
B143	Books		$21.00	High
B144	Books		$10.00	Low
B145	Books		$20.00	High
W724	Books		$11.00	Low
		Avg.Price	$11.71	

Invoices — Auction Item Statistics

The Avg.Price field is a summary field located in a sub-summary part of the layout.

The Relative Price field is a calculation field containing the formula "If(GetSummary(Avg.Price,Class)≥Price,"Low","High")." In other words, it tells FileMaker Pro to look at the value in the Avg.Price field when the records are sorted by the Class field. When records are sorted on the Class field, FileMaker Pro determines whether the Avg.Price field's value is larger or smaller than the value in the Price field, and then displays "High" if the price is higher than the average shown in the summary field, or "Low" if it's lower than the average shown in the summary field.

This example shows the Avg.Price field in a summary part of the same layout, but we could use the Relative Price field in other layouts that didn't include the Avg.Price field, and it would still make the right calculations as long as the records are sorted by the Class field.

If you want the calculation to occur for all the records in the file at all times, use the summary field's name as the break field name as well. In the above layout, for example, we could compare each item's price against the average price of all items sold, regardless of class, with the formula

"If(GetSummary(Avg.Price,Avg.Price)≥Price,"Low","High")"

Since the GetSummary function relies on the calculated result from a summary field, FileMaker Pro must first calculate the summary field data before it can be made available for the GetSummary function. That means summary function calculations take a long time and will slow down the performance of your files. When it needs to make a summary function calculation, FileMaker Pro displays a progress box to let you know. You can press ⌘. to cancel the calculation if it isn't important to you at the time. Finally, if your summary field appears in a sub-summary part and only calculates if the file is sorted in a certain way, then you'll have to re-sort the file each time you add a record or make another change that could affect the sort order.

Logical Functions

Logical functions apply a mathematical or logical test and then produce one of two results depending on whether the test is true. FileMaker Pro 3 has five logical functions, but the operation of logical functions can best be described through the If function. The If function is the basic mechanism for having FileMaker Pro make decisions, and it has a wide range of applications. The format of an If formula looks like this: "If(test,result if true,result if false)."

The If function must always have the format above. The first parameter of the argument is the test, the second parameter is the result if the test proves true, and the third parameter is the result if the test proves false.

Here's an example:

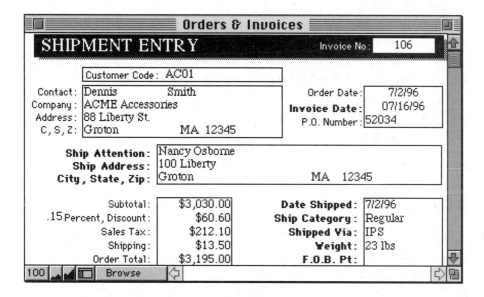

```
┌─────────────────────────────────────────────────────────┐
│▊▒▒▒▒▒▒▒▒▒▒▒▒▒▒▒ Orders & Invoices ▒▒▒▒▒▒▒▒▒▒▒▒▒▒▒ ▣│
│ SHIPMENT ENTRY          Invoice No :    106        ⬆│
```

In this layout, the Shipping field in the lower left corner is a calculation field using the If function. The amount displayed in that field depends on whether or not a certain condition is true. In this case, the formula in the Shipping field is "If(Ship Category="Regular",13.50,19.50)."

This a simple example, where the If function tests for the presence of the word "Regular" in the Ship Category field in the lower right corner. If the word is there, it places the amount 13.50 in the Shipping field. If not, it places the amount 19.50 in the Shipping field.

Notice that the text inside the formula is in straight quotation marks so FileMaker Pro knows this is a text string. Without the quote marks, FileMaker Pro would look for a field named Regular, and we'd get an error message when we tried to finish defining the calculation field.

If you're testing for a particular word (like "Regular" in the example above), use a pop-up list or menu to prevent spelling errors when that word or others are entered. If someone mistakenly entered "Reglar" in the Ship Category field above, for example, the calculation formula would produce the wrong result.

TIP

The above example tests for one condition, but you can combine, or *nest* If formulas inside one another or use FileMaker Pro's logical operators to make far more complex decisions. Whenever you use If formulas, however, be sure the calculation field you define is set to the proper result type, and that the field or fields included in the test have the proper data types. In the layout above, for example, the formula only works if the Ship Category field is a text field. If it's a number field, the words "Rush" or "Regular" will both be evaluated as 0 by the If formula, and the test will always prove false no matter what text is in the field or even if the field is blank.

Now, let's look at all the logical functions in order.

Case(test1,result1 [, test2,result2,default result]...)

This function allows you to test for one or more conditions and specify corresponding results. You can also include a default result that appears if none of the conditions proves true. For example, suppose you want to generate comment reports from a file of student grades. The layout might look like this:

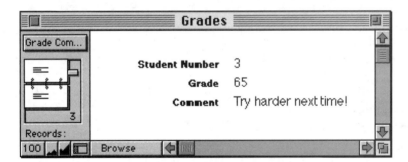

The Comment field in this layout contains this formula:

"Case(Grade≥85,"Great work!",Grade<85,"Try harder next time!")."

The text of the comment depends on the quality of the grade. The result type for this field must be set to text.

Choose(test,result0 [, result1,result2]...)

Use the Choose function to produce a series of different results based on the value of just one expression. In the previous example, there were two different expressions, or tests, to be evaluated. With the Choose function, you have just one expression, but based on whether it is true or false, you can have FileMaker Pro choose from a list of results.

Use the Choose function when the result of an expression or a field contains one of a handful of results. For example, suppose you want a field to indicate the shipping method based on the value entered in a Shipping Option field, like this:

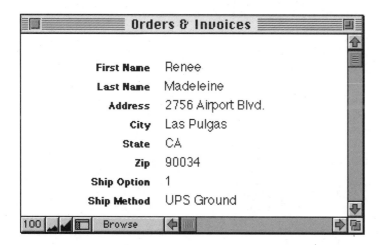

Here, the Ship Option field contains the formula: "Choose(Ship Via,"Will Call", "UPS","Air")." If the Ship Option field is left blank, the Ship Method field displays *Will Call*. If the Ship Option field contains the number 1, the Ship Method field shows *UPS Ground*, as above. If the Ship Option field contains a number 2, the Ship Method field shows *Air*.

If(test, result one, result two)

We covered the If function in some detail at the beginning of this section, but here are two more examples that show the function's versatility.

Discount=If(Product Subtotal≥5000,Product Subtotal*.05,If(Product Subtotal≥2500, Product Subtotal*.02,0))

This formula uses a nested If function to apply a second test if the first test proves false. This formula, which might be used to calculate a discount rate in a sales-order file, checks the Product Subtotal field's amount. If the amount is greater than or equal to 5000, then the discount is 5 percent. If the amount is less than 5000, it then checks if the amount is greater than or equal to 2500, and if it is, the discount is 2 percent. If the amount is less than 2500, there's no discount.

You can nest as many If functions inside a formula as you like, up to the 32,767-character limit of calculation field formulas, but at some point it gets a little ridiculous. When you want a field to automatically contain one of several different results based on the entry in another field, a lookup field is more practical. (See *About Lookups and Relational Databases*, in Chapter 11.)

In this layout we've used the following formula to compute the amount of vacation time: "Vacation Time=If(Hire Date<TextToDate("12/01/87") And Attendance≥97,"3 Weeks","2 Weeks")."

Here, we've used the And operator to apply two different tests at the same time, as opposed to applying a second test if the first one fails. In this case, the employee's hire date must be earlier than December 1, 1987, *and* the employee must have an attendance rating of 97 or better to qualify for three weeks' vacation. If either of the conditions is not met, the employee gets two weeks' vacation.

Notice that the And operator is separated from the other parts of the formula by spaces. Operator names must always be set off from field names in a formula. Without the extra spaces in this case, FileMaker Pro wouldn't recognize And as an operator name, but would assume it was part of the Attendance field name. And, not finding a field called "AndAttendance," FileMaker Pro would show an error message when we tried to define the field with this formula.

Also, notice that the date information inside the TextToDate argument is in quotation marks so that FileMaker Pro knows it's text. Using the TextToDate function here allows us to enter a formatted date as a constant in this formula. Otherwise, we'd have to enter the date's numeric value. (See *Date Functions*, earlier in this chapter.)

IsEmpty(field)

The IsEmpty function checks to see whether a field has anything in it. It returns a True value (1) if the field is empty, and a False value (0) if the field contains data. You might use this function to see if a particular field is filled in. For example, to report whether the Zip field in an address record is filled in, you would use the formula "IsEmpty(Zip)." If the Zip field was empty, this calculation would return a 1.

IsValid(field)

The IsValid function reports whether or not the entry in a field is valid (date data in a date type field, for example), or whether the specified field is missing (a related field might be missing, for instance, because the related file wasn't opened).

Here's an example:

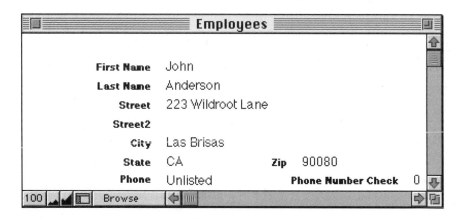

In this case, the Phone Number Check field returns a 0 because it checks the validity of data in the Phone field. The data entered in that field is text, but the field's data type is set to number.

These are just a few of the ways you can use logical functions. It takes some fiddling with these formulas to get them right, but the more you use them, the more you understand them, which makes it easier to use them to automate data entry and improve the accuracy of your database files.

~~~~~~

Numeric Functions

FileMaker Pro includes an assortment of standard mathematical functions you can use for a variety of purposes. As with many other FileMaker Pro functions, these let you perform calculations with a database that you would ordinarily have to do with a spreadsheet program.

IMPORTANT NOTE

In FileMaker Pro, the Exp function is listed as a numeric function, but as it primarily relates to trigonometric calculations, we'll discuss it under *Trigonometric Functions*, at the end of this chapter.

Abs(number)

The Absolute Value (Abs) function converts the value inside the argument into a positive number. Use this function when the calculated value from one or more other fields may produce a negative number, but you'd rather see it as a positive number in the layout.

This function is mentioned in the sections on date and time functions elsewhere in this chapter. Since later dates or times are represented by higher numbers, you need always subtract earlier dates or times from later dates or times to produce a positive number. However, if you want to subtract a later date or time from an earlier date or time, you can use the Abs function to remove the negative sign from the result, like this:

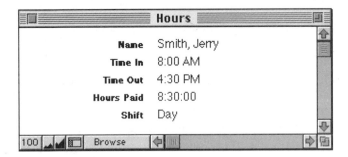

Here, the formula in the Hours Paid field is "Abs(Time In-Time Out)," and a time result type is specified. Since we're subtracting a later time from an earlier one (or a larger number of seconds from a smaller number of seconds), this should be a negative number, but we've used the Abs function to make it positive.

Remember, since times are stored as the number of seconds since midnight, defining this field with a Number type result would make FileMaker Pro display the number of seconds in the Hours Paid field rather than the formatted hours and seconds as shown.

Int(number)

The Integer (Int) function turns a decimal number into an integer, chopping off any digits to the right of the decimal point in the value supplied. This function comes in handy when you're dividing one value by another, so the result will frequently be a decimal number, but you're only interested in the integer amount.

If you bill clients by the hour and you don't include fractions of an hour, for example, you might use the Int function to reduce the hours reported for each client to a whole number, like this:

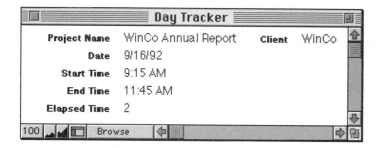

Here, the formula in the Elapsed Time field is "Int((End Time-Start Time)/3600)." The time values (which are values in seconds, remember) are divided by 3600 to return the number of hours. Here, the actual elapsed time is 2.5 hours but the Int function has eliminated the decimal fraction.

The Integer function always returns a value less than or equal to the argument. Use the Round function to make a decimal value "round up" to the next higher value. Use the Truncate function to eliminate a specific part of a decimal number without rounding. See *Round*, and *Truncate*, below.

TIP

Mod(number,divisor)

The Modulus (Mod) function calculates the remainder when you divide one number by another. The number in the argument is the value you want divided, and the divisor is the value you want to divide it by. For example, the formula "Mod(8,3)" is equal to 2, because after you divide 8 by 3, the remainder is 2.

Use this function when you're dividing values and it's important to know the remainder when values don't divide evenly. In a contractor's job database, for example, it might be important to know how much concrete is still needed on a job after the total amount is divided by the amount per full truck, like this:

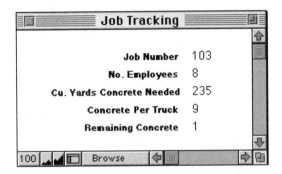

Here, the Remaining Concrete field contains the formula "Mod(Cu. Yards Concrete Needed,Concrete Per Truck)." In this case, the remainder is 1 cubic yard. Knowing this, the contractor would probably decide to supply the remaining yard with a portable mixer rather than order another 9-cubic-yard truckload.

NumToText(number)

When you use the NumToText function, the number, expression or data from the numeric field referenced in the argument is converted to text. When it converts a number to text, FileMaker Pro removes any leading zeroes, dashes or other delimiters from the original value, so you can use the NumToText function to eliminate these elements from data when you don't need it.

For example, suppose you originally created an inventory file that contained part numbers in a numeric field, and those part numbers were entered with leading zeroes. Using the NumToText function, you could convert those part numbers to new numbers in a text field, and the leading zeroes would be eliminated, like this:

ItemNo.	New ItemNo.	Name	Category	Item Count
000-1011	1011	Junior football	Balls	22
000-1012	1012	Regulation NFL Football	Balls	28
000-1013	1013	Official NBA Basketball	Balls	11

Here, the ItemNo. field contains the original numbers with leading zeroes, and the New ItemNo. field contains the formula "NumToText(ItemNo.)," so it converts the numbers to text and eliminates the leading zeroes.

Unless you know you'll want to calculate numbers, define your fields as text. This includes fields with number data such as zip codes, part numbers, and employee numbers. Although the data is numeric, you'll never need to calculate it so you should store it as text. You can still sort numbers in ascending or descending order in text fields.

TIP

Random

The Random function has no argument. When you use this function in a formula, it generates a random number between (but not including) 0 and 1. Use this function when you want to produce random numbers in a field. When you include the Random function in a formula, FileMaker Pro produces a new random number whenever you create a new record or whenever you change a value in one of the other fields referred to in the same formula.

Use the Random function whenever you want to have FileMaker Pro make a random choice. For example, suppose your office has a dozen employees and only one really great parking place. With the Random function, you can have FileMaker Pro assign the space randomly every month, like this:

The Employee Number field here contains the formula "Int(Random*12)+1." To reassign the parking spot each month, you would create a new record in this file. The random number is generated with each new record and multiplied by the number of employees. Since the Random function always produces a decimal fraction between 0 and 1, the Int function eliminates the decimal fraction from the product of (Random*12) to produce an employee number from 1 to 12.

It's necessary to add 1 to the product of Random*12, because the Int function evaluates any value below 1 as 0. In this case, any number between 1 and 2 will make the value 1 appear in the Employee Number field.

Round(number,digits of precision)

The Round function tells FileMaker Pro to round off the result of a calculation. The Round function rounds numbers up at .5 and down at .49. The digits of precision value in the argument specifies the number of digits you want to remain. Positive values apply to digits to the right of a decimal point, and negative values apply to digits to the left of a decimal point.

For example:

"Round(2987.4531,2)" = 2987.45

"Round(2987.4561,2)" = 2987.46

"Round(2947.4531,-2)" = 2900

"Round(2987.4561,-2)" = 3000

You can use the Round function to eliminate or reduce decimal fractions in calculated numbers, or to round off integer amounts. With decimal fractions, for example, you may want to force FileMaker Pro to produce numbers with fewer decimal digits. Normally, FileMaker Pro calculates every number to 22 digits of precision. Even if you've formatted a number field to display only two decimal places, FileMaker Pro still calculates with full precision, and it remembers the full numbers. So, if you use a field as a reference in another calculation, the full-precision number will be used in the calculation, and that may cause problems.

For example, suppose you want to divide the profit on a sale among three salespeople, like this:

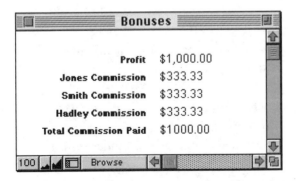

As you can see, these values are formatted as currency with two decimal places. The formula that figures the commission for each salesperson is "Profit/3." However, because we're displaying the values as dollars and cents, the Total Commission field shows *$1,000.00*, even though it's really $999.99999999999999999.

To show the real total paid, we'd have to change the formula that figures each salesperson's commission to "Round((Profit/3),2)." This tells FileMaker Pro to round each commission to two decimal places so these figures match the dollars-and-cents figure in the Total Commission Paid field. Once we do that, the layout shows the actual total, like this:

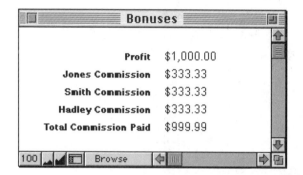

You may also run into situations where you want to round a large number off because the tens and hundreds don't matter. If you want to export sales commission figures to a spreadsheet for comparative charting, for example, you could round off each commission figure to the nearest thousand, like this:

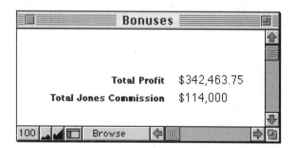

Here, the Total Jones Commission field's formula is "Round((Total Profit/3),-3)."

Sign(number)

The Sign function produces either 1, −1, or 0 depending on whether the value in the argument is positive, negative, or zero, respectively. For example, suppose you want to have FileMaker Pro determine what sort of gift to send your customers, based on the change in their purchasing volume this year over the previous year. You could use the Sign function to help make such a choice in a layout like the one below:

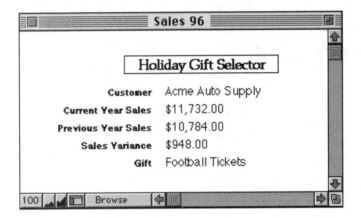

Here, the Gift field contains the formula "If(Sign(Sales Variance)=1,"Football Tickets",If(Sign(Sales Variance)=0,"Cheese Ball","Card Only"))," and the field is set to display a Text result. The Sales Variance field simply subtracts the Current Year Sales field's amount from the Previous Year Sales field's amount. In the example above, the Sales Variance amount is positive, so its sign equals 1, and the Gift field shows the text *Football Tickets*.

TIP

You could accomplish this same calculation by simply looking at the Sales Variance amount and determining whether it was less than or equal to zero in a formula like this: "If(Sales Variance>0,"Football Tickets",(If(Sales Variance=0, "Cheese Ball","Card Only")))."

Sqrt(number)

The Sqrt (Square Root) function calculates the square root of the value supplied in the argument. Square root is used to determine the slope (or hypotenuse) of a triangle and is an important function in many other types of calculations. For example, a painting contractor might want FileMaker Pro to determine the size of ladders needed for each job, like this:

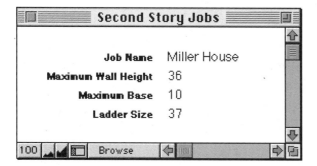

In this layout, the Ladder Size field contains the formula "Sqrt(Maximum Wall Height^2+Maximum Base^2)." The square of the hypotenuse of a right triangle is equal to the sum of the squares of its two other sides, so by calculating the squares of the wall height and the maximum base length, adding them together, and calculating the square root of the sum, you get the length of the hypotenuse, which is the ladder size.

Truncate(number, precision)

Rather than rounding off a number (as with the Round function) or storing only the integer portion of a number (as with the Int function), the Truncate function simply chops off a decimal number at the specified number of decimal places. The precision value in this function's argument indicates the number of decimal places you want the number to have. The decimal point in a number equates to 0. Everything to the right of the decimal point is a positive number, and everything to the left of it is a negative number. Here are some examples:

NEW FEATURE

"Truncate(456.8990,0)" = 456

"Truncate(456.8990,2)" = 456.89

"Truncate(456.8990,-2)" = 400

"Truncate(456.8990,8)" = 456.8990

Repeating Field Functions

Repeating field functions apply only to repeating fields. Unlike aggregate functions, which are mostly used with repeating fields but can also apply to groups of nonrepeating fields, these functions can only be used with repeating fields.

Extend(non-repeating field name)

The Extend function tells FileMaker Pro to reuse, or extend, the value in a non-repeating field so it can be calculated properly in the same formula with all the values from repeating fields. If you don't use the Extend function and you use a nonrepeating field value with repeating field values in a formula, the calculation will only take place with the first of the repeating field values.

For example, let's look at a grade reporting layout like this:

Grades			
May Day Quiz			
Student Number	**Grade**	**Adjustment**	**Adjusted Grade**
1	94	3	97
2	83		86
3	79		82
4	90		93
5	68		71
6	74		77
7	88		91
8	82		85
9	85		88
10	81		84

| 100 | Browse |

Here, the teacher has decided to adjust every student's grade upward by 3 points. The Adjustment field is a nonrepeating numeric field, so the Adjusted Grade field contains the formula "Grade+Extend(Adjustment)." As a result, the Adjustment field's value is added to every value in the Grade field. Without the Extend function in the formula, the Adjustment field's value would only be added to the first value in the Grade field, not to all of them.

GetRepetition(repeating field, number)

NEW FEATURE

The GetRepetition function extracts the data from a specific repetition of a repeating field. You specify the repeating field name and the number of the repetition whose data you want. For example, suppose a Shift field contains three repetitions, like this:

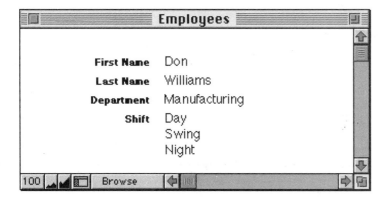

In this file, a calculation field containing the formula "GetRepetition(Shift,2) would return the value *Swing*.

Last(repeating field name)

The Last function returns the last valid entry in a repeating field. Use this function when you're using a repeating field to collect a series of values over time and you want to know at a glance which was the latest value entered. For example, in a layout that tracks estimated completion dates for a project, you'll always want to know the latest estimate, like this:

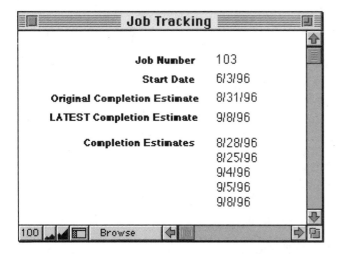

The Completion Estimates field is a repeating field in which different estimated completion dates are entered, one below the other, as the estimate changes. The

Latest Completion Estimate field contains the formula "Last(Completion Estimates)," so it always shows the last date entered.

Although this layout shows all the entries in the repeating field, the layout could be shorter so that the Latest Completion Estimate field showed a date that is otherwise offscreen. In fact, the Completion Estimates field could even be on a different layout or in a related file.

IMPORTANT NOTE

The Status Function

NEW FEATURE

The Status function is used to display information about the operation of FileMaker Pro. Typically, you would use this function with different arguments to determine the current status of operations in FileMaker Pro while performing scripts. For example, a script might need to know which field is currently selected, or the name of the current file, and you could use a status function to supply that information.

We won't go into great detail about using the status function here, but here's a quick rundown of the arguments you might use with it and what they tell you about FileMaker Pro's operation.

Status(CurrentAppVersion)

This displays the version number of the copy of FileMaker Pro you're running.

Status(CurrentDate)

This displays the current date, as determined by your Mac's internal calendar.

Status(CurrentError)

This is for diagnosing errors in complex scripts. You would typically use the CurrentError argument in a Status function with the Set Error Capture [On] script step. Common errors in FileMaker Pro scripts are assigned specific numbers, and when an error occurs in a script, this function displays the number of that error. To see a list of error numbers and further examples of how to use this function, look up the Status(Current Error) function in the FileMaker Pro Help system's index.

Status(CurrentFieldName)

This reports the name of the field that currently contains the insertion point.

Status(CurrentFileName)

This reports the name of the file that is currently active.

Status(CurrentFileSize)

This reports the size (in bytes) of the current file.

Status(CurrentFoundCount)

This reports the number of records in the current found set.

Status(CurrentHostName)

This reports the user name of the person currently hosting the file. (The user name reported is the one registered on the host's Mac.)

Status(CurrentLanguage)

This reports the current language setting on the Macintosh system.

Status(CurrentLayoutCount)

This reports the number of layouts in the active file.

Status(CurrentLayoutName)

This reports the name of the current layout.

Status(CurrentLayoutNumber)

This reports the number of the current layout. (Layouts are numbered from 1 up, starting at the top of the layout pop-up menu.)

Status(CurrentMessageChoice)

This displays the text of the current error message that will be displayed when a script encounters an error.

Status(CurrentMode)

This reports which mode the file is currently in. The function returns a number: 1 for Browse, 2 for Find and 3 for Preview.

Status(CurrentMultiUserStatus)

This reports a number that represents the multi-user status of the current file, as well as the location of a multi-user file. It returns 0 if the file is set to single-user, 1 if the file is a multi-user file running from the host computer, and 2 if it's a multi-user file running on a guest's computer.

Status(CurrentPageNumber)

This shows the number of the page currently being printed or previewed. It displays 0 if no pages are being printed or previewed.

Status(CurrentPlatform)

This determines whether the current file is running on a Mac or a Windows computer. It displays 1 if the machine is a Mac, and 2 if it's a Windows PC.

Status(CurrentPortalRow)

This reports the number of the row in a portal that's currently selected. If no portal row is selected, this function displays a 0.

Status(CurrentPrinterName)

This reports the name and other information about the printer that's currently set for use with the file. On a Mac, this argument shows the printer name (as shown in the Chooser), the type of printer, and the network zone where the printer is located. Under Windows, this argument shows the printer name, driver name, and the name of the selected printer port.

Status(CurrentRecordCount)

This reports the total number of records in the file, not in the found set.

Status(CurrentRecordNumber)

This reports the number of the current record.

Status(CurrentRepetitionNumber)

This reports the number of the current (selected or active) repetition in a repeating field. If the field is not a repeating field, a Status formula with this argument displays the value 1.

Status(CurrentRequestCount)

This reports the total number of find requests currently defined for the file.

Status(CurrentScreenDepth)

This reports the number of bits needed to display one color on the screen on the current system. The value 1 means the screen is black and white; 2 means the screen can display 4 colors; 4 means the screen displays 16 colors; and 8 means the screen displays 256 colors.

Status(CurrentScreenHeight), Status(CurrentScreenWidth)

These report the height and width, respectively, in pixels of the current display screen. For example, on a system using a screen set to 640 by 480 resolution, the Status(CurrentScreenHeight) function would report 480.

Status(CurrentScriptName)

This reports the name of the script currently running.

Status(CurrentSortStatus)

This reports a value representing the current sort status of the file: 0 if the file is unsorted, 1 if the file is sorted, and 2 if the file is partially (or semi-) sorted.

Status(CurrentSystemVersion)

This reports a value representing the operating system version of the current system. For example, it returns 7.5 on a Macintosh running System 7.5, and 4 on a system running Windows 95.

Status(CurrentTime)

This reports the current time in hours, minutes, and seconds (HH:MM:SS) as reported by your Mac's internal clock.

Status(CurrentUserCount)

This reports the number of users currently working with the file.

Status(CurrentUserName)

This reports the name of the current user, as shown under the General settings in the Preferences dialog box. (See *General preferences*, on p. 39 in Chapter 3.)

Text Functions

FileMaker Pro's text functions let you locate, compare, and otherwise manipulate individual characters or groups of characters (called strings) automatically. You use text functions to manipulate data in text fields.

How FileMaker Pro manages text

FileMaker Pro manages text in three ways, depending on which text functions you use and how you refer to your data.

- If you want to use the entire contents of text fields, you can refer to the field names.

- If you're comparing text inside fields, you can have FileMaker Pro look for exact matches in which every character in the string is the same as one you supply and has the same case (upper or lower).

- You can also have FileMaker Pro locate or identify text according to its position from the left, right, or middle of a field.

When you create any formula containing text calculations, be sure to check the result type for the calculation field before you finish defining it. Usually you'll want the result of a text calculation to be text, but there are exceptions, as explained below.

IMPORTANT NOTE

Elsewhere in this chapter, some formula examples include the text operators & and " ". In this section, we'll see how to use FileMaker Pro's text operators and functions to perform a variety of tasks.

Exact(original text,comparison text)

The Exact function lets you compare text in a text field with text you supply. When you use this function, FileMaker Pro makes a case-sensitive comparison of the two text strings in the argument, and then displays a Boolean true (1) if they match or a false (0) if they don't.

This is a case in which you'd want the text formula's result type to be Number.

For example, if the Customer field in a record contains *ACME* and the Ship Name field in the same record contains *Acme*, then the formula "Exact(Customer,Ship Name)" will equal 0: The text in the two fields doesn't exactly match, so the formula proves false.

IMPORTANT NOTE

Since the Exact function calculates a Boolean result, you'll typically use it along with the If function. (See *Logical Functions*, on p. 362 earlier in this chapter.) For example, suppose you want to make sure all the state addresses in your personnel file are entered as uppercase two-letter codes (*CA* rather than *Ca*). You could create a calculation field that posted a reminder notice like the one below:

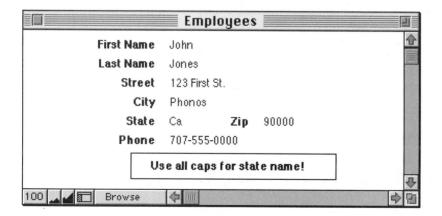

The text in the box at the bottom of this layout is from a calculation field containing the formula "If(Exact(State,Upper(State)) And (Length(State)=2)," ", "Use all caps for state name!")." This tells FileMaker Pro to check whether there are two uppercase letters in the state field, to display nothing if the data matches (the formula proves true), and to display "Use all caps for state name!" if the data doesn't match (the formula proves false).

Notice that, as with all text functions, the reminder text constant has been entered inside quotation marks. If you don't enclose text constants in quotes, FileMaker Pro thinks the text is a field or function name, and (because no such function or field name exists) it won't let you complete the formula. (See the sections on the *Upper* and *Length* functions later in this chapter for more information on this.)

Left(text,number), Right(text,number)

These two functions extract part of a text string from a field by counting the number of characters from the left or right end of the string. The text parameter in the argument is usually a field name, and the number parameter is the number of characters of text you want FileMaker Pro to extract, counting from the left or right.

Used alone, these functions can extract portions of text for use in a different field. For example, you could use the Left function to create a customer code from the first four letters of a company name and the numbers in a zip code field, like this:

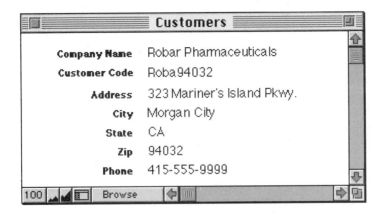

Here, the Customer Code field contains the formula, "Left(Company Name,4) &Zip," so FileMaker Pro takes the first four letters from the Company Name field and concatenates them with the Zip field's data.

If you use both five-digit and nine-digit zip codes, you could use the Left function to extract only the first five digits of the code, like this: "Left(Company Name,4)&Left(Zip,5)."

TIP

LeftWords(text,number of words), RightWords(text,number of words)

The LeftWords and RightWords functions are very useful when you want to separate data in one field into two or more fields. For example, if all your employee name data has been entered into a single Name field, you can use the LeftWords or RightWords function to separate the data into two fields called First Name and Last Name, like this:

NEW FEATURE

In this case, the First Name field contains the formula: "LeftWords(Name,1)." The formula tells FileMaker Pro to look in the Name field and extract the first word, counting from the left. In this case, we could also use the formula "RightWords(Name,2)" to produce the same result, since that formula would extract the second word counting from the right. The Last Name field in this example contains the formula: "RightWords(Name,1)."

Length(text)

This function returns the number of characters in the text string (or, more typically, the field) in the argument. For example, the formula "Length(State)" would equal 2 when the State field contained "NY."

TIP

If you've specified a text field in the argument, the Length function counts all characters, including spaces between words. However, if you've specified a number field, the function only counts numbers, not spaces or dashes. For example, the formula "Length(Phone)" will equal 7 if the Phone field contains 555-1111 and is defined as a number field, but the same formula will equal 8 if the Phone field is defined as a text field.

The Length function comes in handiest when you want the length of text in a field to be determined and used inside a larger formula. For example, if you have a mailing label layout in your Customers file, and you know there's only enough room on the layout to display 25 characters in a customer name, you could have FileMaker Pro display a message alerting users that they'll have to abbreviate the name when it's too long. Below is a customer data entry layout with the reminder notice:

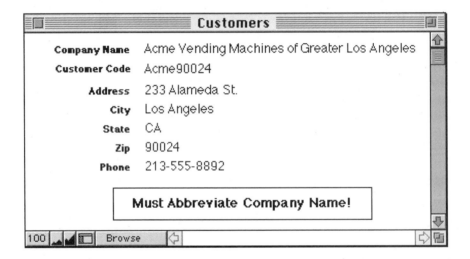

Here, the reminder notice comes from a calculation field that contains the formula, "If(Length(Company Name)>25),"Must Abbreviate Company Name!"," ")."

Lower(text), Upper(text)

These two functions convert every character inside the referenced field to either lower- or uppercase. You can use it to change text to all caps or all lowercase, or you can use it to determine the case of text and then use that information for something else. Here are two examples.

If the information in a State field has been entered haphazardly, sometimes with upper, sometimes with lower, and sometimes with mixed case letters, you can standardize it quickly by creating a new field called State1 containing the formula "Upper(State)," like this:

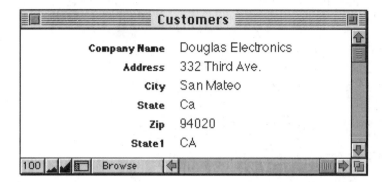

The State1 field's formula will read the data from the original State field, make it all uppercase, and display it in the State1 field.

After you perform a conversion like this, you can then change the State1 field to a text type so it no longer makes calculations, delete the State field, and rename the State1 field State. (However, if you're already using the State field in another text calculation, you'll have to change that formula first to refer to the State1 field so that the calculation remains valid.)

TIP

You could also combine the Upper function with the Exact function to determine whether spellings are in uppercase letters. For example, in an address file where you want to remind data entry operators to use uppercase letters in the State field, you could create a reminder field containing the formula:

"If(Exact(State,Upper(State)))," ","Please use all caps for state information!"."

Compare this formula with the one under the Exact function discussed earlier. The formula there looked for exact uppercase spellings and state codes that were two characters long.

Middle(text,start,size)

Rather than working from the left or right (see *Left* and *Right*, earlier in this chapter), the Middle function extracts characters from somewhere in the middle of a text string. To use this function, you enter the field reference or text constant, the position number (counting from the left) where you want FileMaker Pro to start extracting characters, and the number of characters you want extracted.

For example, suppose you want to extract the area code information from a file of domestic customers. Let's say the area codes have parentheses around them, so you can't just take the leftmost three characters from the Phone field in every record. Instead, you'd use the Middle function in this formula: "Middle(Phone,2,3)."

This formula tells FileMaker Pro to start with the second character from the left and extract three characters. So, if the Phone field contains *(415)555-1212*, this formula will return *415*, as in the Area Code field, like this:

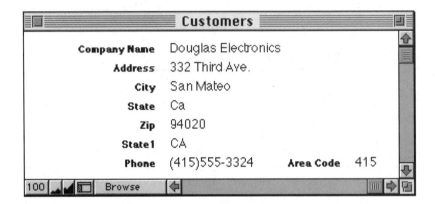

Of course, if your database contains some records with local numbers (no area code), the formula above extracts the second, third, and fourth characters from every record, area code or not, so you'll end up with some data you don't want. However, you can use the If function to make FileMaker Pro more choosy in a formula like this: "If(Left(Phone,1)="(",Middle(Phone,2,3)," ")." This tells FileMaker Pro to extract the area code only if the first character in the field is a parenthesis. Local numbers won't begin with a parenthesis, so FileMaker Pro will skip them.

MiddleWords(text, starting word, number of words)

MiddleWords extracts words, rather than characters, from a text string in a field. You specify the field as the text value, the number of the starting word (counting from the left), and the number of words to extract. For example, suppose your database has names in one Name field. You could use the MiddleWords function to extract the last name and title from the Name Field, like this:

Here, the LastTitle field contains the formula "MiddleWords(Name,2,2), which tells FileMaker Pro to look in the Name field and extract two words, counting from the second word from the left.

PatternCount(text,search string)

This function calculates the number of times a particular pattern of text characters occurs in a field. You specify the field name as the text parameter, and the text string representing the pattern as the search string parameter. For example, if a text field called Product contained the words "Action Faction Battalion," the formula "PatternCount(Product,"tion")" would produce the result 3, because the string "tion" occurs three times in the Product field.

**NEW
FEATURE**

Position(text,search string,start,occurrence)

The Position function scans the supplied text (or text field) for a specified occurrence of the search string you enter, and then reports the numeric position at which that search string begins. If the search string isn't found, the formula returns a zero. The start parameter in the argument tells FileMaker Pro where to begin scanning text or a text field, starting from the left.

So, for example, the formula "Position(Customer,"ing",1,1)" would return 10 when the Customer field contains "Acme Plating & Engineering," because the *i* in the first occurrence of "ing" is the tenth character from the left. If the Customer field contained "Ingersoll Engineering, Inc.," this formula would return 1. If the Customer field contained "Acme Toys," this formula would return 0.

Proper(text)

Proper is another function you can use to standardize the spelling of data. It converts the text in the argument so the first letter of each word is capitalized and all the other letters are lowercase.

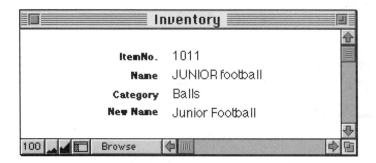

In the file above, for example, the New Name field contains the formula "Proper(Name)," so it converts the haphazardly capitalized data in the Name field into proper capitalization.

This function is the best way to clean up capitalization in a file. You'll have to create a new calculation field in which to enter a formula containing the Proper function, but once you do, all the data in the referenced field will be copied into it with the proper capitalization. If you were trying to accomplish this in the example above, you would then delete the original Item Name field, rename the calculation field, and change its type to Text. (Of course, if the original Item Name field is used in any other formulas, you'll have to change them to refer to the new field before FileMaker Pro will let you delete the original field.)

Replace(text, start, size, replacement text)

The Replace function lets you replace certain parts of a text string with other text you specify. It locates the text (or text field) you specify, counts over to the start position you enter, and then removes the number of characters you indicate in the size part of the argument and replaces them with the replacement text in the argument. The replacement text you specify can be shorter, as long as, or longer than the text it replaces, but remember to enclose it in quotation marks so that FileMaker Pro knows it's text.

TIP Use this function when you want to replace part of the text in a field. (If you want to replace *all* the text in a field, use the Replace command. See *Replacing data in several records at once*, on p. 78 in Chapter 5.)

For example, suppose one telephone prefix used by your customers has been assigned to a new area code. You could use the Replace function combined with the If function to test for the number prefix that has been moved to the new area code, and then replace the old area code with the new one, like this:

Here, the formula in the New Phone field is: "If(Left(Phone,8)="(415)946", Replace(Phone,1,5,"(510)")," ")."

This formula tests for phone numbers with the 946 prefix in the 415 area code, and then converts them to the 510 area code. It checks the first eight characters from the left in the Phone field, and if they equal "(415)946," it replaces the first five characters with (510), so the area code is changed. In records where the 415 area code and 946 prefix aren't found in the Phone field, the New Phone field will remain blank, so users will know to continue dialing the old number.

Substitute(text,search string,replace string)

The Replace function lets you replace a specific text string, as indicated by its position in a field, but the Substitute function searches for text that matches a search string and then replaces it wherever it occurs in a field.

NEW
FEATURE

For example, suppose you moved your mail-order sporting goods firm from Alabama to Florida, and you want to change all the product descriptions that include "Alabama" in the name so they include "Florida" instead, like this:

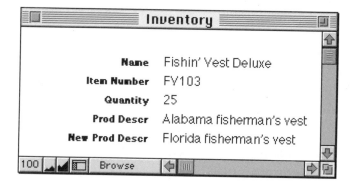

In this file, the original description is in a field called Prod Descr, and the revised description is in a new calculation field called New Prod Descr, which contains this formula: "Substitute(Prod Descr,"Alabama","Florida")."

TextToDate(text)

The opposite of DateToText, this function turns a formatted date (which FileMaker Pro treats as text) into the number of days FileMaker Pro needs to calculate the date. Using this function is the only way you can enter a date constant into a formula (unless you happen to know the number of days since January 1, 0001, that represents the date you want to use).

When you use the TextToDate function, the date information in the argument must be entered in MM/DD/YYYY format and must be enclosed in quotation marks (so FileMaker Pro knows it's text). For example, suppose you want a calculation field named Reminder to display a birthday reminder notice on June 15, 1996. The formula might read,

"Reminder = If(Date=(TextToDate("06/15/1996")),"Jan's Birthday!"," ")."

Although this example shows text entered in MM/DD/YYYY format, this text could also be supplied from several fields or calculated results, all of which were concatenated into one text string. For example, the MM part of the string might come from one date field (the result could be converted to text using the DateToText function), the day portion from a calculation field result set to text, and the year portion from another field. As long as the three results were concatenated using the & operator and slashes divided the portions of the date, the result would be the same.

(For more on the If function, see *Logical Functions*, on p. 362.)

TextToNum(text)

The TextToNum function converts numbers in text strings into real numbers so you can calculate with them. You can use this function to extract a number from the middle of a text string or simply to convert a number expressed as text into its numeric equivalent so you can use the number in a formula.

For example, suppose an editorial database lists articles by length in a text field, and you want to compute an average article length. Because the values are expressed as text, you need to use the TextToNum function to convert the values to numbers first, like this:

Here, the Words field contains the formula, "TextToNum(Length)."

This function works best when you know there's only one string in the named field that looks like a number. If there's more than one numeric string in a text field, FileMaker Pro concatenates them. For example, if the Length field above contained *1500 Words, 4 photos*, the Words field would contain *15004*.

**IMPORTANT
NOTE**

TextToTime(text)

This function turns text into a time value, so you could enter a time in the HH:MM or HH:MM:SS format as a constant in a formula and have FileMaker Pro calculate it. FileMaker Pro can transform any text in the HH:MM or HH:MM:SS format into a time value, even if the text has AM or PM after it. This function is the simplest way to enter a time constant into a formula. Otherwise, you have to enter the number of seconds since midnight that equals the time you want to specify.

For example, suppose you have a file that charts your progress as a runner, and you want to set a goal of 1:15:30 for the time it takes to run a certain course. With the TextToTime function, you could enter this time as a constant in a logical formula that compares your real time against it, like this:

Here, the Note field is a calculation field containing this logical formula:

"If(Elapsed Time≤TextToTime("01:15:30"),"Good Job!","Slacker!")."

The formula compares the value in the Elapsed Time field and displays *Good Job!* if it's less than or equal to 1:15:30, and *Slacker*! if it's greater than that. The TextToTime function tells FileMaker Pro to evaluate the text entry 01:15:30 as a time value.

Trim(text)

The Trim function removes extra spaces from before and after the supplied text. You'll use this function mostly when you've imported data from another program and there are extra tabs or spaces before or after the data once it appears in your file.

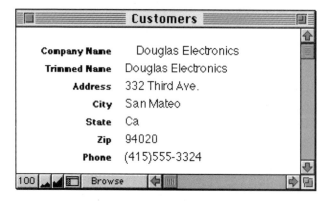

Here, for example, the Company Name field entry has some extra spaces in front of it, and the Trimmed Name field eliminates them with the formula "Trim(Company Name)."

WordCount (text)

NEW FEATURE

This function simply counts the number of words in a field or text expression. For example, if you hold a contest in which customers are asked to describe the virtues of your new floor wax in 25 words or less, you could create a database file with a field that shows each entry's word count, like this:

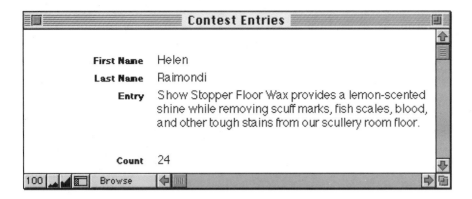

In this case, the Count field contains the formula "WordCount(Entry)."

Time Functions

Like dates, FileMaker Pro stores times as numbers so it's easier to calculate them. FileMaker Pro measures time to the second on a 24-hour clock. Since there are 86,400 seconds in a day (60*60*24), any given time is equal to the number of seconds since the previous midnight. For example, 12:05:00 AM is equal to 300.

FileMaker Pro recognizes data in time fields in the HH:MM or HH:MM:SS formats, and you can even add AM or PM to times you enter and FileMaker Pro will still understand them. So, 1:15 is understood as 1:15:00 hours, and 1:15 P.M. is understood as 13:15:00 hours.

Because FileMaker Pro stores times as numbers, you can add and subtract them easily. In the job tracking file below, the Elapsed Time is a calculation field containing the formula "End Time-Start Time."

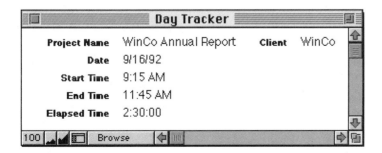

This example only calculates the proper elapsed time if both the start and end times are on the same day.

The Elapsed Time field has been set to a Time result so it shows the HH:MM:SS format. If this field were formatted as a number, it would show the number of seconds in 2.5 hours, or 9000.

Since FileMaker Pro keeps track of time in seconds, it's best to subtract earlier times from later times to make sure the result is a positive number. (If you don't want to do this for some reason, you can always convert a negative number to a positive one with the Abs function. See *Numeric Functions*, earlier in this chapter.)

Now, let's look at the time functions.

Hour(time), Minute(time), Seconds(time)

These three functions return the hour, minute, or second number from the specified time. For example, the formula "Hour(Start Time)" equals 1 if the Start Time field contains the time 1:15 A.M. (FileMaker Pro uses a 24-hour clock, so if the Start Time field contains the time 1:15 P.M., the result of this formula would be 13.)

If you use the Seconds function and the time supplied is in the HH:MM format, then the formula result is 0, because no seconds are specified.

Use one of these functions when you want FileMaker Pro to extract only the hour, minute, or second number from a time. For example, suppose all a company's workers start on two shifts, between 6:00 and 8:00 A.M. on the day shift, and between 4:00 and 6:00 P.M. on the night shift. A personnel file for the company could use the Hour function to determine the hour each employee starts work and then use that information to automatically display which shift the employee is on, like this:

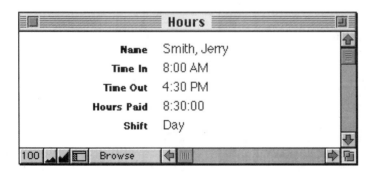

In this case, the Shift field is a calculation field containing the formula "If(Hour(Time In)≤8,"Day","Night")." This tells FileMaker Pro to look at the hour of the Time In and to display *Day* in the Shift field if it's less than or equal to 8, or to display *Night* in the Shift field otherwise.

Time(hours,minutes,seconds)

This function returns the formatted HH:MM:SS time when the appropriate numbers are supplied in the argument. For example, the formula "Time(2,23,30)" would produce 2:23:30.

Use this function when you want to collect individual hour, minute, and second values from one or more other fields and display them as a formatted time. For example, suppose you had a database of race results that included separate fields for hours, minutes, and seconds. A fourth field could produce the formatted time, like this:

In this case, the formula in the Total Time field is "Time(Hours,Minutes,Seconds)."

If the numbers supplied as the second or third parameters are more than 60, FileMaker Pro automatically increments the minute or hour value to compensate. Thus, the formula Time(2,62,70) would produce 3:03:10. If any of the three fields is blank, FileMaker Pro enters a zero for that portion of the formatted time.

TIP

TimeToText(time)

This function converts a time value to text so you can include the formatted time in a sentence created by text in a calculation field. In a calendar file, for example, you might include a layout with a follow-up note to remind customers of upcoming appointments, like this:

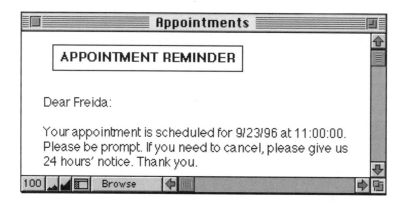

Here, the text in the body of the note is produced by a calculation field with this formula:

""Your appointment is scheduled for "DateToText(Date)&" at "&TimeToText (Time)&". Please be prompt. If you need to cancel, please give us 24 hours' notice. Thank you.""

As you can see, the formula includes the text as well as functions that turn values from the Time and Date fields in this file into text that becomes part of the message. Without the TimeToText function, the time 11:00:00 would be expressed as the number of seconds since midnight.

TIP

You can avoid using the TimeToText function here by including the Time field as a merge field. See *Adding Fields*, on p. 130 in Chapter 6.

Trigonometric Functions

We won't go into much detail with these functions, because this is a book about FileMaker Pro, not about trigonometry. If you know enough trigonometry to understand what these functions do, then the descriptions that follow should be more than enough to allow you to use them in FileMaker Pro.

Atan(number)

The Arc Tangent (Atan) function calculates the inverse tangent, or arc tangent, of the number supplied. The result is the angle, in radians, whose tangent is equal to the number in the argument. For example:

Atan(1) = .785398

Degrees(Atan(1)) = 45

Cos(number)

The Cosine (Cos) function calculates the cosine of the number supplied in the argument, as long as the number is an angle expressed in radians. For example:

Cos(1.047) = 0.5

Cos(Radians(60)) = 0.5

Degrees(number)

The Degrees function converts the supplied number from radians to degrees. The rest of FileMaker Pro's trigonometric functions produce values in radians, so this function converts radians to degrees. For example:

Degrees(Atan(1)) = 45

Degrees(1.0472) = 60

Exp(number)

The Exp function calculates the value of the constant e (2.7182818, or the base of the natural logarithm), raised to the power of the number supplied in the argument. This function is the inverse of the Ln function (see below). For example:

Exp(1) = 2.71828182845904

Exp(Ln(2)) = 2

Ln(number)

The Ln function is the inverse of the Exp function described above. It calculates the natural (or e-base) logarithm of the supplied number. For example:

Ln(2.7182818) = 1

Ln(Exp(5)) = 5

Log(number)

The Logarithm (Log) function calculates the common (or 10-base) logarithm of the number supplied, as long as the number is positive. For example:

Log(1) = 0

Log(100) = 2

PI

The PI function has no argument. When you use it in a formula, it supplies the value of the constant Pi (π), or approximately 3.14159. PI is often used in calculations involving circles. For example:

PI(Radius^2) = area

(PI/180)*n Radians = n degrees

Radians(number)

The Radians function converts the value supplied in the argument into radians. Use this to convert degree values to radians for use in other FileMaker Pro calculations. For example:

Sin(Radians(30)) = 5

Radians(45) = .785398

Sin(number)

The Sin function calculates the sine of the supplied number, when the number is an angle expressed in radians. For example:

Sin(Radians(60)) = .748

Sin(.610865) = .5736

Tan(number)

The Tan function calculates the tangent of the supplied number, when that value is an angle expressed in radians. For example:

Tan(.13) = .1307373

Tan(Radians(34)) = .6745085

Troubleshooting

Because calculation formulas are so flexible, there are lots of potential pitfalls when you create them. Let's look at some common problems and solutions.

FileMaker Pro shows an alert when you click OK to enter a formula.
FileMaker Pro will display an alert box when you make an error in defining a formula. The alert box appears when you click the OK button to finish defining the formula. There are different alert boxes, depending on the nature of the error you've made, as shown on the next page:

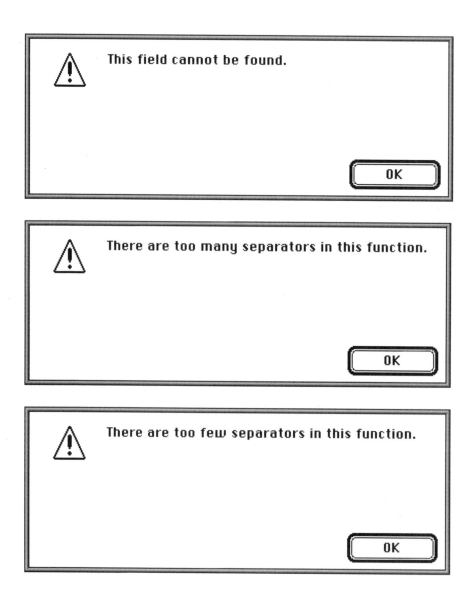

These alerts are always caused by errors in the syntax, or format, of the formula. After you click the OK button in one of these alerts, FileMaker Pro returns to the calculation options dialog box and selects the part of the formula where it thinks there's a problem, like this:

IfGrade =

If(Grades)>90,"Good Work!","")

Here, the field name specified is Grades rather than Grade, and FileMaker Pro can't find a field with that name. FileMaker Pro always tries to highlight the portion of a formula where there's a problem, but it isn't always right. Consider this example:

Bonus =

`If(Salary>25,000,10██,500)`

Here, FileMaker Pro has warned that there are too many separators (commas) in the formula (there are three commas, and the If formula's syntax calls for only two.) The program highlights the portion of the formula shown above, but the real problem is that the value 25,000 contains a comma and it shouldn't. Commas can only be used in formulas to separate one part of a function argument from another, so FileMaker Pro is confused here by the comma separator in 25,000.

The only way to resolve problems like this is to carefully review the formula and check the format of the function(s) you're using. Specifically:

- Make sure there aren't any missing or extra commas or parentheses in the formula. Don't use commas to separate thousands in numbers. Be sure there are as many left parentheses as right parentheses in the formula. Check all zeros in numbers and make sure you've typed the zero key (0) and not the capital *O* to indicate each zero.

- FileMaker Pro doesn't care whether or not you have a space between expressions, constants, field or function names, or operators. FileMaker Pro will ignore unnecessary spaces. However, you *must* use spaces to separate function names, field names (or parts of field names), and operator names from one another. If a formula refers to a field called ProductSubtotal, for example, FileMaker Pro would look for a field with that name. If the real field name was Product Subtotal, FileMaker Pro would display an error saying the field couldn't be found.

- Always separate function names from their arguments with parentheses. If a formula said "IfSalary," for example, FileMaker Pro would look for a field named IfSalary.

- Enclose all text in straight quotation marks. Otherwise, FileMaker Pro will assume the text refers to a function or field name (depending on where it occurs in the formula), and will report an error because it can't find a function or field with that name.

Summary function calculations don't appear.

Summary function calculations depend on the results from summary fields and on the sort order for the file. If a summary function calculation doesn't produce a value, check the following:

- Make sure the summary field itself is producing a value. If the field was defined to produce a value that's weighted by values in another field, and there are no values in that other field, the summary field may not contain any values. Also, if the summary field is in a sub-summary part of the layout and the file must be sorted in a certain order for the value to appear, it won't produce a value unless the file is sorted properly. Check the summary field's definition to see what's required for the field to produce a value.

- Make sure the file is sorted on the proper break field. The second part of a summary function argument specifies the break field on which the file must be sorted for the calculation to occur. Make sure the file is sorted on that field.

A calculation field's value is displayed as 0 wherever the field appears.

There are three potential problems here:

- You're using a logical formula with a numeric result, and the logical test proves false (which equals 0) in every case.

- You've set the field's result type to number, but the formula produces text (FileMaker Pro always evaluates text as 0).

- One or more of the values or field references in the formula is zero (0), based on the data in your file. For example, the formula "Tax*Subtotal" will equal zero (0) if either the Tax or Subtotal field is empty.

16 Using Summary Fields

- Where You Can Use Summary Fields
- Which Records Are Summarized?
- Summary Field Functions
- Summary Field Limitations
- Troubleshooting

Summary fields calculate data across a group of records, rather than within one record. When you create a summary field, you specify the type of calculation and the field on which you want it made.

As you tab through a layout in Browse mode, FileMaker Pro skips over summary fields because you can't enter data into them. But like calculation fields, you can select data in summary fields and copy it to the Clipboard.

To define a summary field, choose the Summary field type in the Field Definition dialog box, and then click the Create button. (See *Defining summary fields*, on p. 61 in Chapter 4 for the procedure.)

Where You Can Use Summary Fields

Typically, you'll use summary fields in summary parts of layouts so they produce totals, averages, or other basic calculations for reports. When you use a summary field in a summary part, however, you must sort the database on a particular field to make the calculation work. You can also use summary fields in the body of a layout. Let's look at two examples.

In this report layout, a summary field called Total Price creates the boldface totals for each item category and for the Total Donations amount at the bottom.

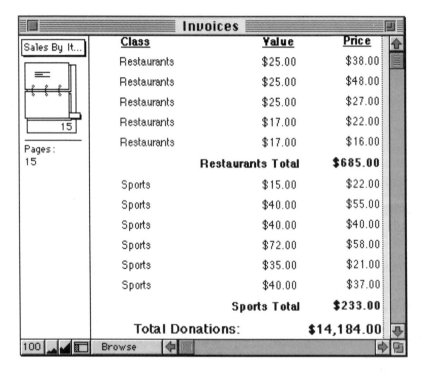

In this layout, the category totals are in a sub-summary part and the Total Donations amount is in a trailing grand summary part. The report is shown in Preview mode because that's the only way to make the sub-summary part appear. Also, this file is sorted on the Class field, because that's the way sub-summary part is defined—if records weren't sorted by class, FileMaker Pro couldn't calculate total donations by class.

In the second example, there are three summary fields in a single-record layout:

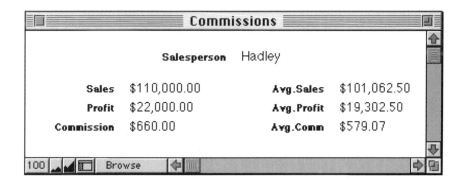

The Sales, Profit, and Commission fields show these amounts for the salesperson shown at the top of the record. At the right, three summary fields display the average sales amount, profit, and commission paid for all the salespeople in the file. Having these summary fields in the single-record layout enables us to compare one salesperson's totals with the averages for the whole sales force.

Which Records Are Summarized?

The specific group of records upon which a summary calculation is made depends on where you put the summary field in a layout.

- If you use the summary field in the body of a layout (so it appears in every record) or in a grand summary part, the summary formula calculates every record in the current found set.

- If you use the summary field in a sub-summary part, the formula calculates only the records summarized in that part, and the calculation only takes place if the records are sorted on the proper field. (See *Troubleshooting*, at the end of this chapter.)

As we look at the summary field functions below, you'll see why you might want to use summary fields in different layout parts. For more ideas about using summary fields in summary parts, see *Using Summary Parts*, in Chapter 9.

Summary Field Functions

FileMaker Pro offers seven summary functions: Total, Average, Count, Minimum, Maximum, Standard Deviation, and Fraction of Total. When you choose the Summary field type in the Field Definition dialog box and create a new field, the Summary Options dialog box appears, like this:

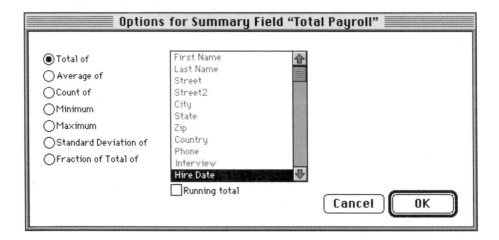

After you select a summary function, select the field whose data you want to calculate from the list at the right. Notice that, as in the above example, fields set to text or container types can't be calculated with summary functions, so they're dimmed in the list.

Depending on which function you choose, you may have additional options for that function. Here, for example, the Total function is selected at the left, and the Running total option appears below the field list.

Let's look at each summary function now.

Total

Total is probably the most common function in summary fields, which is why it's the default option in the Summary Options dialog box. It sums the values in a specific field from several records. When you define a summary field and choose the Total function, you also have the option to calculate a Running total (or a cumulative total) by clicking the checkbox beneath the function name.

ItemNo.	Name	Category	Count	Unit Cost	Value
B101	Junior Football	Balls	22	$7.95	$174.90
B102	Regulation NFL Football	Balls	28	$12.95	$362.60
B103	Official NBA Basketball	Balls	11	$18.98	$208.78
	Cumulative Total:	**$746.28**	**Category Total:**		**$746.28**
C101	Speedy Special Race Car	Cars	8	$44.95	$359.60
C102	Gloria Glamor GoMobile	Cars	3	$35.25	$105.75
	Cumulative Total:	**$1,211.63**	**Category Total:**		**$465.35**
D101	Apple Annie Doll	Dolls	24	$29.37	$704.88
D102	Baby Wetnaps	Dolls	12	$23.32	$279.84
D103	Giant George	Dolls	5	$74.50	$372.50
	Cumulative Total:	**$2,568.85**	**Category Total:**		**$1,357.22**

In the inventory report above, the Category Total and Cumulative Total amounts are calculated with summary fields. The Category Total field uses the Total function to sum the Value field for each category of items. The Cumulative Total field uses the Total function with the Running total option to produce a running total of the overall value of the inventory. As you can see, the Cumulative Total amount increases after each category of merchandise. If we were looking at the very last category in this report, the Cumulative Total field would show the total value of the inventory.

Average

The Average function lets you calculate the average value of items in a field. For example, the following report contains a summary field showing the average price of items bought at a charity auction:

```
┌──────────────────── Invoices ────────────────────┐
│                Auction Item Statistics            │
│                                                   │
│   Item No.  Class                        Price    │
│   B137      Books                        $1.00    │
│   B138      Books                       $10.00    │
│   B139      Books                       $10.00    │
│   B140      Books                        $9.00    │
│   B141      Books                       $21.00    │
│   B142      Books                       $21.00    │
│   B143      Books                       $21.00    │
│   B144      Books                       $10.00    │
│   B145      Books                       $20.00    │
│                          Avg.Price      $11.71    │
│ 100 ▁▃▟▤  Browse    ◁ ▥                  ▷ ▣     │
└───────────────────────────────────────────────────┘
```

The Avg.Price field here is a summary field, and because it's in a sub-summary part (and the file is sorted on the Class field), it computes the average price paid for items in this class. (If the field were in a grand summary part or the body of the layout, it would calculate the average price for all items in the file.)

IMPORTANT NOTE

When computing averages, FileMaker Pro doesn't include records in which the designated field is empty.

When you choose the Average function, the Weighted average option appears. If you click the Weighted average option, you'll see a second list of fields, like the example at the top of the next page:

Using the second list, you choose a field whose values you want used to weight the average. (Notice that you can choose a related field from another file by using the pop-up menu above the list.)

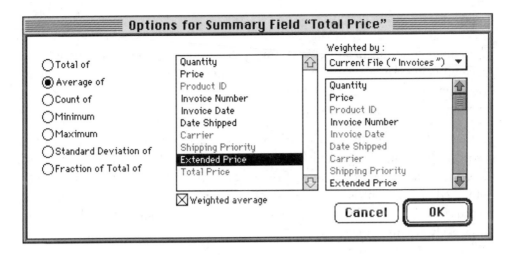

For example, suppose we want to compute the average unit cost for each item in an inventory file. In the following example, the simple and weighted averages are both shown in a sub-summary part.

The Avg.Cost field on the right just averages the values in the Unit Cost field in each category. The WtAvg.Cost field on the left weights the average by the Item Count field. In the Dolls category, you can see that because there are relatively few expensive dolls, the average cost per unit drops when the average is weighted by the item count.

Count

The Count function produces a count of the number of records in which the specified field contains data. The record counter in Browse mode always shows how many records there are in the current found set, so at first glance the Count function doesn't seem too useful.

However, the Count function applies to a particular field, and it only counts the records where the designated field contains a value. Therefore, you can use Count to quickly see how many of the records in a found set have a particular field filled in. You can also use the Count function to display the total number of records in a found set right inside a record or report, by counting a field that you know is always filled in.

In the personnel file below, for example, there's a record for each employee. The Last Name field always contains data, so counting this field would show the number of employee records, and thus the number of employees. The Review Done? field shows whether or not each employee has had an annual performance review. The box at the bottom of the layout contains two summary fields: the 5 is displayed by a summary field that counts the Review Done? field, and the 7 is displayed by a summary field that counts the Last Name field. This way, we know at a glance that only five of seven employees has had an annual review.

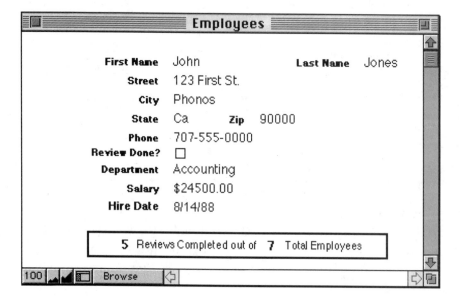

The Running count option appears when you define a summary field with the Count function. If you use a running count, the summary field shows the number of the current record in relation to all the records counted in the found set. For example, in an election database, you might use a running count in a summary field to show which of several precincts is reporting, like this:

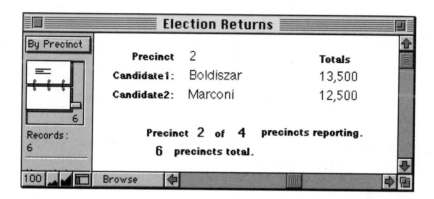

There are three summary fields in the bottom two lines in this layout. The *4* is displayed by a summary field that counts the Totals1 field (the total for Candidate1), so it shows the total number of records in which a result has been reported for the first candidate. (Even if Candidate1's total is entered as 0, this field is still counted. But for records where results haven't been entered, this field is blank so the precinct isn't counted.)

The *2* is calculated by a summary field with the running count option defined for the Totals1 field, so it shows that this particular record is the second of four records where the Totals1 field contains a value. The *6* is calculated by a summary field that counts the Precinct field, so it shows the total number of precincts. Notice that it matches the record counter number in the status area.

FileMaker Pro doesn't increase the running count value when a record doesn't contain a value. In the layout shown below, for example, the same three summary fields are used as in the layout on the previous page. However, the running count value doesn't change in the records for precincts 3 and 5. Because there's no vote count value in the Candidate1 field in each of these records, the running count number is simply carried forward from the previous record.

```
╔══════════════════ Election Returns ══════════════════╗
║                                                          ║
║   Precinct      Candidate1    Candidate2                 ║
║                                                          ║
║   1              26,000        22,500                    ║
║   Precinct  1  of  4   reporting precincts, out of  6   precincts total.
║                                                          ║
║   2              13,500        12,500                    ║
║   Precinct  2  of  4   reporting precincts, out of  6   precincts total.
║                                                          ║
║   3                                                      ║
║   Precinct  2  of  4   reporting precincts, out of  6   precincts total.
║                                                          ║
║   4              14,000        15,600                    ║
║   Precinct  3  of  4   reporting precincts, out of  6   precincts total.
║                                                          ║
║   5                                                      ║
║   Precinct  3  of  4   reporting precincts, out of  6   precincts total.
║                                                          ║
║   6              18,750        16,000                    ║
║   Precinct  4  of  4   reporting precincts, out of  6   precincts total.
║                                                          ║
║  100  ▲◢□  Browse                                        ║
╚══════════════════════════════════════════════════════╝
```

Minimum and Maximum

These two functions show the lowest or highest value in the field from all the records in the current found set. They're useful for several purposes, including finding the smallest order in an orders file, the highest grade in a grade report file, the lowest count in an inventory file, and so forth. In the following example, two summary fields in a sub-summary part show the minimum and the maximum prices paid at an auction.

```
┌─────────────────────────────────────────────────────┐
│ ▣▤  ═════════════ Invoices ═════════════  ▣▤       │
│ ┌──────────────────────────────────────────────┐ ⬆ │
│ │           Auction Sales Report                │ ▤ │
│ │                                                │   │
│ │  Item No.  Class                     Price    │   │
│ │  ────────  ─────                     ─────    │   │
│ │  B137     Books                     $1.00     │   │
│ │  B138     Books                    $10.00     │   │
│ │  B139     Books                    $10.00     │   │
│ │  B140     Books                     $9.00     │   │
│ │  B141     Books                    $21.00     │   │
│ │  B142     Books                    $21.00     │   │
│ │  B143     Books                    $21.00     │   │
│ │  B144     Books                    $10.00     │   │
│ │  B145     Books                    $20.00     │   │
│ │  Low Price        $1.00  High Price $28.00    │ ⬇ │
│ 100 ▂▃▆ ▣ │ Browse │ ◀▥        ▶ ▣            │
└─────────────────────────────────────────────────────┘
```

By showing the lowest and highest prices paid for a category of items, you can see at a glance whether the price paid for a particular item is relatively low or high. If you showed these summary fields in the body of a single-record layout, you could easily compare each item's price with the highest and lowest prices for items in its class (by finding only records in that class), or in the whole database (by finding all records in the file).

Standard Deviation

Standard deviation is a statistical function that calculates the average deviation from the mean, or average value in a group. This function is handy when you want to know whether an individual record's value is or isn't "in the ballpark" when compared with other records' values in that field.

In a database of auction item sales, for example, you might want to know whether individual prices are higher or lower than those of the typical sale.

Using the Standard Deviation function, you could calculate the standard deviation from the average price, and then use it to establish a range into which most prices fell, like this:

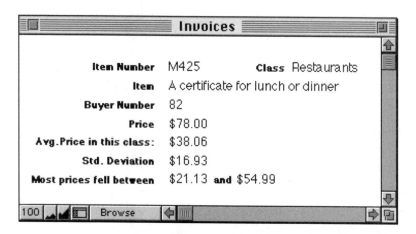

In this record, for example, the $78.00 value shown in the Price field is not only higher than the average of prices paid for Restaurant items, but it's also higher than the upper end of the range indicated in the "Most prices fell between" line. Here's how the standard deviation function is used to calculate the upper and lower limits of the price range in the "Most prices fell between" line:

The value $21.13 is the lower end of the range determined by the standard deviation. This value is produced in a calculation field that subtracts the Std.Deviation field's amount from the Avg.Price field's amount ($38.06 – $16.93).

The value $54.99 is the upper end of the range determined by the standard deviation. This value is produced in a calculation field that adds the Std.Deviation field's amount to the Avg.Price field's amount ($38.06 + $16.93).

This example also shows the GetSummary function at work. Since the Std.Deviation and Avg.Price fields are themselves summary fields, we can't use their values directly in the calculation formulas that produce the lower and upper ends of the price range. Instead, we must use the GetSummary function. To calculate the lower end of the price range, for example, the formula is "GetSummary(Avg.Price,Class)-GetSummary(Std.Deviation,Class)." The GetSummary function tells FileMaker Pro to extract the calculated values from the Avg.Price and Std.Deviation fields when the file is sorted on the Class field (the break field). For more on *The GetSummary Function*, see p. 360 in Chapter 15.

Fraction of Total

The Fraction of Total function lets you see quickly what percentage of the whole database (or found set) is represented by a single record's value. In an inventory database, for example, it might be useful to know how much of your inventory costs are tied up in any one item, shown below.

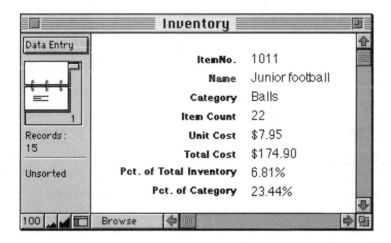

The Pct. of Total Inventory field here is a summary field that uses the Fraction of Total function.

When you use the Fraction of Total function, you get the option Subtotaled. When you choose this option, you see a second list of fields, as shown on p. 411 earlier. You must choose a field on which to sort the database for the subtotal to appear. In the layout above, for example, the Pct. of Category field uses the Subtotaled option. This field only shows a value when the database is sorted by the Category field, and then it shows the percentage of the category's total represented by the value in this one record.

Summary Field Limitations

Summary fields are easy to create, and it's almost impossible to define a formula that won't work. However, the summary may not produce the calculation you want, and there are some important limits to keep in mind when you create summary fields and use them in layouts.

- When you define a summary field, you can only select a field with a number, date, or time result as the field to be summarized. You can't use text, global, or container fields, and you can't use other summary fields. These field names are dimmed in the list of field names in the summary options dialog box.

- You can't use a summary field name in a calculation field formula. As explained in the Standard Deviation function example shown earlier, you must use the GetSummary function when you want to use the value produced by a summary field as part of the formula in another calculation field.

- Summary field results in sub-summary parts aren't displayed in Browse mode. To see summary values, display the layout in Preview mode.

Troubleshooting

You want to select a certain field for calculation in a summary field, but its name is dimmed on the list in the Summary Options dialog box.
If a field named is dimmed in the Summary Options dialog box, it's because you can't use that field in a summary calculation. Summary field calculations can only deal with numeric results, so the field you select must be a field containing a numeric value. Here's how to check:

Put the Summary Options dialog box away, and then look at the field's type in the list of fields in the Define Fields dialog box. The field's type must be Number, Date, Time, or Calculation, and Calculation fields must also be set to a number, date, or time result to be available for summary field definitions. (To check the result type of a calculation field, double-click on the field's name in the Define Fields dialog box and then check the Calculation result is pop-up menu at the bottom of the Specify Calculation dialog box.)

Sometimes your file will contain text fields that store numbers, such as zip codes or phone numbers. However, even though a field contains numbers, it must be defined as a numeric field for you to use it in summary calculations. To change a field's type from text to numeric, just select the field in the Define Fields dialog box, click Number or press ⌘N, click the Save button, and then click the Done button. (See *Adding or Changing Fields*, in Chapter 5 for more information.)

You define a new summary field, but the calculated value doesn't appear.

There are several things to check when this happens.

1. Are you viewing the layout in Preview mode? You must be in Preview mode to see the summarized values.

2. If you still can't see the values, check the field's placement on the layout. Switch to Layout mode and make sure none of the field's borders are touching or overlapping the boundary between the body, header, footer, or any summary parts. When a summary field overlaps a part boundary its values can't be displayed.

3. If you're sure about the field placement, make sure the records in the found set do in fact contain numeric values in the field you're trying to summarize. If the field you're trying to summarize contains text, FileMaker Pro will evaluate the text as zero and you'll likely see a zero (0) in your summary field. If the field contains dates or times, FileMaker Pro will use the underlying date or time numbers in its calculations. (See *Date Functions* and *Time Functions*, in Chapter 15.)

4. If your summary field relies on another field for its calculation (the Weighted average option in the Average function or the Subtotaled option in the Fraction of Total function), make sure there are numeric values in those fields (for weighted averages) or that the records are sorted on the correct field (for fractions of the total).

Index

~~~~~~

S

More from Peachpit Press

Excel 5 for Macintosh: Visual QuickStart Guide

Maria Langer

Microsoft Excel is a wonderfully versatile spreadsheet program and Excel 5 has added an array of new features that add not only to its power, but to its complexity as well. Rather than plowing through heavy-handed manuals, Excel users will find Peachpit's *Excel 5 for Macintosh: Visual QuickStart Guide* an easier self-teaching tool. Like all the books in the *Visual QuickStart Guide* series the reader is presented with the most helpful kind of information—detailed illustrations and screen captures showing exactly what you'll see on your computer. Once you've learned the program, the book serves as a valuable reference to specific functions and features. *$16.95 (272 pages)*

FileMaker Pro 3 for Macintosh: Visual QuickStart Guide

C. Ann Brown

FileMaker Pro 3 for Macintosh: Visual QuickStart Guide offers users easy-to-follow, step-by-step instructions for getting the most of Claris' FileMaker Pro 3. This book is filled with hundreds of screen-shots and loads of tips. As with all the *Visual QuickStart Guides*, information is presented in a straightforward, graphic fashion, so you'll find what you need, understand it, and get right to work. *$16.95 (248 pages)*

The Little Mac Book, Fourth Edition

Robin Williams

Now a worldwide bestseller (over 350,000 in print in 13 languages), *The Little Mac Book* covers the basics of operating a Mac. It explains how to use the mouse and menus; what windows, files, fonts, folders, and icons are; and much, much more. This edition adds a wealth of new information as well as a gaggle of cartoons and illustrations by the ever-amusing John Grimes. Includes a tutorial for new users. *$17.95 (408 pages)*

The Little System 7.1/7.5 Book

Kay Yarborough Nelson

This book is a concise introduction to System 7.1 and 7.5's virtual memory, desk accessories, Finder, Control Panel, and other features. It covers TrueType, tricks for multi-tasking, and ways to customize your system. "There's just enough hand-holding to keep beginners from getting lost, but not so much that experienced users will lose interest. That said, this is also a great little book for more advanced users." —MacUser *$13.95 (208 pages)*

The Macintosh Bible, Sixth Edition

Jeremy Judson, editor

With over 1,000,000 copies in print, more people turn to *The Macintosh Bible* for answers to their Mac questions than any other book. The completely updated and revised Sixth Edition draws upon the knowledge of 12 Mac experts and over 50 contributors to bring you information on the latest hot Macintosh topics like the Internet, System 7.5, PowerBooks, Mac Clones, Troubleshooting, and using the Mac in a Home Office environment. In addition, you'll learn the valuable tips, tricks, and techiques (such as, accessing the Internet, finding the coolest Web sites, networking your Mac to other Macs, and starting a second business at home using your Mac) for which *The Macintosh Bible* is well known. This is the Mac reference to keep next to your Mac and to turn to again and again for reliable, accurate, and insightful information. Discover why THE NEW YORK TIMES has praised previous editions as "like having a Macintosh expert at your side whenever you need one." *$29.95 (1000 pages)*

The Macintosh Bible Guide to ClarisWorks 4

Charles Rubin

ClarisWorks is one of the best-selling integrated software package for the Macintosh. Version 4 boasts more than 100 significant enhancements. *The Macintosh Bible Guide to ClarisWorks 4* offers a clear, no-nonsense approach to getting the most out of this power-packed, yet accessible, package. It shows in great detail how to work with each of the six applications that comprise ClarisWorks— word processor, spreadsheet, database, drawing, painting, and communications—and how to work with them together. It's full of tips and trouble-shooting advice. It also features a large section on advanced techniques, making it ideal for beginning to advanced users. *$24.95 (520 pages)*

The Macintosh Bible Guide to Excel 5

Maria Langer

The Macintosh Bible Guide to Excel 5 gives beginning through advanced readers a no-nonsense, real world approach to getting the most out of version 5. Now, cross-platform users can enjoy the same features and functions available in the windows version: new Help Wizards, improved interface, and OLE (Object Linking and Embedding) 2.0 for editing documents. *$24.95 (496 pages)*

The Macintosh Bible Guide to Games

This thorough, highly entertaining book/CD package is the ultimate reference to games on the Mac: virtually every Mac game—past, present and future—is covered. The accompanying CD-ROM is crammed with goodies, many unavailable elsewhere: game demos; shareware and freeware games; patches and cheaters, slide shows and QuickTime movies of games currently in development. *$34.95 (600 pages, w/CD-ROM)*

The Macintosh Bible Guide to Word 6

Maria Langer

Whether you're a beginning or experienced user of Microsoft Word for the Macintosh, this book will bring you up to speed with version 6. With step-by-step recipes, you'll create newsletters, invitations, display advertising, and more. Provides plenty of details on Word's newest features, including how to add annotations, graphs, and QuickTime movies to documents. *$24.95 (750 pages)*

The Macintosh Bible "What Do I Do Now?" Book, Third Edition

Charles Rubin

The third edition of this bestseller (over 143,000 in print) includes new material on repair software as well as information on troubleshooting for all Macs. It also covers common problems in widely used programs like Word, Excel, PageMaker, and QuarkXPress. "No longer will you have to crawl on hands and knees to beg at the altar of the local Macintosh guru; it's all right here in this book." —MacTalk *$22 (416 pages)*

The Macintosh Font Book, Third Edition

Erfert Fenton

The newly revised edition of this lively typography primer demystifies fonts for beginning through intermediate Macintosh users. It provides clear, simple-to-follow instruction in basic typography concepts. Plus it gives the low-down on new font technologies, new ways to buy type, TrueType, and expanded coverage on legal issues. Containing 50 percent new information, *The Macintosh Font Book* reflects new procedures in System 7.5 without neglecting those of earlier versions. *$24.95 (400 pages)*

Microsoft Office: Training on CD

Quay2 Multimedia

No more expensive training courses; no more fumbling with video cassettes. As with the others in our *Training on CD* series, you can watch hundreds of narrated live-action demonstrations by an experienced Macintosh instructor, right on your own computer. Office covers the details of Microsoft's Word, Excel, and PowerPoint. Word topics covered include: formatting, tabs, setting styles, special characters, page numbering, headers and footers, multiple columns, reports, graphics, tables, mail merge, envelopes, labels, and Autotext. Excel topics covered include: navigating, filling cells, selection techniques, entering data, formatting, data analysis, charts, macros, views and panes, linking, and using formulas, operators, references, and functions. PowerPoint topics covered include: working with slides, entering text, formatting text, bullets and colors, adding graphics, adding charts, and creating templates. *$99.95 (CD-ROM)*

The QuarkXPress Book, Fourth Edition for Macintosh

David Blatner and Eric Taub

If you're serious about QuarkXPress, this is the book to have. It's the highest rated, most comprehensive, and best-selling QuarkXPress book ever published. Now totally updated and rewritten to cover version 3.3, it includes a handy tear-out card showing keystroke shortcuts. Includes XTensions, EfiColor, and AppleEvent scripting. Winner of the Benjamin Franklin Award, Computer Book Category, and runner-up for the PUBLISH Readers' Choice Award, Mac Book Category. *$29.95 (778 pages)*

QuarkXPress Tips & Tricks, Second Edition

David Blatner, Phil Gaskil, Eric Taub

All the smartest, most useful shortcuts and techniques from Peachpit's best-selling *QuarkXPress Book*, plus many more, are packed into this book. *QuarkXPress Tips & Tricks* provides quick answers to common questions, as well as insights on techniques that will make you a power user. Each chapter covers a distinct aspect of QuarkXPress, such as document construction, type and typography, copy flow, color, and printing. An excellent companion for any QuarkXPress user. *$34.95 (425 pages, w/CD-ROM)*

WordPerfect 3.5 for Macintosh: Visual QuickStart Guide

Rita Lewis

A quick and efficient manual to guide you through the new twists and turns of WordPerfect 3.5. This handbook is task-oriented, easy-to-grasp, highly-visual and menu-driven. Nearly 300 screen captures and succinct to-the-point instructions reduce complex maneuvers to a series of easy-to-follow steps. WordPerfect 3.5 for Macintosh quickly helps you master the first word processor native to the PowerMac and the only one fully compatible with System 7.5. *WordPerfect 3.5 Visual QuickStart Guide* shows you around all the upgraded features including new automated short cuts (such as QuickCorrect), the powerful macro language, and an extensive array of buttons and tool bars for easy command access. *$16.95 (272 pages)*

For online information about these and other Peachpit books and CD-ROMs— plus excerpts from our latest titles—visit our Web site:

http://www.peachpit.com

Order Form

USA **800-283-9444** • **510-548-4393** • FAX **510-548-5991**
CANADA **800-387-8028** • **416-447-1779** • FAX **800-456-0536** OR **416-443-0948**

Qty	Title	Price	Total

SUBTOTAL		
ADD APPLICABLE SALES TAX*		
SHIPPING		
TOTAL		

Shipping is by UPS ground: $4 for first item, $1 each add'l.

*We are required to pay sales tax in all states with the exceptions of AK, DE, HI, MT, NH, NV, OK, OR, SC and WY. Please include appropriate sales tax if you live in any state not mentioned above.

Customer Information

NAME

COMPANY

STREET ADDRESS

CITY   STATE   ZIP

PHONE ( )   FAX ( )
[REQUIRED FOR CREDIT CARD ORDERS]

Payment Method

❏ CHECK ENCLOSED   ❏ VISA   ❏ MASTERCARD   ❏ AMEX

CREDIT CARD #   EXP. DATE

COMPANY PURCHASE ORDER #

Tell Us What You Think

PLEASE TELL US WHAT YOU THOUGHT OF THIS BOOK: _____ TITLE:

WHAT OTHER BOOKS WOULD YOU LIKE US TO PUBLISH?

MAC   **PEACHPIT PRESS** • 2414 Sixth Street • Berkeley, CA 94710